W9-CHO-895

To: Robb
Christmas 2003
With Love
From: Bob + George

THE ART OF LANDSCAPE DETAIL

NIALL KIRKWOOD

THE ART OF LANDSCAPE DETAIL

Fundamentals, Practices, and Case Studies

JOHN WILEY & SONS, INC.

New York • Chichester • Weinheim • Brisbane • Singapore • Toronto

This book is printed on acid-free paper. ∞

Copyright © 1999 by John Wiley & Sons. All rights reserved.

Published simultaneously in Canada.

Graphic design by Jay Anning, Thumb Print.

Library of Congress Cataloging-in-Publication Data:

Kirkwood, Niall G.
    The art of landscape detail: fundamentals, practices, and case studies / Niall G. Kirkwood.
        p.   cm.
    Includes bibliographical references and index.
    ISBN 0-471-14044-9 (alk. paper)
    1. Landscape design.   I. Title.
SB472.5.K57   1999
712—dc21   98-51756
                                  CIP

Printed in the United States of America.

10 9 8 7 6 5 4 3

CONTENTS

PART THREE
CASE STUDIES 221

ACKNOWLEDGMENTS

THE TITLE OF THIS BOOK and a large part of its content derive from a lecture course of the same name that was first offered in the spring of 1993 in the Department of Landscape Architecture at the Harvard Graduate School of Design. The high level of interest in the subject shown by subsequent classes of students suggested that further study in this area was long overdue. Since then, the course has been expanded in length to include issues of durability, weathering, and detail craftsmanship. In developing this manuscript, I have added these topics along with information arising from the ongoing academic concerns of instruction and research into the subject.

Landscape detail as an aspect of landscape architecture has been overlooked in recent studies of site planning, landscape history, design theory, and professional practice. As a result there is a lack of published information on the subject. This situation echoes a note made in 1917 by Henry Vincent Hubbard and Theodora Kimball in the reference section of their classic book, *An Introduction to the Study of Landscape Design*. At that time they instructed student readers to turn to books on engineering because of the lack of writing in English on modern landscape construction. Some 80 years later, landscape design projects and current practitioners in landscape architecture have created a small amount of analysis and commentary in the field to which students can turn. I have not ignored these resources when they have been useful in introducing specific detail issues. Spacemaker Press of Washington, D.C., for example, should be noted as a growing source of landscape design detail in their project and practice monographs. There are, however, as an introduction to the subject, two previous sources in editions of *Landscape Architecture* magazine that should be identified. Here I am particularly indebted to the published articles on landscape detail by Albert D. Taylor written between 1922 and 1936 and, in more recent times, by Linda L. Jewell. Their illustrated articles and practice notes on a wide range of topics in landscape implementation and detail design were a welcomed addition to the modest amount of published material. Taylor's articles comprising "landscape construction notes" and, later, "garden details" focused on the private gardens and estates of that time, elegantly documenting the state of office and detail construction procedures for other practitioners in the field. In contrast, 50 years later, Jewell's published work in the 1980s and 1990s addressed a different professional circumstance. These articles cataloged details and landscape materials associated with construction technologies that were undergoing profound changes of application and production, in particular those connected with the complex interdisciplinary projects found in urban landscape construction—for example, transitways, streets, and plazas. In this book I intend to build on their work, but in doing so, to offer a quite different perspective on the subject. A more thorough analysis of the design approaches and themes that produce landscape detail will be covered, as well as a more critical investigation on the currently accepted roles of design and technology in the broader conception of landscape architecture and design.

I would like to acknowledge a number of design teachers and practitioners who served in my own training as a source of inspiration through their concerns for the quality of detail design. In addition, they possessed an ability to transfer these concerns to their artistic endeavors in daily practice, including consideration of design at the detail scale. Of these, the most significant is Professor Trevor Dannatt of London, England. I would also like to mention Dr. Ron Brunskill and Donald R. Buttress at the University of Manchester, England, the late John Shaw of London, and Robert M. Hanna and Sir Peter Shepheard, at the Graduate School of Fine Arts at the University of Pennsylvania in Philadelphia. I note particularly Sir Peter's evening lecture series "Elements," which will be fondly remembered by his students as a model of reflective practice in landscape design at the detail scale.

In addition, I am indebted to a number of people who have encouraged and assisted in the development of particular strands of thought in the evolution of this manuscript: within the Graduate School of Design at Harvard, Gary Hilderbrand and Charles Harris, as well as Tim Mackey, Matt Gaber, and Patricia Bales. Special thanks are extended to Quentin Caron and Sally Coyle, who assisted in the area of emerging and innovative detail materials and their applications.

The following practitioners who participated in the case studies and gave freely of their own time, and the resources and time of their offices and staff, were crucial to the demonstration of contemporary detail practice. They are, in alphabetical order, Henry Arnold, Susan Child, Stuart O. Dawson, Dan Kiley, David B. Meyer, Laurie D. Olin, Mario Schjetnan, Martha Schwartz, Ken Smith, Michael Van Valkenburgh, and Peter Ker Walker. Their immense contributions are noted.

Discussions with Daniel Winterbottom, ASLA, of the University of Washington, and Richard Burck, ASLA, helped to clarify many of the ideas developed in this book. The ongoing dialogue with Alistair McIntosh, ASLA, RIBA, over the precise nature of the making of a landscape has proved to be

one of the most rewarding aspects in this endeavor. I would like to note his immense contribution, which he would immediately discount.

Members of the John Wiley & Sons staff in New York provided support, especially Margaret Cummins, Aquisitions Editor, Janet Feeney, Associate Editor, and those who guided the project in its early stages, Dan Sayle, Senior Editor, and Tracy Thornblade, Assistant Editor. I wish to acknowledge those people who read the manuscript and gave critical comments, Alistair McIntosh, RIBA, ASLA, Alan Ward, ASLA, and Sonali Soneji, who made corrections to the initial manuscript draft.

Research assistant Raphael Justevitz of the Graduate School of Design diligently transcribed all the practitioners' taped discussions and implemented the planning of the case studies under the author's direction. Further research on the case studies was carried out by graduate students Nick Tobier, Sara Peschel, and Reshma Singh. Mme. Gilberte Brassaï and the estate of G. Brassaï, Paris, are thanked for permission to reproduce the photograph on the cover.

The preparation of this book was assisted by a grant from the Graham Foundation for Advanced Studies in the Fine Arts, which I wish to thank for its support.

Finally, I want to thank my wife, Louise, a landscape architect in her own right, and my daughter, Chloe, for their constant support and encouragement, each in her own way.

PREFACE

THE ART OF LANDSCAPE DETAIL concerns the subject of landscape detail and its relationship to landscape design. It addresses the role of landscape detail in the landscape design process and examines its form and expression not only as a means of understanding landscape design work, but as a source of creative expression in the fields of landscape architecture, urban design, and site architecture. The various chapters of this book introduce readers to the scope, concerns, approaches, and practices of detail form and design. In addition, it is intended to prepare students and young practitioners who are beginning their initial training in design offices in regard to the role of landscape detail in the formation of contemporary built landscape space and the detail ideas and themes that are to be found there.

Before addressing the topic of landscape detail and the detail design process, two notes of explanation are necessary. First, it should be understood that this book is concerned with selected aspects of landscape detail, for example, those dealing with detail aesthetics and expression, rather than a broader and more comprehensive survey of the subject. Second, the primary goal of this book is to advocate for the development of the specific detail parts of conceptual ideas in landscape design, simultaneously with the general. Landscape architecture's strength as a design discipline derives largely from the incorporation of diverse and complex social, cultural, environmental and aesthetic concerns into holistic solutions. I have therefore highlighted detail ideas and built forms that are consistent in their artful use of landscape detail or predict new ways of interconnecting the detail parts with the whole. Thus, landscape design work is seen and understood to evolve simultaneously at both scales.

This book is inspired by the exemplary landscape detail of built landscapes throughout the world, ranging from the Montmartre Steps in Paris illustrated on the cover and within, to the detail design work of landscape architects featured in the case studies. These include projects by contemporary landscape architects such as Dan Kiley, Martha Schwartz, Mario Schjetnan, and Susan Child. It has also been deeply influenced by the more humble details

found in the vernacular landscapes of towns and communities, in the ordinary roads and squares, in neighborhood parks, playgrounds, and street corners. Here, notable details do not always have to be part of beautiful or exemplary landscapes, although that is always a bonus, nor do they have to be rare or precious in their execution. What matters is the quality and art that is brought to them. That is the spirit of this book, and it is also the manner in which the subject of landscape detail will be examined.

As noted earlier, the primary audience for this work is landscape architectural students and landscape designers starting their careers in the design profession. The limited coverage in the curricula of undergraduate and graduate landscape architecture schools and departments on the subject of landscape detail suggests that along with the insufficient amount of general technological training given to students, the neglect of this subject will continue in the foreseeable future. It is therefore timely to also offer a reevaluation of landscape detail within landscape architectural education and to reconsider its role in the practice of contemporary landscape design.

In 1976, Gary O. Robinette, ASLA, noted in the preface to his textbook, *Landscape Architectural Site Construction Details*:

> In all that has been written about the history, the development, the theory and the philosophy of landscape architecture and environmental development, all too little attention has been paid to the basic element of the ultimate "particle" in the continuum—the site construction detail. This is a first attempt to rectify that shortcoming. It is not being done by producing a definitive text on the *processes, methods and techniques* (which is admittedly needed), but by collecting and illustrating a series of examples or "case studies," if you will, of how site details have actually been executed in a number of specific instances. ... *What is actually needed is a definitive book on landscape detailing which gives the history, the philosophy, the various techniques, materials and expense and which shows photos of the constructed project alongside a drawing of the detail* (emphasis added).

PURPOSE OF THE BOOK

This book identifies the general processes of landscape detail, emphasizing the evolution of detail practices where no single solution is at hand and the designer must investigate alternative approaches for a range of project types and site conditions. It also examines more critically specific detail ideas and motifs that have constituted the artistic core of designers' investigations into the subject.

The intention is to prepare students and entry-level practitioners to fully develop their conceptual design ideas through the medium of landscape detail. In the range of professional and working opportunities students and entry-level practitioners will likely first encounter in the profession, there is still opportunity to evolve outdoor spaces that are sensitive to the conditions resulting from the changing social and legal environment, while demonstrating the very best in progressive ideas in landscape architecture. The objectives of this book are, therefore, as follows:

• To broaden the vocabulary and detail construction language of the built landscape environment.

• To unite the activity of landscape detail design with progressive site planning.

• To impact and rectify the poverty of generic landscape detail form found within current professional literature and academic instruction.

Over the last 20 years a range of landscape technology books have been published that provide a catalog of generic landscape details and/or reproduce drawings of isolated site details implemented in practice. These books are identified in the bibliography, and so this ground will not be covered again. This book still belongs, however, to the mainstream of research and writing on site construction and landscape technology, through its insistence on relating the design processes, methods, and techniques of landscape detail to the requirements of the professional design office and construction site as well as to the classroom.

The book is organized into three parts: *Fundamentals, Practices,* and *Case Studies;* together, they address four questions:

• What is landscape detail?

• Why is it important to landscape architects in the design and development of outdoor space?

• How is it carried out by individual designers?

• What is its significance in the built environment?

In answering these questions, the various chapters focus on basic core knowledge about the subject and the development of landscape detail forms. It should be noted, however, that this is not a "handbook" or a source of landscape detail ideas that can be lifted and applied in an arbitrary fashion to any site project, nor is it concerned with listing technical solutions to landscape design problems. Rather, it focuses on introducing and developing work habits in the designer that allow an individual to recognize and distinguish conditions and opportunities in landscape detail design. It is the author's

intention that those who have an interest in this subject will be encouraged to perform further work and research. Topics in specialized and advanced landscape detail are identified and briefly described as subjects for further study in Chapter 6.

There is no single identifiable theory (or theories) of landscape detail that sustains landscape detail practice. It has remained a product of either the design office or the site, where landscape details and detail ideas have evolved over time as a result of a process of trial and error or because of changing code and statutory requirements. In the design office, landscape details have often been repeated through the tradition of "rules of thumb" that are institutionalized through professional office standards and company manuals. Rules of thumb are best described as practices derived from certain tried and tested detail forms and material applications used over and over again. Alteration to the detail form or substitution is made only when necessary, based on new information from the field. In many cases, there are no records as to how these rules of thumb evolved or when they were first proposed, and there are instances in which certain supposedly good detail practices have been shown, over time, to be wrong or inappropriate, or have been altered to achieve better results. There are also instances in which changes in codes, standards, and regulations make previously standard details unworkable and obsolete—for example, in the areas of universal accessibility and the detail forms of pedestrian safety barriers.

The following considerations are relevant in the study of landscape detail:

- The practice rules of thumb are being supplanted through economic and professional changes within the discipline of landscape architecture. These include computer information technologies that alter the way documentation is processed, changes in legislation and codes regarding the built environment (for example, the American Disabilities Act of 1990 (ADA)) and the increasing specialization of design work with the advent of project and site construction management.

- Detail information that is developed in practice is rarely communicated to, and thus not integrated into, teaching, and information that may be developed in design schools is rarely conveyed to the profession.

- Landscape detail and the methods of generating detail form have rarely been considered to be a subject for concentrated academic study or part of any ongoing research into landscape aesthetics or design by landscape design educators and practitioners.

The traditional method of addressing the subject of landscape detail within design courses, if covered at all, was within the technology sequence of undergraduate and graduate landscape architecture programs. At the initial stages of this book, I made a survey of landscape technology courses offered within these programs in North America. A particular emphasis of the survey was the scope and topics covered in the areas of landscape detail and construction. Among the questions asked were the following:

- What are the general approaches covered in courses of instruction in landscape technology?

- Are they derived from landscape technology as a supporting subject or one separate from studio design instruction?

- How do you classify landscape detail (if at all) within your current courses: by material, (stone, wood), by element, (paving, walls), by condition (changes of level), or by category (surface, boundaries)?

- What methods of instruction, if any, do you currently use in the teaching of landscape detail?

The results of the survey showed that existing landscape technology courses focused almost exclusively on the review and application of site implementation techniques or on simulating the processes and production of sets of working drawings. It should be recognized that there were a few individual teachers who had developed inventive and challenging landscape detail and construction courses using, for example, design/build and field research exercises or detail precedent studies, but these were rare.

The following were identified as Key Issues and Detail Study Techniques used in existing courses, or were considered significant to the instructors if not actually covered.

Key Issues

- Materials, their character, selection, and application

- Weathering, time, and detail design

- Custom details

- Detail making, how things are made and go together in the design process

Detail Study Techniques

- Documentation of detail design processes

- Keeping of detail sketchbooks

- Precedent studies of existing detail projects

- Measured drawings of existing site details

The Key Issues and Detail Study Techniques identified in the survey are addressed within this book.

Students and educators in landscape architecture will find this book a primary text to support teaching and study in the area of landscape technology and design. In addition, those in related design fields will also find it a source of information on particular aspects of the built environment: landscape planners, urban designers, environmental designers, public artists, garden historians, and preservation and restoration consultants. Among those who may also find the book useful are public agencies; city officials; conservation, neighborhood planning, and historic groups and committees; and individuals and groups who administer or are involved in the design review of outdoor space and who are called upon to make decisions at a detailed scale in the built landscape.

It is assumed that students have completed basic introductory courses to acquire knowledge of landscape design and studio practices, as well as an introduction to drafting, drawing, sketching, and basic survey techniques prior to starting studies in this area. Those professionals and officials seeking advice who have no background in landscape design or site execution should consult one of the general introductory landscape implementation textbooks noted in the bibliography or, better still, consult with a licensed landscape architect in their locales.

This book is intended to be appropriate for use across varied climatic, geographical, and cultural regions and landscapes. With one exception, the detail case studies are drawn from the United States and from within private landscape architectural practice. This is a result of personal focus by the author and does not suggest that the subject is limited to such a narrow area. It is hoped that case studies in landscape detail for all regions, in both the public and private sectors, will be developed in the future. The restricted sampling from which they were drawn do not, however, invalidate the conclusions about detail design. The intention is to demonstrate that a designer in any locale is faced with a series of general detail conditions with specialized local concerns and issues.

The author's main interest in landscape detail lies in the following areas:

- The role of landscape detail as an art form

- The range and types of landscape detail processes used today by contemporary designers

- The future uses of landscape detail form in progressive site design

Landscape detail is considered here through work created in both the large corporate landscape architectural office and in the studio of the single practitioner. The sources of information range from designers' personal sketchbooks to manufacturers' literature, from those who design landscapes to the people who maintain them and the public that uses them. I reflect on the influence of weather and weathering on details—ice, heat, rain, and wind—the issues of amenity and safety, and especially the concerns of detail construction, durability, and failure. All this has been done to demonstrate to the reader the breadth of the subject as a determinant in the physical form and experience of outdoor social space.

Finally, this book is based on a simple proposition: every designer sees the subject of landscape detail in a fresh light, not simply because these individuals transform the built environment to suit the specific needs of clients and programs, but also because each one's vision of that landscape comes from a particular motivation. Design in detail should be a source of pleasure as well as an occasion for discovery and new insights into the design process. Landscape detail itself constitutes a potent source of inspiration for contemporary designers in their search for purposeful and expressive forms in the landscape. For this reason, *The Art of Landscape Detail* is offered as a celebration of the exemplary detail work that has gone before, and what may be created by designers in the future.

N. K.
Cambridge, Massachusetts
September 1998

INTRODUCTION

A DESIGNER FOR WHOM I WORKED soon after leaving design college started each project in a similar manner. Upstairs in his cramped office he would tape a single piece of paper onto a small portable drafting table. Working in graphite and colored pencil, he would quickly move his hand across the surface, marking the general spatial configuration, structure, and organization of the spaces in plan and sectional sketch drawings. In the bottom left-hand corner of the paper, a full-size or half-size detail drawing, usually in section, was emerging at the same time. This detail was developed, manipulated, and explored with the same clarity and precision as the major design expression of the plan form. Throughout the subsequent development and elaboration of the project, this single detail element remained intact and established the further development of a detail language for the entire project. On this drawing was also found the information about materials, finishes, and textures by which a language of detail construction could be established, shaped, and articulated. Here was clearly illustrated a holistic approach from project inception to completion, from concept to implementation.

I have constantly returned, in my own landscape practice and teaching, to this early formative experience. It is significant not only in helping to carry out and explain an integrated approach to the complex and often ill-defined processes of design, but also in assisting design students to understand the relationship between design ideas, the development of these ideas at the detail scale, and the translation of details into a built reality on-site.

Looking over his shoulder, which was a frequent activity for an entry-level employee at that time, I was able to witness the entire scope of this practitioner's design process at work and to marvel at the ease and clarity with which it seemed to be carried out. Although I later had the opportunity to work with other gifted designers, this initial lesson remains today the clearest exposition of a complete approach to design, simultaneously moving from concept to detail, from detail to landscape, landscape to detail. I also believe it is the single most important aspect of design and the processes of detail form that can be learned from practice.

1

At the beginning of any career in design, there are certain formative moments that stand out as being significant in helping to shape a designer's working methods. Events like these are often overlooked or even completely forgotten because they appear, at first, too small, too humble. Others stay with the individual, growing in importance as the designer's mind and hand develop and mature, and as the engagement with daily professional work becomes ever more complex and intricate.

How landscape details are developed, and what distinguishes the worthy from the inadequate, is important not only to seasoned practitioners and their clients, but also to design students and young professionals at the start of their careers. Details are ultimately judged successful or unsuccessful by designers, based on an understanding of their conceptual ideas, the evolution of their physical forms, how these forms may alter and age, and the meanings attributed to them over time. This is not a matter of personal whim or left to chance; it falls to the designer to make clear, informed detail decisions.

Conceptual ideas in landscape detail derive from a range of sources: artistic innovations, the specifics of a client's program and site, the regulations and codes that govern public built environments and outdoor spaces, and design ideas that support or distinguish cultural values—for example, interpretations of the phenomena of the natural landscape or those of civic identity. To landscape detail is brought immense artistic endeavor, invention, and thought. It is the specific area in which the activity of landscape design is carried out at the human scale.

DETAIL AS AN ELEMENT OF DESIGN?

In the evolution and implementation of landscape architectural projects, the landscape detail has a narrow but significant role—narrow because it concerns the smallest perceived part of the landscape, significant because the project at the human scale is dependent on the execution and durability of a reasoned detail form.

In reviewing the subject of landscape detail through previous writings, publications, and textbooks, the reader can see marked differences in the way the topic has been treated. Landscape detail has been identified either as the practical outcome of some earlier design decision about the site or program, or as the embellishments of outdoor space. In his textbook on landscape detail, *Site Design and Construction Detailing*, revised in 1992, Theodore Walker begins by stating:

> It is assumed that the reader is familiar with the basic principles of design and these will not be discussed.

While this notion is echoed in a number of other standard landscape construction textbooks, he clearly suggests that the subject of landscape detail and the processes of detail design are to be considered separately from the activities of landscape design.

Other authors and designers see detail as design elements that embellish public or private outdoor spaces. This is particularly true of those who work in urban landscape design and urban planning. Landscape details are often likened to minor accessories, features, or furniture added to the structure of parks, plazas, and streets, which play a role in their success or failure as social spaces. Allan Jacobs, in *Great Streets* (1993), writing about the form, spatial character, and expression of public streets throughout the world, notes:

> Details contribute mightily to the best streets: gates, fountains, benches, kiosks, paving, lights, signs, and canopies can all be important, at times crucially so. At the same time, some contribute less than might be thought. The most important of them deserves special attention.

He then describes what he considers some that might merit attention — streetlights, paving and paving patterns, benches, small fountains, signs and awnings — but concludes:

> Alone, great fountains, or gates, or paving, or lights are not enough. Details are the special seasonings of a great street.

Landscape details, having been identified as "special seasonings," are not considered during the initial design phases. In the formation, creation, and shaping of outdoor space, they are considered elements in the menu of "ingredients" to be added according to the individual taste of the designer or their availability or "strength." This concept thus excludes the possibility that the ordinary elements of the street — the curbs, road surfaces, ramp transitions, and boundary walls — the details considered not special, have any value in this regard. Such separation is symptomatic of the continuing perception of landscape detail as the final part of the design process, which, as such, can be added and taken away at will.

In *Site Planning* by Kevin Lynch (1986), detail is also seen as the minutiae of the larger landscape, the "furniture" of exterior spaces, in which he includes the following additional elements:

> Seats, traffic signals, signs, utility poles, light poles, meters, trash cans, fireplugs, manholes, wires, lights, plant containers, alarms, newsstands ...

This listing of elements—man-made artifacts in an urban landscape— emphasizes the multitude of site details that

> affects the appearance of the whole, and if it accumulates without design, as it usually does, it can create a sense of clutter.

He continues, pointing out that there is a need both to organize and plan the many separate detail parts and to establish which are significant, which are not, and more important, which details the designer has control over. Absent from this list are, again, the ordinary detail elements of sidewalks and paved surfaces. However, Lynch makes three useful general observations in regard to how details may actually be advanced and created:

> Details require an investment of design and supervision if they are to be finely shaped, and the effect for the user should justify that investment. Most details are normally left to the customary operations of many separate agencies. This may be successful where there is a strong tradition or when the particular detail is not crucial. The designer focuses on the details critical for the perception and use of the site.

An alternative view to those outlined by Walker, Jacobs, and Lynch will be presented here. Although it will be concerned with the "perception and use" of landscape detail, it sees the process of developing details as integral with, and part of, the design process. Landscape detail is a design activity, not an afterthought or embellishment.

Two issues are central to this viewpoint of landscape design and detail. First, the "art" in the title *The Art of Landscape Detail* lies in the evolution of landscape detail and the design processes involved in that evolution, as much as in the end result. Second, the underlying motivations in landscape detail are aesthetic, concerned with the resolution of design ideas at the detail scale. In short, we cannot design well if the way detail is conceived is not considered an active part of how we envision, organize, and achieve the original aesthetic intentions of any landscape design proposal.

Working from the detail or the particular toward the general reverses the traditional way in which the landscape design process is normally taught and carried out. The relationship between part and whole, the fragment and the completed work, the detail and the landscape, therefore, becomes more significant in the landscape architect's creative processes.

THE READER

To date, scant attention has been given to this issue in the training and education of designers, so that students have little opportunity of understanding, let alone mastering, the subject prior to entering design offices. For the student of landscape architecture or the young practitioner who has just left design school, it is a daunting task to tackle a subject that has a deeply demanding practical side and yet is based on a knowledge and expertise built up over a lifetime of design work and site experience.

For student readers approaching the subject for the first time, this book offers an introduction to the aesthetic concerns, language, and expression of landscape detail as a way of understanding exemplary past and present landscape design work, as well as a source of design ideas for their own design studio work. Young designers who may already be familiar with the activity of detail design through working in a design office will be able to broaden their knowledge and understanding of the vocabulary and detail language of landscape architecture and to reevaluate their own built work and the work of others. Finally, educators will be supported in their coursework and teaching through establishing connections between landscape detail and the processes of design and rectifying the poverty of generic landscape detail currently found within design literature and instruction.

Here, the areas of concern in landscape detail are introduced, an explanation of the general practices and techniques of the landscape detail process is outlined, and case studies of designers and their built landscapes illustrate the application of these practices within the constraints of the professional office. The case studies have been selected to demonstrate how landscape detail relates to the broader conception of design theory, particularly in the design of the contemporary built environment. The course of study has three distinct bearings:

- It sets out to demonstrate *the significance of landscape detail* in the built landscape.
  This is accomplished through an introduction to the elements, language, and expression of landscape detail form, tracing the scope of their influence in the making of the built environment today. Why details work or do not work, and what ultimately makes them right or wrong for a particular landscape condition, are examined.

- It introduces and describes *how details have been achieved* within the current design and site implementation practices of landscape architecture.
  Detail design and detail processes are presented through built examples and case studies of exemplary practice within a range of open space types: the public park, the corporate plaza, the civic memorial, the water edge promenade, and the urban square.

- Finally, it *advocates for new research into landscape detail design* to be carried out within the changing world of design practice.

Together, these three directions of study establish an overview of the circumstances in which detail and detail design were implemented in the past, describes the detail issues and concerns of the present, and speculates about the forms of detail design practice that may emerge in the future.

STRUCTURE OF THIS BOOK

The book begins with the *fundamentals* of landscape, continues with a series of detail *practices* that are encountered in their use, and concludes with *case studies,* aspects of detail design. These illustrate the issues and problems of carrying out landscape detail design within professional, economic, and site constraints. General approaches are linked by particular facts to their application in practice; these approaches are then discussed. The book is divided into three parts:

- **Part One, Fundamentals** (Chapters 1 through 3).
  Introduces the background, scope, approaches, and themes present in landscape detail practices. Summary remarks and issues arising during the detail design processes are included for student readers at the end of Chapter 3.

- **Part Two, Practices** (Chapters 4 through 6).
  Reviews and demonstrates the issues, opportunities, and problems of detail practices in a range of conditions. These include the vocabulary and language of detail making and craft of realizing a design idea in built form, the issues of climate and weathering, the researching of landscape details through case studies, and the use of detail precedents in landscape design. A summary suggests possibilities for future detail work and study.

- **Part Three, Case Studies** (Chapter 7 and Postscript).
  Presents an overview of current and emerging topics to be considered in landscape detail, through discussions with contemporary designers and detail design case studies in exemplary landscape projects taken from their professional design offices. A postscript provides concluding remarks on the interrelationship of built landscapes, design ideas, and the medium of landscape architectural detail.

METHOD OF STUDY

Parts One and Two, with individual Chapters 1 through 6, constitute a sequential method of approaching and studying the subject of landscape detail design. At the same time, they can be read as individual essays on various landscape detail topics. Conceived as short lessons, they start with a discussion of the main points, then continue with examples, supporting information, and an explanation of the issues related to design and practice. The general topics covered in each chapter are listed at the beginning, with a short summary of the chapter's intent and scope. At the end of each chapter is a list of definitions of key words and terms. A series of classroom exercises are included to allow instructors to formulate individual assignments related to the chapters and to tailor them for local and regional variations. A short list of references for further reading and study are provided for readers who want to continue to explore a specific topic. Together, the chapters build into a group of short introductory essays concerning aspects of design relevant to the subject of landscape detail, followed by illustrated landscape detail case studies. These can form the basis for custom-designed lectures, seminars, or workshop presentations. Further background reading and information on each designer and case study can be found in the appendix.

CASE STUDIES

The case studies, which form Part Three, are the core segment of this book. The current poverty of information or illustration of landscape projects as living, dynamic processes of design, with the accompanying dead-ends, backtracking, leaps of imagination, and periods of absolute dark desperation, has meant that there are few available sources of drawn and written material on detail design from which to draw. There are, however, many designers who have been able to talk very clearly about this area of their design work. The discussions with the designers were specifically held for this book and have not appeared in print before. Any existing drawn and written information on their projects is currently maintained in the private records, files, and archives of design offices, individual designers, or public planning and design agencies. Many sets of initial sketches, working drawings, specifications, progress prints, glass plate and slide photographs, and correspondence files are either already lost or destroyed or are located in basements and locked storerooms, where they continue to grow more fragile. Exceptions are those documents and personal papers presented to universities or foundations as scholarly archival material, for example, Thomas Church's and Garrett Eckbo's papers at the University of Berkeley, California, A. D. Taylor's at the University of Illinois at Champaign-Urbana, and Lawrence Halprin's at the University of Pennsylvania, Philadelphia. Microfiche and computer storage have replaced or recorded the documentation of only the most recent project work. It should be noted that in 1997 the archives of Frederick Law Olmsted and the subsequent Olmsted offices located at the Olmsted National Historic Site in Brookline, Massachusetts, one of the most significant collections in landscape architecture, still contains 50,000 individual pieces yet to be cataloged and archived. Olmsted Job #120 Standard Details has not been conserved and is not available for research access. Acknowledging the enormous effort already undertaken by the National Park Service and by archivist and librarian Linda Genovese in cataloging the collection to date, we can appreciate the enormous task ahead when considering less well known but worthy practices and practitioners throughout the country.

The case studies are presented as the first of what is intended to be a growing library of illustrative material that explores the making of landscapes rather than simply presenting photographic documentation of completed built design work. As a course of study, it is intended that this will lead to the development of a more vital and creative approach to landscape detail and one that will ultimately encourage and support students, educators, and practitioners in the pursuit of more progressive forms of designed landscape space. There can be no claims, however, that the material covered here is comprehensive in scope. The subject is a immense one, covering not only landscape detail, but also the broader areas of landscape technology and design and the changing nature of technology in society. Previous publications and textbooks on the subject are listed in the bibliography at the end of this book. Readers are advised to examine for themselves how the subject has been treated in the past as a way of understanding both its current strengths and shortcomings.

Now let us briefly examine the role that detail plays within the broad area of technology and the influences on landscape architecture that were exerted by the changing relationships of technology to landscape design and detail.

LANDSCAPE TECHNOLOGY, DESIGN, AND DETAIL

The term *technology* is defined as:

> The application of science, especially to industrial or commercial objectives. The entire body of methods and materials used to achieve such objectives.
>
> *The American Heritage Dictionary of the English Language*, 1971

Derived from the Greek *technē*, meaning "art or craft," application of *technology* to the design field is quite recent, starting just after the middle of the nineteenth century. It has been applied to all of the so-called practical arts, including engineering, mechanical design, and site construction. In his essay "The Idea of 'Technology' and Postmodern Pessimism" in *Does Technology Drive History? The Dilemma of Technological Determinism* (1994), Leo Marx outlines the pre-1850 usage of the complementary terms *mechanic arts* and *fine arts*. He states, "The artifacts, the knowledge, and the practices later to be embraced by 'technology' would continue to be thought of as belonging to a special branch of the arts variously known as the 'mechanic' (or 'practical,' 'industrial,' or 'useful') — as distinct from the 'fine' (or 'high,' or 'creative,' or 'imaginative') arts." Therefore, building roads, bridges, and parks belonged to the "mechanic" arts, oil painting and sculpture belonged to the "fine" arts. A plantsman who planned and installed a garden for a client was a mechanic artist; a painter who documented that garden for aesthetic and creative purposes was a fine artist. Marx continues, "Ever since antiquity, moreover, the habit of separating the practical and the fine arts had served to ratify a set of overlapping and invidious distinctions: between things and ideas, the physical and the mental, the mundane and the ideal, female and male, making and thinking, the work of enslaved and of free men." By extending this line of thought to landscape design and implementation, it is clear that landscape architecture had roots in both the "mechanic" arts and the "fine" arts as they were described; in fact, the strength of the field derived, in part, from the combination of both. However, by separating aesthetic or creative concerns from the areas of work concerned with *technology,* that term used to describe the practical and the useful, the landscape discipline was broken into two distinct categories. The first category was closely associated with the creative act of design and the study of design aesthetics. The second was concerned with the forming and implementation of design ideas.

Thus, ideas about landscape design were separated from ideas about making landscapes, in short, forming a disconnection between "making" and "thinking." Does this mean that artistic or aesthetic judgment is solely the province of the designer who conceives the initial idea? In the case made earlier of the garden, the plantsman's skill and work were not considered to have an aesthetic or creative nature in themselves, but only the possible results of the work through another more discerning person's eyes, description, and appreciation. During the course of this book we will return to this question and speculate about the changing relationship between "mechanic arts" and "fine arts" as it is now realized in the practice of landscape architecture, some 150 years later. It is the contention of this book, however, that the mechanic arts and fine arts can be clearly unified through the subject of landscape detail, where the pragmatic concerns of construction and making are linked with the aesthetic concerns of ideas and thinking. There is a clear interrelationship between detail, design, and technology, in which landscape detail links the concerns of the "fine" and "mechanic" arts found in landscape architecture.

One of our main contributions as designers is not the scale at which landscape projects are conceived and executed, or the scope of the work, but, rather, the quality of design thought and precision of design execution that are brought to the detail parts. To this end, we return to the relationship between concept and detail in design and consider them together in the design process as being of equal importance. We will broadly examine the background of landscape detail and design and then explore detail practices that are necessary for students and younger designers to become familiar with, and to work with, in landscape design. It is with these readers in mind that we now introduce the fundamentals of landscape detail.

FUNDAMENTALS

A fundamental inquiry into any aspect of reality is the relationship between the part and the whole, the fragment and the complete, the detail and the invisible unity of a deed, of an object, of a thought.

BIANCA ALBERTINI & SANDRO BAGNOLI,
Carlo Scarpa, Architecture in Detail, 1988

Detail design in landscape architecture results from two factors: first, the need to establish and develop conceptual ideas in landscape design; second, a concern for the issues of making built landscapes. The working processes of design practitioners vary widely in the balance between these two factors; however, it is the presence of both that characterizes the resultant landscape detail form.

The relationship between these two factors is introduced in Chapters 1 to 3 through an overview of the fundamentals of landscape detail. A review of definitions associated with, and given to, landscape detail is followed by examples demonstrating the design purpose and significance of landscape detail in the built environment, and then an examination of how landscape details are achieved within the processes of landscape design.

In Chapter 1, "Landscape and Detail," the relationships between landscape detail and design form the background to a study of the subject of detail. Chapter 2, "Detail Concerns," addresses the wide range of practice and professional issues that influence and direct the detail design process. Chapter 3, "Approaches and Themes," focuses on the detail process itself, with a review of general methods and techniques.

CHAPTER 1

LANDSCAPE AND DETAIL

THIS CHAPTER INTRODUCES the role of landscape detail in the built land-scape. It addresses the issues of quality, aesthetics, creativity, and implementation in landscape detail through an examination of its relationship to the landscape design process. Our concern at the outset is to establish a sensibility toward landscape detail as a significant activity of the designer's work and its central role in the shaping of the final form of any constructed landscape project. The roles and various definitions given to landscape detail in professional practice and design education are addressed. Student readers will gain an introduction to the core subject of landscape detail and the key elements that constitute the focus of a designer's attention.

1. INTRODUCTION

Let us start by considering two questions: what is landscape detail, and what are the many forms it takes in the built landscape? Landscape detail is a process of design. As a major determinant in the final form and expression of built work in landscape architecture, landscape detail is first and foremost a design activity, a way of pursuing ideas about landscape form and space at a particular scale. However, landscape detail has a very particular appeal for designers working in landscape architecture, one that is not fully explained either simply as a means of developing design ideas or by the role it plays in the final representation and implementation of design projects. It is the aesthetic and artistic possibilities that landscape detail presents which, in the end, constitute the most significant consideration for designers. These possibilities include matters of landscape expression and the search for a traditional, as well as a contemporary, landscape detail language.

Landscape detail translates design ideas into a built landscape, establishing the overall scope and character of the parts, how they will be formed and assembled, with which combinations of materials, and how their finished properties are to be established. This activity includes addressing the con-

12

cerns of form, structure, design language and expression, material choice, dimension, and texture, and the demands of implementation, climate, and maintenance. In short, landscape detail establishes scale, articulates space, and both contains and expresses design ideas at the scale of detail resolution.

The relationship between landscape and detail is, therefore, one that is central to design ideas and their evolution, is fundamental to the work of a design office in terms of the evolution and production of built work, and, most important, is a deeply evocative and personal means of design expression for the designer.

Landscape detail results in a wide variety of forms, ranging from those located below the ground, including subsurface drainage and foundations, to those aboveground, including minor structures, pergolas and pavilions, fences, walls, and gates. In addition, landscape detail forms address unique and complex installations, for example, planting over concrete structures or on roof decks and in other special conditions, such as the use of porous granular paving systems for surface drainage, custom-designed lighting, and individual water elements and fountains. The entire range of landscape detail forms would constitute an immense catalog of natural and man-made elements, all parts of which are necessary for the study and practice of landscape design and landscape architecture.

The focus here, however, will be much narrower, concentrating instead on the built landscape details of social spaces—including parks, squares, and streets—those most closely associated with the detail work of landscape architecture and landscape design in cities, towns, and other communities. Detail forms include horizontal paved surfaces, steps, ramps, walls, and overhead structures. Although a majority of the built landscapes we will examine are the result of private resources, for example, those created by business corporations and commercial institutions, the audience for and users of the external landscape spaces in this book are public. The use of these spaces is therefore as open and democratic as possible. They are for the convenience and delight of diverse groups of people of all ages and backgrounds, and the landscapes support both individual and collective activities. Our emphasis here is on this type of designed space and the forms of landscape detail that provide for the larger, diverse, and, ultimately, more demanding user groups. We will find detail inspiration in the built landscapes of streets, lanes, alleyways, parks, cemeteries, ball fields and recreation areas, shopping centers, schoolyards, public waterfronts, and stairways.

Designers today have to learn an immense quantity of information about the changing methods of landscape installation, landscape materials and their qualities, and the regulations and codes covering the issues of public health and safety. In the process, a large body of detail expertise has vanished unnoticed. What has gone is considerable, but unquantifiable: how to shape

13

landscape details and make them significant in a landscape, how to do specific details (for example, simple surfaces), how to reveal joints and edges and make them meaningful, how to carry out detail transitions on-site (for example, turning corners). In short, there is a lack of knowledge about how to create a group of landscape details that are singular and identifiable within a built landscape, but are also able to support a larger collective design idea.

From older landscapes we receive immense satisfaction, a sense of continuity over time between the completed built landscape and the detail parts. In regard to built landscapes constructed in the last 25 years, many of which fail to pass on that sense of continuity, this seems like an unobtainable goal. For the designer or design student preparing to enter the field, this may cause a certain amount of anxiety. What will be the role of landscape detail in the future? Will opportunities exist for the designer in the future to develop ideas to a detail scale, and how will the design expression at the detail scale, be made visible?

Let us start to examine these questions and the large body of detail expertise by first describing an example of an older landscape, a set of public stairs built in the last century, and then go on to look more carefully and critically at the detail issues and ideas that are found to be at work there.

The Montmartre Steps: A Description

We start by identifying and describing the detail parts that comprise a particular landscape. The image on the front cover of this book and in Figure 1.1 illustrate the context in which this urban landscape is found.

The black and white print on the cover entitled "The Steps of Montmartre," taken by the photographer Brassaï in 1936, documents a public stairway located between Rue Azais and the Place Suzanne-Valadon in the Montmartre district of Paris. In the photograph a sequence of landscape detail elements can be seen: flights of well-worn stone steps (266 in all) recording the passage of feet continuously moving up and down, generous landings formed in a small-patterned block, inserted at 45 degrees and framed by stone bands, and a well-rubbed metal handrail placed in the center of the steps to direct movement and provide much needed support on the long ascent and descent. The handrail is connected to vertical gas mantle poles, which give discrete pools of light on the landings where people stop to rest. The gradient is marked by sloped sides formed with Belgian block (which shows rough patching and filling, a sign of recent repairs) and two rows of aligned and matched mature canopy trees. The steps on one side abut sheer vertical stone tenement walls, and the entire scene is rendered in the photograph as one that is robust, plain, and gritty and yet displays an elegant spareness and beauty through the clarity of the landscape detail forms. It demonstrates this through what we will call "the art of landscape detail."

Figure 1.1
The Steps of Montmartre,
Paris. View from Place
Suzanne-Valadon.

The photograph depicts a built landscape of striking physical and spatial qualities, made up of simple parts put together with attention to the issues of detail scale and a visual, tactile, and material richness. Detailed with *precision*, *scaled* appropriately (but including an extraordinary detail transition), and powerfully *executed*, it contains these haunting and luminous qualities for us still, through the photographer's art. It should be pointed out that the landscape contains these detail qualities not because it is old or was thought to have been a worthy subject for this particular photographer but, rather, because it exemplifies a built landscape that has transcended the ordinary through the nature of its landscape detail forms. Elements and materials were assembled, formed, and shaped in the most direct of ways. Here a commonplace detail language was pursued instead of the idiosyncratic, both as a design response rooted to a place and as a pragmatic solution to use and climate.

The stairway is little changed today from Brassaï's time. It is remarkably intact as a built landscape, although all the trees have been replaced over time and the stonework repatched. The stairway is still in daily use by residents taking children to the local school at the foot of the steps, or tourists scorning the adjacent modern funicular to climb to the cathedral located on the top of the hill.

The art of landscape detail has the ability today to encompass the conception, articulation, and implementation of built landscape spaces such as this, and to articulate and develop similar qualities that are found there: those of *detail precision* and *detail scaling*, and those arising from the matters of *detail execution*.

It is not a question, however, of simply copying or blindly lifting exemplary detail forms of the past to use in current work. Even if it were physically and technically possible, with the use of traditional tools, labor, and materials, it would serve little purpose. The detail forms of the Montmartre Steps illustrated in Figure 1.2 were developed for this particular place and altered over time only to address specific concerns arising from the site, for example, context, form, function, expression, weathering, durability, and maintenance.

Figure 1.2
Handrail and step detail
form, Montmartre Steps,
Paris

16

It is not important whether the details of the Montmartre Steps are right or wrong, appropriate or inappropriate, good or bad (however that could be judged). What is ultimately of more interest to the designer today is what is possible in a design situation such as this and what can be *learned* from this particular group of detail forms and their expression.

Why were certain details selected and others not? What is the relationship between those details and the completed landscape as a whole? Given the wide range of design choices that accompany a built work of this type, a simple flight of steps, what is to be considered by the designer during detail design? Finally, what aspects of detail form are to be given significance during the detail development process and in the implementation period?

No information is available today about the intentions of the original "designer" of the Montmartre Steps, however loosely the term *designer* is used, whether it was an engineer, architect, contractor, or city official. In addition, there is no information available describing the conditions under which the project was carried out, or the subsequent alterations and repairs to it over time. This is typical of the many ordinary and extraordinary public landscapes that are encountered on a daily basis, and which remain unstudied and therefore little understood.

Detail qualities result from the properties or detail characteristics that distinguish one particular built landscape space from another and how they have been developed for that particular place through detail design.

It is often easier to recognize in a built landscape the absence of particular detail qualities than to recognize their presence or to describe the development of detail qualities used in an ongoing piece of design work. There are many people, both trained in design and untrained, who are able to make such judgments, including residents of dysfunctional parks, streets, and neighborhoods; city and municipal authorities; design critics; and journalists.

The design qualities of the Montmartre Steps derive from the simplicity, visual richness, and expression of the built landscape detail. Let us briefly review the detail qualities of this landscape from the three points of view identified previously and examine how they contribute to the physical and spatial detail qualities present in the space. These are the nature of *detail precision*, the appropriate *detail scale* of the space, and the concerns of *detail execution*.

Detail Precision

Here, precision in landscape detail does not concern the accuracy of site installation practices with guidelines for the use of materials and rules for tolerances, joints, and cutting dimensions. Rather, it is concerned with the precise expression of the conditions of the site context and the specific requirements of this external set of steps. The alignment of ascent and descent is straight, the shortest way from top to bottom of the slope and back again. It is a repetitive order calculated over its entire length, a rhythm of steps, risers, and landings. The sequence of railings and vertical lamp poles, the geometry of paired and matched canopy trees—all reinforce this order. It is a landscape structure derived from the detail parts, with each element separate but at the same time contributing to and supporting an overall built form.

This "structure" organizes the spatial order while establishing the location, placement, and hierarchy of the detail parts. It is composed *in response* to the change of grade as well as forming a *measure* of that original change (the order of the number of steps in each flight of stairs and the number of flights of stairs and landings in the overall rise). In this lies the detail response to the function of the place and the qualities of detail precision that result from it.

Detail Scale

The detail resolutions of handrails, steps, and lamp poles are sized to the pedestrian scale. Railings break at landings to allow the cross-over and circulation of foot traffic between the individual flights. The steps are centered in the space but extend only partially across the width of the passageway. A detail transition connects the steps to the edge of the space through exaggerated and overscaled stairway cheeks and curb edges. The series of steeply tilted stone planes modulate, bend, and flatten as the stairway moves up and down. The surfaces are populated and marked by the two rows of paired and matched canopy trees set into canted circular openings in the stones. The extension of the step edge therefore becomes the single detail moment that turns an ordinary landscape detail into an extraordinary detail transition.

Detail Execution

Execution is defined here as the design methods by which landscape detail forms can be made on-site, and which are initially considered and developed during the early conceptual stages of detail design. The Montmartre Steps can be thought of as resulting from two forms of detail execution, one a construction achieved through sculpting the plastic and malleable material of the ground surface and its slope, the other, a more mechanical approach that assembles, on the slope, a series of smaller modular stone elements.

In the first instance, the original ground surface, which was bare eroded earth or sparsely planted, is uncovered as bedrock and viewed as an overlay of a thick stone placed on the ground surface, into which a set of treads, risers, and landings are cut. To either side of these cut steps the stone lies unworked, and set into this angled surface are a double file of trees. Manufactured metal light and railing fixtures are attached to the newly worked ground surface. The second form of detail execution is a combination of separate detail pieces—cubes and cut blocks of stone, lengths of metal bars, posts, cast metal lamp bases—all brought to the site and fitted together in a structural order.

Conceived initially as a passageway with the use of an elongated solid riser and tread over the full width, the stairway is, however, restricted in its width. The rest of the stairway width is stretched to the face of the walls on both sides as an extended and articulated curb edge. This results from the requirements of ascending and descending a steep incline, which include the need to use, or to be close by, a railing for safety and comfort, the economy of a centrally located post, rail, and lights determining two small lanes of travel, up and down, with crossings at landings, and the ability to handle transitions at the edges to a variety of conditions: walls, other steps, and landings.

Is this built landscape made out of a large mass of sculpted material, or is it made up of a series of individual parts brought together and assembled on-site? The answer is that both views are correct. During the early stages of detail design these are simply ways to visualize how landscape detail forms are to be established and how they will eventually be realized on-site.

Summary of Detail Qualities

The value for landscape design in beginning to study landscape detail is based on the belief that one of our main contributions as designers is not the scale at which landscape projects are conceived and built, or the scope of the work, but rather the quality of design thought and the precision, scale, and concerns of execution that are brought to the detail parts.

The Montmartre Steps are realized as a work of landscape architecture through the use of spare and economical landscape details, using commonly recognizable materials. They consist of a series of undistinguished detail elements made remarkable through their particular combination and repetition. The requirements of program and site are combined with aesthetic and design considerations to form an austere yet sensuously articulated built landscape. Although most of the landscape detail design effort concentrates on the serial form of the rise and fall of steps, the landscape detail that most closely identifies the Montmartre Steps is the tilted curb edge. Imagine how different the form and appearance of the space would be if the steps extended the full width of the passageway, with two or three intermediate handrails placed in parallel. Imagine again, if the steps were placed to one side or the other, with or without canopy trees, how the nature of the space would be altered. At the Montmartre Steps one of the ordinary detail parts, the elongated curb, is elevated to make something that is quite out of the ordinary. Thus, it establishes the detail character of the stairway, which, in turn, identifies this particular place.

Figure 1.3
Bunker Hill steps, 1992,
Los Angeles. Designer:
Lawrence Halprin.
Courtesy of Hanna/Olin
Ltd.

Other Steps and Forms of Landscape Detail

The Bunker Hill Steps in Los Angeles by landscape architect Lawrence Halprin (Figure 1.3), completed in 1992 at a cost of $12 million, illustrates a more contemporary form of the public stairway. The tree-lined stairway connects the financial core, including the Central Library, to a new business district at the top of Bunker Hill. It is made up of scalloped flights of poured concrete steps, landings, and side walls, with a centrally located raised water runnel fed from an upper pool. In this case, however, the steps, landings, and other elements present up and down its length, as well as the accompanying railings and artwork, are entirely different in their detail nature, layout, material use, and detail expression from those of the Montmartre Steps. They present a quite different set of physical and spatial detail qualities. In response to the issues of *detail precision*, the appropriate *detail scale* of the space, and the concerns of *detail execution*, they diverge from the Montmartre Steps in the use of a more personalized and idiosyncratic detail language. This language derives from combinations of themes and motifs from the natural (rock-lined water channels) and the classical (inflected symmetrical flights of steps), all derived from sources beyond the immediate context of the site.

The study of past examples of built landscapes results in an understanding of detail precedents, material selection, and installation practices. To alter the built environment through ordinary landscape detail design, while acknowledging that certain occasions call for the detail level to be sharply intensified, should be a goal of the designer.

In describing the landscape of the Montmartre Steps, the landscape details were considered as a clear and identifiable part of the total built work. They were the design intent of the stairway at the detail scale, the sum of the ideas contained within the detail forms. But was there a clear understanding of what landscape detail is? There was a recognition of what constituted the landscape detail of the stairway, the intent and process of resolving design ideas at detail scale, and the resultant detail forms of, for example, step and handrail. However, this may not be perceived by everyone outside the field of landscape architecture, let alone those within. Do those who are designers view landscape detail differently from those who commission, implement, or maintain built landscapes? Do individual types of landscape design work, whether new projects or the preservation of existing landscapes, involve landscape detail in a different sense?

The way in which the term *detail* is often applied in landscape design and the various meanings of the word itself have created a misunderstanding of the role of landscape detail in landscape design. Let us now examine the term *landscape detail* itself and the various and sometimes contradictory meanings currently attached to it.

The Term *Landscape Detail*

The use of the term *landscape detail* occurs in a variety of ways within landscape architecture, and it carries with it a range of uses and definitions. These fall into one of two general groups: *landscape implementation details* or *landscape design details.*

Landscape implementation detail. This term identifies construction practices of built landscapes realized at a detail scale and the documentation of landscape materials, assemblies, and their subsequent performance on-site. It covers a range of terms frequently used in design offices, including *construction details, working drawing details,* and *site details.* These communicate how a particular detail part is to be realized on-site and establishes in words, sketches, and technical drawings the materials and the degree of skill and workmanship that are required during execution. Although replacement of traditional drafting methods by computer aided design, storage, and display techniques is increasingly becoming the norm, the use of *landscape detail* files persists in the new digital medium.

Landscape design detail. The second definition of *landscape detail* is concerned with design ideas and the detail themes, moods, and motifs that are established during the development and evolution of landscape proposals as part of the process of landscape design. Landscape design details can form part of a more expansive design concept or may emerge during the initial evolution of that design concept. In addition, *they may also constitute the design concept itself,* and its resolution as a specific detail type or condition: such as a step, wall, or handrail. They are established graphically and spatially in the process of cutting site sections or developing site plans at a 1 to 5 scale or larger. A designer can also produce freehand design details as entries in a sketchbook or on yellow trace, much earlier in the process as part of a pattern of working in detail.

In this book the production of landscape detail through the design process is considered one of the most deeply creative practices that a landscape architect undertakes and an artform of the highest order. For the rest of this book the use of the terms *detail, landscape detail,* and *detail process* will refer to the second definition "landscape design detail," or design practices at a detail scale. In addition, the term *designer* will refer to those involved in the design and development of built landscapes. These are people trained and licensed as landscape architects, but they may also be site artists, site architects, or other design professionals.

The major focus here will be on the *processes* that enable conceptual landscape design ideas to evolve and mature. These processes will be examined to present a broader understanding of detail design and the actions of articulating detail ideas through a vocabulary of built detail form.

Finding the Starting Point

What is landscape detail design, and why should it be considered an art? Landscape detail design is the process that gives form and expression to the ideas of landscape architecture. The art of this process, which is considerable, arises from the ability of landscape detail to be both an individual entity and also part of a collective built form and design concept.

The work of Frederick Law Olmsted and Calvert Vaux in the creation of Central Park, New York, demonstrates one aspect of this art form through an attention to the scale, materials, craft, and the quality of detailed design present in the United States during the second half of the nineteenth century. In Figure 1.4 one of the transverse road bridge structures that separate pedestrian and vehicular circulation establishes an individual detail condition, as well as forming part of a larger detail language throughout the park. A minor element in relation to the scale of the whole park, it is given as much consideration as larger, more visible and public parts, such as the Bethesda Terrace and Fountain, with its ornate and highly textured balustrades, parapets, and basin. However, examples of less well known but as considered landscape architectural elements exist throughout the country that illustrate landscape detail as part of an individual and collective form.

Figure 1.5 illustrates such a landscape architectural element in a paved stone ramp found in the environment of an open-air fruit and flower market. Here local designers and builders directed and shaped the construction of their particular environments, whether market squares, parks, or streets, with a true regard for function, form, materials and the need to build for future generations of use.

Figure 1.4
Transverse road bridge, Central Park, New York, 1858. Olmsted and Vaux.

Figure 1.5
Detail in local environment, ramped paved surface.

The everyday use of landscape detail form as part of the landscape architect's working process is, however, often misconstrued. It is often viewed as the final resolution of landscape elements, carried out within the project drawings and implementation phases of landscape architectural work.

A thick folder of photocopies or blueprints of standard drawings, sketches, and technical information found near the drafting board are the most common images of landscape detail and the detail process in design offices.

One of the first tasks likely to be given to a young designer entering a professional landscape office is to assist in the preparation of project drawings. These tasks may vary as to where they occur in the design process or in the overall scope of work. The drawings represent and develop initial landscape concepts through to their final detail form and implementation. This sequence starts with an existing group of rough freehand sketches that outline the basic parts and relationships of a project in plan, section, or perspective. Figure 1.6 illustrates a typical group of such early sketches from the notebooks of landscape architect Mario Schejtnan. The sketches are then taken from this evocative, though loosely defined and unscaled, state through a detail process that

Figure 1.6
Freehand landscape design sketch by Mario Schjetnan, Landscape Architect. Courtesy of Mario Schjetnan.

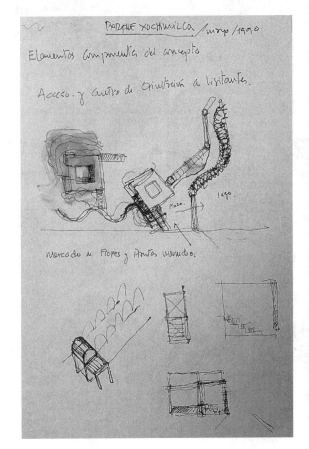

24

refines their general form and appearance into a constructional language and then establishes and controls the specifics of their final expression, assembly, and implementation. This is known within the design process as either the *schematic and design development* or the *detail design* phase of a project.

As the newest and least experienced member of a professional office, the entry-level designer is likely to be ill-prepared to carry out this task. Any previous training or preparation in this area of landscape design and landscape technology will probably have been extremely restricted in scope and depth. Landscape design studios, because of their limited time frame and teaching focus, are rarely able to cover the development of sketch design proposals beyond preliminary drawings and models for "final presentation" in studio. As described in the preface to this book, courses in landscape technology only survey basic construction materials and standard construction solutions for landscape site features, and provide an introduction to documentation and site implementation procedures.

Another sequence of design thinking, with the resultant documentation of drawings and sketches, is required to take place between the production of sketch design ideas, as exemplified by the design studio, and a completed built project. This is the evolution of a detail language. This activity is termed *landscape detail design* or the process of *landscape detail.*

In taking our first steps toward creative yet usable and sensibly built landscape details, let us attempt to define *landscape detail design* more closely, starting with the role of landscape detail as an art form.

Landscape Detail As an Art Form

The art of landscape detail is found partly in the generation of innovative forms from existing landscape detail forms and partly in their evolution into a contemporary built language.

The role of detail has a long and rich tradition in the fine and applied arts. Landscape detail is quite distinct from the detail practices found in the fine arts (for example, sculpture or painting) or the applied arts (for example, furniture, ceramics, or industrial design). Landscape detail derives its strength and character from a reconfiguring of the form and expression of *existing types* of landscape detail found in the built environment and the redefinition of their individual and collective functions and meanings.

Landscape detail shares with other fields of applied design — for example, architecture, interior architecture, furniture design, textile and industrial design — a requirement to be an evolutionary rather than a revolutionary process.

In furniture design, for example, in the design of a chair, a clear connection is made between its general purpose for sitting, which has changed little over time, and the need for the structure to give human support, the selection of materials, which is now more open for experimentation, and the detail design process. The fabrication and assembly of the individual parts, the joints and fixings, and the final built object all result from a series of detail decisions made early on in the design of the chair. Its final form, profile, and sculptural shape are a result of detail decisions made during the process and are related to issues of precedent, scale, dimension, fabrication, production, economics, and the accompanying search for a designer's personal design expression and a compatible language of built form.

In the case of a chair and other objects at that scale, all design decisions are detail decisions.

Landscape detail is often viewed as an extension of the detail practices of architecture. This is the case when the particular landscape design concepts evolve as an extension of architectural principles, such as a structural column grid, entry axis, or sequence to and from a building. Edward Allen, in *Architectural Detailing: Function, Constructibility, Aesthetics,*[1] identifies the concept of detail "patterns" in connection with architectural detail.

> Detail patterns are elemental fragments that are present in all successful building details. They represent an accumulation of centuries of wisdom about what works in building construction and what doesn't. Many of the patterns are firmly grounded in scientific fact. Others are based just as solidly on common sense and the realities of human performance. The experienced architect employs all of these patterns automatically, as if by instinct, when designing details.

Although this statement has some relevance to landscape detail, particularly regarding the sources and application of detail patterns, there are clear differences in the purpose and types of landscape detail. The most obvious is that landscape details are predominantly located outdoors, or where the conditions of climatic change (sometimes extreme) are present on a daily and seasonal basis. The actions of sun, wind, rain, humidity, and ice alter external landscape details, affecting the way they are initially conceived. The scale and size of built landscapes are also factors, particularly with the emphasis on the horizontal ground plane and its manipulation and modulations. Finally, in the practice of architecture every part of the building is considered and details are worked out over the total built form. Wall, floor, and ceiling surfaces, details associated with furnishings and fittings, and hardware for doors, windows, lighting fixtures, and utilities are a few of the areas that are the focus of special attention. In landscape architecture attention to detail to this extent is rarely seen or achievable across an entire project. This does not mean that areas are overlooked in a built landscape, simply that this amount of studied attention is rarely necessary to describe and form the detail elements of an overall landscape proposal. There are fewer detail parts, and the repetition of certain key elements means that there are fewer intersections and junctions between different materials and detail forms. With the exception of restoration and conservation work on historic landscapes, the built landscape becomes overfussy and cluttered when detail design is given the same studied attention as found in architecture detail design.

It is wrong, therefore, to directly associate the two types of detail design, landscape architecture detail and architectural detail, as deriving from similar concerns and processes. Within architectural curricula, detail practices are firmly embedded in both technology and design sequences of workshop courses and design studios. In landscape architecture education, the situation is quite different. The topics of landscape detail and detail processes have been considered of minor importance in relation to the primary subjects within a core curriculum, which include design theory, ecology, planning, history, plants, and representation. In order to explore possible ways to expand and develop the influence of landscape detail on design instruction, let us now examine how the subject has traditionally been taught.

2. BACKGROUND TO LEARNING ABOUT LANDSCAPE DETAIL

Landscape Detail Within an Academic Curriculum

Landscape detail is associated most closely with the technology and construction sequences in undergraduate and graduate design schools in landscape architecture. It is also briefly addressed in the related design fields of architecture, urban design, public and land art, and environmental design. It is likely to be encountered by landscape design students in one or more of the following settings:

- *The design studio.* Studio problems that require site sketch design proposals to be developed to a detail scale of resolution. Examples range across all types of sites and programs, including parks, gardens, and other public spaces.

- *Landscape technology or implementation courses.* Lectures, workshops, and assignments review and develop individual detail solutions or carry out the production of sets of detail drawings and specifications.

- *History and design theory.* Examples of past and contemporary landscape design work and practitioners are illustrated through their design projects, that include built detail forms.

- *Professional practice.* The topics of implementation documentation, drawings and specifications, professional liability, site observation, postimplementation evaluation, and state licensing examinations address detail practices and their contractual, legal, and professional implications.

There are further opportunities within the landscape curriculum to observe or study landscape detail. These occur during field visits as part of design studio, landscape technology, or implementation courses, or during summer internships.

- *Field visits.* Observation of landscape sites and the implementation of site-work elements include the viewing of test panels or mock-ups on-site, as well as visits to material sources provided either through extraction and processing procedures (for example, quarries, sand and gravel pits, lumber yards) or manufacturing plants (including brick and precast concrete factories).

- *Summer office internships.* An internship can include the copying, or preparation and execution of, design development and working drawings, as well as researching technical literature, detail products, materials, and companies.

Although "landscape technology" includes subjects like grading, drainage, materials, structural mechanics, construction and site practices, and working drawings, landscape detail is more commonly found in the documentation and implementation areas, those dealing with the completion and execution of a design project, for example:

- Site engineering systems and structures

- Site materials and elements

- Preparation of working drawings

- Introduction to specification writing

- Introduction to cost estimation

- Site techniques and practices

- Site project management and organization

Landscape detail within the technology sections of a landscape curriculum is viewed here as part of the implementation and execution of a built landscape.

Let us review again more closely *studio design,* the area of instruction in which landscape detail and detail form have potential to play a more significant role in landscape design.

Studio Design: Detail and Design

Rarely does the landscape detail process occur in a design project within the setting of a design studio, unless as an afterthought. Yet this appears to be at odds with the idea that the process of landscape detail is a design activity. The requirement for the preparation and illustration of "two typical site details" usually means a rushed effort during the last few hours before a project is due. Its purpose, of course, is to convey the idea that site planning and landscape design concepts will, if given the time not usually available within a studio, be developed to the smallest of parts. Landscape design is viewed as starting with a range of strong conceptual ideas and site planning and spatial organizational strategies and eventually arriving at the detail forms. Landscape details are typically adapted or copied straight out of the standard textbooks and bear little relationship to the initial conceptual design, the given site and its context, or the individual program and design elements at hand. Landscape detail as described here is less part of a process of evolved design thinking, but more a search for generic detail solutions that can be quickly modified and applied.

There are, however, specific types of studios whose primary objectives are concerned with working initially at the detail scale. Two examples of this type are those associated with a *site furniture project* or a *design/build project.* In a site furniture project, the site furnishings (movable or fixed) and built elements (kiosks, seats and benches, fountains, gateways, temporary tent structures) constitute the main design focus of a small outdoor private or public space. A design/build project includes the design, documentation, and subsequent implementation of a landscape project as shown in Figure 1.7, in which students, faculty, and community interests are interconnected with the resolution on site of detail site problems and working methods.[2]

The design/build project also allows the possibility of examining earlier detail decisions made in the studio as to the ease or difficulty of resolving detail conditions on-site. This is irrespective of any skill required by the students in handling tools, materials, or assembling detail elements.

Figure 1.7
Design/build project,
Department of Landscape
Architecture, University of
Washington University.
Courtesy of Daniel
Winterbottom.

29

We must now turn our attention back to the term *detail* itself, to understand its many interpretations within the context of landscape design, its relationship to the design process, and how it is to be addressed in the rest of this book.

3. CLASSIFICATIONS AND DESCRIPTIONS

The Range of Definitions of *Landscape Detail*

Landscape detail has a number of parallel and sometimes contradictory meanings within landscape architecture and the design and manufacturing fields. No single definition can therefore be agreed upon by the various parties who use it.

Advice from Manufacturers

Consider these three fragments taken from advertisements for landscape products found in the back pages of *Landscape Architecture* magazine:

- "Add character, *detail* and cohesiveness to any design project."

- "Installation under turf. Please copy this *detail* to your plans."

- "*Details:* Design, Engineering, Tooling, Manufacturing, Finishing and Assembly. 10,000 installations in a decade."

As these fragments of advertising illustrate, the term *landscape detail* can comprise a wide group of meanings and descriptions. First, detail is considered to be an attribute that is added to a project. Next it is considered to be a drawing that contains pertinent technical information. Finally, it is part of a process, in this case, the making and assembly of a component part—a lighting fixture.

Advice from Designers

What does the term *landscape detail* mean as you currently understand it? This question was posed by the author to groups of landscape design students who were starting to study landscape technology and detail design.[3] There was little to distinguish their answers from those of the manufacturers' advertising copy. Examples include the following:

- "A seventies style *drawing,* of a bench or curb at a scale close to full size."

- "Some small *special point* in the landscape."

- "How a specific joint or connection is *built.*"

- "*Design* at the microscale."

Combining interpretations of the term from these two sources, a range of potential definitions can be established. Any of these descriptions can serve as a starting point in understanding the range of meanings given to *detail* or describe the extent of the categories that fall under the subject. These are summarized in the following list:

1. *Landscape detail as a drawing.* Identifies the broad category of individual and enlarged drawings that, together with plans and sections, form a set of working drawings. They are usually combinations of the conventions of cross section and plan that describe minutely a particular part of a built landscape or provide specific information at key points throughout the site implementation process.

   A group of such drawings associated with a design project is referred to as "the details," "the detail sheets," or the "construction details." As noted earlier, with the rise of computer drafting the techniques of representing and working with this information has changed, but the basic terminology has not.

2. *Landscape detail as an instruction.* Specific instructions provided with a drawing; dimensions, notes, and/or written specifications. They are also the means by which design ideas are transmitted to builders to carry out a design intent.

3. *Landscape detail as a singular part of a design.* A common assignation in describing a usually less significant or diminutive part of a whole. The issue of size is relative; a detail of a larger site or region may represent hundreds of acres. This term is, however, usually referred to within a smaller or more closely defined site or project area. An example is a gateway entrance to a public park, including boundary elements, paving surfaces, signage forms, and lighting details.

4. *Landscape detail as an artifact.* Parts of the built landscape that are clearly identifiable as discrete objects. For example, a curb, bollard, or any manufactured object can be referred to as the detail or site detail.

5. *Landscape detail as a term for ornamentation.* This term is more commonly used in reference to illustrative or applied decoration, ornament, or trim that is more typically seen in mass-produced clothing or architectural embellishments. Its roots derive from the French *de,* meaning "apart" and the verb *taillier,* meaning "to cut." It was more commonly used in the nineteenth century to describe applied decoration used to break down the monumentality of the mass and scale of vertical wall surfaces. Here again detail is considered to be an accessory that is added or removed from a design.

6. *Landscape detail as an element of site implementation. Construction detail* and *site detail* are common terms used to describe a particular task of site execution or piece of work.

7. *Landscape detail as a process.* The process itself, of developing a landscape design idea or intent, is usually referred to by the verb (to detail), as are all aspects of that process found in a design studio or office. These include drawings, scales of operation, and type and quantity of information. It is also considered a stage in that process where the developed design is worked out, the activity of taking a landscape design down to a detail or "microscale," during which the essence of a design is worked out within a piece of the whole.

Throughout this book we will be primarily using the definition of *landscape detail as a process* as that which is most closely allied to our intent to bring together the practical and the poetic.

4. ASPECTS OF THE DETAIL ART

In notable outdoor spaces in the world—Piazza San Marco, the Tuilleries in Paris, Central Park in New York, the Kyoto Gardens—designers with sketchbooks and cameras have painstakingly recorded the results of a landscape detail process. Many of these detail images in bound sketchbooks or color slides are destined to be pinned above drawing boards in drafting rooms, filed in plastic sleeves, or, more likely, left in unopened vacation sketchbooks on dusty shelves. The use of precedents in detail practices, however, is still a time-honored tradition in the training of a designer. Observation of detail and detail practices is important in recognizing and understanding exemplary detail forms. To conclude this chapter, the physical evidence of several landscape forms are examined. Some are found in historic parks and piazzas, others in more contemporary settings, such as new urban squares and plazas. Certain details can be traced to the work of specific designers who are named, but many remain anonymous.

The focus is on a simple condition in the built landscape—the movement of water over a built landscape surface. This condition is central to the landscape discipline in these instances and constitutes a primary focus during the development and resolution of detail forms in the landscape design proposals. We will review these detail forms using criteria similar to those used in the earlier discussion of the Montmartre Steps and examine how they contribute to the physical and spatial *qualities* present in the landscape detail.

Example of Detail Forms: Movement of Water over a Landscape Surface

In parks, set into gravel walks, is a simple, unadorned little detail—the Parisian drain cover, as shown in Figure 1.8. We know we are in the Northern Hemisphere, because the water flows down the drains clockwise. This mass-produced metal lid, through the shaping of the slots, mimics and guides the rainwater flow with precision, elevating this simple pragmatic activity into a poetic landscape detail. It demonstrates through the detail formation and method of execution both the conceptual means by which it was formed and the results of that process. It locates this place within a larger landscape, at the same time collecting water and taking it away in the most efficient manner.

Figure 1. 9 shows an ordinary detail cut into a set of stone steps. Water from a modest brick path is led down to the public street by a sequence of channels. Here is the puritanical version of the Parisian drain cover, getting things done in a matter-of-fact way, no more, no less. Three grooves are cut into stone, each progressively shallower—which is curious, because you would expect the opposite—as the water accumulates on its downward path.

▲ Figure 1.8
Drain cover, Park Monceau, Paris. Designer: Adolphe Alphand.

◀ Figure 1.9
Drainage grooves, steps, Beacon Hill, Boston, Massachusetts. Designer: unknown.

33

What makes this drain interesting is the qualities achieved by the attention to the scale of this everyday condition. This is the appropriate response for the slow drip, drip, drip of November and March; it is precisely scaled and executed for a slow-wearing and relentless climate.

The drainage of moisture away from a seating ledge is turned into an example of individual detail mastery at multiple scales. In Parc Guell, now a public park overlooking the city of Barcelona, a meandering sculpted platform bench (shown in Figure 1.10) demonstrates the subtle movement of local moisture away from the seating surface. The broken glazed tile surface slightly tilts toward the back of the curved bench to a small dished channel to carry off excess water. The sitter is made aware of the presence of this channel by a series of raised dimples in the bench's surface, which prevent contact between user and water. The moisture is taken away from the open channel through regularly placed openings in the back of the bench to a second channel rim, where it is collected and discharged to the ground below through a series of spouts in the guise of tortoise heads. The draining of the bench becomes a symbolic journey from sky to ground. The rainspout head, one of a series of highly idiosyncratic plant and animal detail motifs found in the park, represents for the designer the imposition of order in a disordered world. The premier focus of

Figure 1.10
Curved tile bench, Parc Guell, 1914, Barcelona, Spain. Designer: Antoni Gaudí. Courtesy of Terrall Budge.

detail attention on this bench to date has been the material qualities of the broken glazed tile finish and the geometrical resolution of the curved bench form. The detail qualities arise, however, as much from the designer's resolution of how the bench is actually to be used, the detail precision of the water movement and drainage, and the patterns of weathering, as from the unified and careful rendition of the surface finishes.

In one of the most quoted and recognizable of urban landscape spaces, the Piazza del Campo in Sienna, Italy, a single landscape detail (illustrated in Figures 1.11 and 1.12) controls the raging downpours during the occasional violent rainfall in southern Europe. Collecting water quickly, up to two feet in depth at its neck, this is a landscape detail that can be ignored in the dry summer as simply an urban ledge for sitting and resting in the Piazza, but when it rains, it is revealed as a practical collector of water scaled appropriately to the size, form, and nature of the space. It stands at the opposite end of the

Figure 1.11
Piazza del Campo main drain—dry. Sienna, Italy. Designer: unknown.
Courtesy of Laurie Olin.

35

▶ Figure 1.12
Piazza del Campo main drain—wet. Sienna, Italy. Designer: unknown. Courtesy of Alistair McIntosh.

▼ Figure 1.13
Piazza del Campo paving—wet. Sienna, Italy. Designer: unknown. Courtesy of Alistair McIntosh.

spectrum to the Parisian drain and the Beacon Hill grooves by elevating the act of collecting and guiding moving water as a significant civic element.

To guide the movement of water during storms, the delicate folded brick surfaces of the Piazza (shown in Figure 1.13) enfold and tip the rainwater into long thin bands of a more durable stone, which lead down to the single drain. The detail qualities arise because this is not simply a pattern in the paving, it is a didactic feature, demonstrating both the process of moving water (ephemeral urban streams) and the means by which it can be achieved, as well as forming an urban stage for city life during the long dry periods between precipitation events.

In the southwest corner of the city of Philadelphia's Independence Park, summer rain showers make this public stone stairway a temporary cascade (Figure 1.14). It is not pleasant to walk up, but visually arresting as a detail condition. The large amount of surface rainwater seeks the lowest point. The steps are evenly laid, so the flow is neither channeled nor directed. This may not be a detail condition that requires repetition, but it can be remembered as a landscape form and transformed through detail design.

Figure 1.14
Stairway in flood.
Independence Hall,
Philadelphia, Pennsylvania.
Designer: National Park
Service.

37

Reappearing as a continuous rendition of the Independence Park steps in flood, the fountain shown in Figure 1.15 in a contemporary public square built in the late 1980s directs water to fall continuously over a ground plane of stone steps and rocks. It demonstrates the visual and tactile properties of water movement with plumes, ripples, and sprays. In this version, the movement of water is, of course, orchestrated and powered by nozzles and pumps. What is of interest in the detail design is the preservation and precise replication of the visual detail qualities of water movement and the mechanical means by which this can be achieved.

The contemporary fountain also alludes to the historical precedent of stepped water in fountains, as demonstrated here in Figure 1.16, in one of the secondary basins at Versailles. The nature of the basin at Broadgate, once the water is turned off—the dry stones and steps and the prominent fountain edge—demonstrate reinterpretation of detail form and the relationship between the visual qualities of the built detail and the concerns of detail precision and execution.

Figure 1.17 addresses again the problem of standing stones in a "fountain" in which water may at times be absent—the wet/dry fountain. A combination of ordinary and distinctive materials, asphalt, water, and selected irregular granite boulders, are placed on a slightly bowed asphalt circle, with the stones in five concentric circles. The tidy surface configuration betrays a complex subterranean infrastructure of powered spray nozzles, mist emitters, area drains, piping, and tunnels. The movement of water is a result of the

◀ Figure 1.15
Fountain, Exchange Square, Broadgate Development, London. Designer: Laurie Olin.

▲ Figure 1.16
Obelisk Fountain, Versailles, France. Designer: André le Nôtre.

action across, around, and onto the surface of the stones. The detail condition of stones placed in water responds to three site influences: the shape of the surface, the direction of the subtle falls to direct drainage movement and avoid standing pools of water, and the scaling of stones in elevation to water jets and sprays. The detail qualities arise from these features.

Whether the final landscape detail evokes natural forms (New England rocky coastlines), gestures from the field of contemporary sculpture, or the design issues of repetitive use of elemental forms and geometries is open to continuous individual review and interpretation.

Figure 1.17
Tanner Fountain, Harvard University, Cambridge, Massachusetts. Designer: Peter Walker with the SWA Group.

40

5. DETAIL CHARACTERISTICS

Although the previous landscape detail examples are varied in location, type, and age, certain characteristics that led to the development of the final detail forms can be determined or speculated about. These characteristics are useful in determining the fundamental issues that have to be addressed in the detail design process. They will also become the starting point in illustrating the methods or steps taken in the process of landscape detail development. Detail characteristics are summarized in the following list:

Detail Precision

1. *The expression of site.* The particular site, place, or context in which the details occur are expressed directly through detail design form, pattern, color, and texture.

2. *The expression of design ideas.* The details clearly express, either singly or collectively, the design ideas that form the larger landscape proposal and support and reinforce these ideas throughout the extent of the project. Rather than being one of a compendium of fragments, each detail supports and explains the larger design concept.

3. *Hierarchy of detail language.* An individual detail is part of a larger system of details on the site, which contributes to the development of a consistent hierarchy of language of details. This can happen over different periods of time or phases of implementation.

Detail Scale

4. *Multiple scales.* A detail works simultaneously at a number of scales—the scale of the human body, the scale of the site, and the scale of the larger landscape beyond.

5. *Spatial continuity.* There is a spatial continuity connecting different aspects of a site through detail in the vertical, overhead, and horizontal planes.

6. *Visual continuity.* There is a visual continuity connecting different aspects of a site through the details of motion, directionality, transparency, and closure.

Detail Execution

7. *Materials and their assembly.* The choice of materials and the assembly and expression of those materials are related either to surrounding indigenous sources (for example, stone, brick, concrete, sand, and plants) or the vernacular use of available or recycled materials.

8. *Ability to accommodate changes.* The details, either singly or together, are enhanced by the changes brought over time by design alterations, addi-

tions, and the effects of weathering. The details also demonstrate concern for appropriate ongoing maintenance.

9. *Restraint.* A project site demonstrating restraint is the result of careful consideration in organizing and making detail form and is not cluttered with extraneous or unnecessary detail elements. It calls for a reductive rather than an additive process, taking away rather than continuously adding.

6. DEFINITIONS OF TERMS

Key terms and phrases discussed in this chapter are defined below.

Landscape detail: a design process that translates conceptual ideas into a built landscape.

Designer: individual(s) involved in the formation, design, and development of built landscapes.

Detail qualities: detail characteristics or properties that arise in individual built landscapes and distinguish one space from another.

Detail precision: expression of the conditions of the site, context, and the specific requirements of a detail element.

Detail scale: detail forms sized appropriately to human dimensions or other specific criteria.

Detail execution: design method by which landscape detail forms will be made on-site and are initially considered and developed during the conceptual stages of detail design.

7. CLASSROOM EXERCISES

These exercises form a series of assignments to be carried out as part of a design studio or within the structure of a course on landscape technology or design in detail.

Assignment 1: Landscape and Detail

1. Examine completed landscape design project(s) in your area through drawings, field trips, and interviews with the designer(s) to understand the general scope and pattern of the design detail forms.

   Determine through examination of private and public, residential and institutional projects: What is the extent of the landscape detail forms? Were they all documented by the designer? Is there a common detail language to be seen, and is it derived from any precedents, local or historic? In addition, are there key detail forms on the site that establish and set the common detail language?

2. Explore other design fields to find examples of the working methods of detail design. For instance, investigate fields such as industrial design, furniture design, naval architecture, or engineering.

   Study other design fields to answer these questions: How does the process of detail design differ from that in landscape architecture as you understand it? What is similar? How do designers in other fields view the subject of detail design?

3. Review current landscape design magazines, including the technical and trade advertisements at the front and back, to see how many different ways detail or details are described or illustrated.

   Collect or photocopy these images and organize them by type. Students may review magazines from other design areas, for example, architecture, horticulture, interior design, or engineering, for comparison.

8. REFERENCES AND SOURCES

Section 1. Introduction

1. Edward Allen, *Architectural Detailing: Function, Constructibility, Aesthetics.* (New York: John Wiley & Sons, 1993.)

Section 2. Background to Learning About Landscape Detail

2. Design/build courses are offered in the Departments of Landscape Architecture at the University of Oregon in Eugene, at the University of Massachusetts at Amherst, Temple University in Philadelphia, and the University of Washington in Seattle, for example. See the following articles describing their work:

   Paul Bennett, "Approaching It Hands-on," *Landscape Architecture* 88, no. 4 (April 1998): 46–51.

   J. William Thompson, "Hands on Education," *Landscape Architecture* 82, no. 9 (September 1992): 49–51.

3. Results taken from a questionnaire administered by the author at the Graduate School of Design, Harvard University, during 1994–1996.

9. FURTHER READING

1. Those interested in reviewing past writings on the subject of landscape detail design and implementation in the United States should start with articles by Albert D. Taylor and Linda L. Jewell in *Landscape Architecture* magazine. They are a rich source of both historical information on landscape implementation practices and materials and commonsense observations and rules of thumb. Examples include the following:

Taylor:

"Notes with Reference to the Construction of Steps and Ramps." 14, no. 1 (October 1923): 43–58.

"Notes with Reference to the Construction of Curbs and Gutters." 14, no. 3 (April 1924): 195–202.

"Notes on Construction of Ha-Ha Walls." 20, no. 3 (April 1930): 221–224.

Jewell:

"Granite Curbing." 71, no. 1 (January 1981): 97–100.

"Curb Ramps at Intersections." 72, no. 6 (November 1982): 87–89.

"Ornamental Metals." 78, no. 8 (December 1988): 121–125.

See also:

Chapter 3 of *The Art and Mechanics of Landscape, Process Architecture* no. 117, entitled "Street Furniture," by Linda L. Jewell, which covers site detail through the furnishings of public space, including bollards, seating, trash receptacles, planters, drinking fountains, light fixtures, mailboxes, fire hydrants, and phone booths.

2. Albertini, Biancia, and Sandro Bagnoli. *Carlo Scarpa: Architecture in Details.* Cambridge: MIT Press, 1988. Introduction to the work of architect Scarpa through investigation of themes and detail language. Good illustrations of a working method of sketch drawing and detail design.

3. Alphand, Adolphe. *Les Promenades de Paris.* Paris: J. Rothschild. 1867–1873. Reprint, Princeton Architectural Press, 1984. Contains illustrations and a vast range of external detail of streets, parks, and public works, which still influence landscape architecture today.

4. Bye, A. E. *Art into landscape Landscape into art.* Mesa, Ariz.: PDA Publishers, 1983. Look at the photographs and plans of walls and the detail ground surfaces.

5. Ford, Edward R. *The Details of Modern Architecture.* Cambridge: MIT Press, 1991. Classic study of key projects in the twentieth century architectural canon. As a study method, it raises questions about the need for a equivalent one for landscape architecture.

6. Wilkinson, Elizabeth, and Marjorie Henderson. *The House of Boughs: A Sourcebook of Garden Designs, Structures, and Suppliers.* Covelo, Calif.: The Yolla Bolly Press, 1985. Glance through this illustrated catalog of landscape detail elements to see the broad range of materials, forms, and detail expression.

CHAPTER 2

DETAIL CONCERNS

THIS CHAPTER ADDRESSES the range of professional concerns that encompass aspects of the aesthetic, legal, and constructional requirements of contemporary landscape detail. It also addresses the more individual aspects of landscape detail practice related to the designer's training and licensing and discusses the particular use of standard and nonstandard detail forms that distinguish the work of one designer or design office from that of another. It should be noted that for the design student, exposure to the entire range of detail forms and their expression may not occur until he or she has been in a design office for a number of years and has performed a significant amount of professional work. The student reader will be introduced to the influences and constraints that act on the development of landscape detail form during the evolution of a design proposal.

1. INTRODUCTION

We now consider the questions, why is landscape detail necessary, and what is its purpose and role in the built landscape? In short, what is the range of detail concerns?

Among the examples of landscape detail work within a person's immediate view at any time in the built environment, a large number of detail forms appear to have been carried out with consideration for the most basic of concerns—for instance, to provide a walking surface, to divert water, or to accommodate changes in grade. These functional concerns are derived from the everyday requirements of use and detail performance. For the designer who wishes to start to acquire good detail practices, it is important to understand the forces that differentiate these landscape detail concerns from those brought about solely by legal or economic requirements, as well as those arising from the individual detail expression of the designer. Thus, the following issues must be addressed. They are also questions that must be considered by the designer at the beginning of each project:

- How are the landscape detail concerns, once they have been established, to be weighed or judged one against another, and which are found to be more important than others?

- Do these concerns change over time?

- Finally, and most important for designers, how can these issues be reconciled during the detail design process?

In addressing these questions, the objective is to understand that although landscape detail and the processes of detail design can be the focus of a considerable amount of effort and energy for a design student or practitioner in landscape architecture, the motivations to carry them out are guided as much by forces outside the landscape profession as those directly related to landscape design.

2. DETAIL CONSIDERATIONS

> Thus the miniscule, a narrow gate, opens up an entire world. The details of a thing can be the sign of a new world which, like all worlds, contains the attributes of greatness.
>
> GASTON BACHELARD, *The Poetics of Space*, 1992

In reviewing the *considerations* that affect detail design and the broad range of concerns, a subject that is often overlooked is the designer's own concerns in professional growth, including development in spatial, contextual, technological, and aesthetic issues. These include the relationship of landscape detail and design *observation,* the issues of *place and context,* the connection between *design and technology* through detail design, and the development of *individual detail expression.*

Training the Designer in the Powers of Design and Detail Observation

Landscape detail describes a new form of spatial imagination by virtue of its dimension and size. This apparent liberation from scale is described by Bachelard in *The Poetics of Space:* "The man with the magnifying glass—quite simply—bars the every-day world. He is a fresh eye before a new object."[1]

Landscape detail is a form of seeing. Landscape detail forms and detail design teach us to observe, as Bachelard notes, to focus at the small scale, to find new ways of looking at the landscape, to rediscover what exists and what has previously eluded our recognition (see Figure 2.1).

The fact that landscape detail is often concerned with the relatively unknown, unperceived, small parts of a landscape does not lessen its importance. The very scale of landscape detail is one of its inherent strengths.

Figure 2.1
Landscape detail is a form of seeing.

46

Defining Place and Context through Landscape Detail

Landscape detail defines the nature or spirit of a place, the "genius loci," within which the piece of work is carried out. Landscape detail forms have the ability to reflect or resonate with the characteristics of the site, place, and context in which they occur and with the scale and character of the surrounding environment. (See Figure 2.2, where a wooden cap is applied to a stone boundary wall of a historic cemetery near Princeton, New Jersey.)

In addition, they reveal the nature and properties of the local geology, soils, vegetation, and climate. The specific nature of the local or regional landscape may be reflected in the choice of plants or in selection of the landscape materials—whether timber, stone, or clay, with their varied qualities of reflectivity, density, color, surface, and texture—and the particular methods of local craft and craftsmanship.

Connecting Landscape Detail to Construction Technologies

Landscape detail design relates to the act of making connections and joints and the pleasure to be found in their design development. (See Figure 2.3 for a contemporary expression of connections and joints as a thin stone vertical screen wall in a public park and its exposed underlying structure.) Many designers today are divorced from the physical realities of the landscape building site, the workshop, or the quarry, or have limited experience in handling the range of raw materials and products that are currently used in site construction.

▲ Figure 2.2
Defining place and context through landscape detail. Timber wall cap, cemetery, Friends Meeting House, Princeton, New Jersey.

◀ Figure 2.3
Connecting landscape detail to construction technologies. Blue Wave Pavilion structural screen in Jardin Atlantique, Paris, 1987, by François Brun and Michel Péna. Courtesy of Joseph Disponzio.

47

▶ Figure 2.4
Parking bollards. IBM
Precinct at Solano, Texas.
Office of Peter Walker and
Martha Schwartz. Courtesy
of Hanna/Olin Ltd.

▲ Figure 2.5
John Fitzgerald Kennedy
Memorial Park, Cambridge,
Massachusetts.

The landscape detail process still requires attention to the making of landscape form and a love of the crafting of materials: their selection, placement, weight, jointing, and finish. The process is carried out, however, as a *design activity* at the conceptual stages of a project rather than as the final implementation of a design proposal. In that way, construction technologies (the "mechanic" arts, the practical and useful) and aesthetic and artistic design activities (the "fine" arts, the creative and imaginative) are combined in the early stages of conceptual landscape design. Here thinking and making are united, allying the creative possibilities of construction technologies with the practical concerns of progressive landscape design.

Toward the Art of Landscape Detail: Finding Individual Design Expression

Landscape details can be assertive and visually active, for example, through the use of highly contrasting forms and repetitive materials, textures, and hues.

For example, see Figure 2.4, illustrating Solano, IBM's headquarters in Westlake and Southlake, Texas, by landscape architects The Office of Peter Walker and Martha Schwartz. Landscape details can be quieter, more passive, harmonizing with their surroundings, and forming part of a background, such as in the John F. Kennedy Memorial Park in Cambridge, Massachusetts, the work of Carol R. Johnson and Associates, as illustrated in Figure 2.5.

The significance of landscape details is related to their ability to both mirror and establish in their physical evolution a remarkable range of design meanings. In short, they can open up a new realm for the designer to both represent and generate design ideas.

Let us continue by looking at the general considerations and concerns of landscape detail, those related to program, function and uses, form and material, structure and expression, interpretation and meaning, and their particular issues and problems.

A landscape design's success or lack of success can be related to the emphasis on sensitive, well-considered details. In developing ideas, a designer develops for each project a group of details that indicate how it will be constructed. The designer has to consider the following questions regarding prospective landscape detail forms to know whether they will accomplish the desired outcome:

• Will the detail forms function as originally intended after implementation, for example, by shedding water, preventing erosion, allowing plants to grow and flourish, or supporting the weight and movement of pedestrians?

• Will they change their structural properties over time?

• Will they withstand the rigors of climate, including extremes of heat and cold, wind and water, salt spray and ice?

• Will they work together as a common group of details intensifying and supporting the overall conceptual ideas and forms of landscape spaces that are produced?

Designers cannot leave these questions unanswered as conceptual detail ideas mature and develop. It is important to understand that landscape detail forms and the processes of detail design require a considerable amount of effort within the landscape design process and continue to exert considerable influence on how the broader landscape design ideas are to be translated into built work. In considering the preceding specific questions, it is necessary to cover a broader group of *detail concerns* governing the way landscape detail design is carried out. These are the basic conditions, related to practice and aesthetic issues, under which detail design is carried out, irrespective of project type, size, or location, as follows:

1. *Historical Background.* This briefly covers the context in which landscape detail forms have previously been executed and the key documents and personalities involved.

2. *Types and Classes of Detail.* The identification of the range and descriptions of landscape detail used in design practice.

3. *Design and Aesthetics.* Spatial and design issues are outlined, arising from the general concerns of generating landscape detail form.

4. *Design Services.* How and where the subject of landscape detail appears within the conventions of standard contractual relationships between client and designer.

49

5. *Liability and Insurance.* The legal issues arising from design work in landscape architecture are examined in relation to the specific concerns of detail design.

6. *Licensing Examination.* Sections and content of the landscape licensing examination that address the issues of landscape detail design and the detail process. Describes how the subject is viewed from within the professional body.

To ensure the successful execution of any project, these concerns must be addressed. In addition, they provide a reliable and effective way of carrying out the following detail activities:

- Analyzing landscape details in existing projects

- Reviewing one's own detail design work, or the work of others, in a design office or studio

- Judging the quality of manufactured elements or prefabricated or off-site landscape forms

- Diagnosing potential problems in existing built landscape work

They are also useful as a way of reviewing the work of previous generations of landscape projects and landscape detail forms to determine their successful and distinguishing features.

3. DETAIL CONCERNS

The Current Landscape

The condition of many built landscapes in the public realm of our cities and towns today raises serious issues for designers regarding the suitability of their landscape details, and the concerns that were addressed in the preceding section of this chapter.

Figure 2.6, showing a set of public steps on an exposed public waterfront pedestrian promenade, illustrates the lack of concern for structure, material selection, the form of the detail resolution of paving elements, joints, and thermal movement, and lack of consideration for the utility of the type of detail in this public, yet harsh, maritime location. The failure of the landscape detail elements, the lack of durability, and the breakdown of materials and methods of construction have required the recent overhaul and rehabilitation of numerous public outdoor spaces in this country, for example, Copley Square in Boston and Pershing Square in Los Angeles. Still more are closed indefinitely for reasons of public safety, including Allied Bank Plaza in Tampa, Florida, an award-winning project only ten years old. Clients such as educational

Figure 2.6
Conditions of the detail landscape in the public realm.

institutions, corporations, public agencies, and town officials challenge the ability of designers to detail outdoor spaces for an expected life of beyond ten to fifteen years, and delegate responsibility to project managers. Beyond regular maintenance, will large expenditure of financial resources and labor be required to counter the failure in detail design practices? Of more significance, how can designers learn to carry out sound detail practices?

4. HISTORICAL BACKGROUND: A BRIEF ACCOUNT OF KEY DOCUMENTS AND EVENTS

A summary of the evolution of landscape detail and landscape detail practices now follows. This account briefly covers those publications, practitioners, and organizations that were mentioned by the designers who took part in the cases studies at the end of this book, as being significant in the evolution of their own thinking about detail design and its practices. In a number of instances they recorded the current state of landscape details or established standards of detail design. This discussion does not identify or describe practitioners or offices that may have been the finest exponents of carrying out detail design or those detail standards. The purpose here is to illustrate that although the role of landscape detail has had a considerable influence on the final form of landscape architecture in past times, its use and development often pass unseen and unrecorded.

This summary follows a simple chronological sequence, some of the designers referring to both ancient and modern influences, with a small number of examples taken from more recent times. Together, they illustrate design periods or cultures that continue to exert an influence (to varying degrees) on current landscape detail design.

The construction of landscapes and the conception and execution of detail design has been carried out, for thousands of years, by unknown and unrecognized laborers and artisans or by other building trades and professionals such as engineers, architects, stonemasons, and carpenters. Patrons and clients from communities, institutions, and governments carried out large-scale landscape works with built site elements such as roadways, flood control walls, pavilions, flights of steps, and balustrades and installed large nursery plantations, orchards, and gardens employing the skills of farm workers, foresters, and master gardeners. A greater number of vernacular landscapes were built by hand with the use of local materials, tools, and techniques.

Of these, the most relevant to the development of landscape detail are early farming and agricultural practices of wall and fence building, pond construction and stream diversion, field drainage and ditch construction, earth moving and soil consolidation, windbreaks and tree plantations.

This legacy of ancient built work in landscape architecture has largely been destroyed or reworked until imperceptible. There are but limited records of the original intent of the design and even fewer of any detail descriptions or complete drawings.

Of greater interest to the current development of landscape detail forms are the following historical periods or landscape types:

- *Roman town planning, road building, and material standards.* These include Vasari's descriptions of construction materials and building techniques, as well as commentary on issues of detail design, proportion, and scale.[2]

- *Arabic or Moorish gardens and courtyards.* Of particular interest is the use of shallow water in contained channels, fountains, runnels, and pools and their detail design, as well as highly articulated patterned floor and wall surfaces in unit tiles and reflective stone.

- *The Italianate villa and garden.* These include the full range of garden and domestic-scale landscape detail elements, with an emphasis on walking surfaces, transitions in the landscape, walls, balconies, terraces, and collections of artwork and iconographic detail forms and symbols applied or integral with wall and ground surfaces.

- *Japanese garden.* The documentation of particular gardens and their design and symbolism was noted. This included layouts of plants, paths, pools, and bridges and their construction and maintenance, as well as detail parts and arrangements in photographs and drawings. Of particular interest to designers was the reductive use of landscape details, in which a restrained palette of landscape materials and the use of clean, articulated forms achieved built works of outstanding spatial balance and aesthetic beauty.

• *The English estate park.* Although the scale of planning and design was often sweeping and extended over a large acreage, detail forms in the landscape nearer the main houses contained inventive transitions and ground surfaces, the most noticeable being the "ha-ha," a walled or ditched transition to exclude livestock and maintain open vistas. In addition, a consistent detail language across entire estate parks required the development of a standard set of detail conventions for barriers, working and decorative surfaces, and small buildings and structures. Many imaginative and workable detail forms found and documented in the stables, barns, and garden areas were inspiration to the designers who formed the case study examples.

• *Early American settlements and communities.* Another group of built landscapes and their detail forms were identified by the designers as proving significant in their personal interest and involvement in detail design. These were of two types: the detail forms, craft, and aesthetic values of religious groups and their built environments, predominantly the Shakers and Mennonites; and the regional variations of landscape detail forms that resulted from early farming practices and the development of land establishment and protection methods. These include security and boundary fences, walls, and structures, as well as a range of interior domestic items in timber, including chairs, benches, and working artifacts.

Selected Publications

The following are an eclectic mix of monographs, art books, and technical documents that contain as their main focus, or included as a section, written and drawn studies, research and recommendations about detail design and landscape built forms. They do not represent the total amount of published documentation about the subject; rather, they illustrate the types of sources that designers have used and are still using in their own detail research.

Les Promenades de Paris, 1867–73 [3]

Adolphe Alphand's book, *The Streets of Paris,* documents the assembly of street furniture, elements, and details that were developed in the Bois de Boulogne in Paris under the direction of Baron Hausman. The collection of park detail elements and street detail forms illustrates a comprehensive language of landscape details developed from mass-produced metal and timber fixtures and forms: benches, tree grates, kiosks, signs. Subjects of interest include the following:

• Roads and paths (Chapter 3)

- Lakes, ornamental lakes and ponds, streams and waterfalls, and details of their construction, and artificial rocks in rubble stone and cement (Chapter 5)

- Architectural works executed in the Bois de Boulogne, including kiosks, signposts, entrance gates, handrails, tree grates, and various models of benches and shelters (Chapter 7)

These elements are seen today on the streets of Paris, and the bench with the replaceable slotted timber back has reappeared in city parks and streets throughout the world. The importance of Alphand's work lies in the comprehensive way in which all the detail parts were worked together into a complete detail language and form related in scale, size, and material use.

Landscape Architecture Magazine Articles, 1911–present

In the early years of this monthly publication of the American Society of Landscape Architects, the editors featured short practice articles, illustrated with drawings and photographs and written by practitioners for other practitioners, on a range of construction and technology issues.

Although the readership was small and the number of articles limited, this publication was important in attempting to formalize certain basic detail activities within landscape design (materials, paths, paving, and walls) and to disseminate this information to the immediate professional body.

The influence of the articles of A. D. Taylor has already been noted. Another example is the writing of Gilmore Clarke, in articles such as "Notes on the Construction of a Park Bench" (vol. 20, January 1930). He also laid out guidelines for the stone facing details of parkway bridges in another article (vol. 21, April 1930). These and other articles of this type stand, therefore, both as an account of the basic approaches and issues of landscape detail that existed at that time and as a record of the detail subjects, some which have entirely vanished from the central concerns of professional work. For example, the details of polo fields (vol. 12, 1917) and croquet lawns (vol. 13, 1924) are rarely featured in most of the daily work of landscape architects. They do, however, offer a glimpse at the seriousness with which landscape architects of the time attempted to document a series of detail standards and practices to be used within the profession.

Over the years the subject of details and detail design has had an uneasy relationship within the journal, reflecting the changing nature of the profession as well as a shifting of editorial emphasis.

In recent years articles about landscape detail forms and materials are found in the "Technique and Practice" section and have covered increasingly more specialized topics, such as computer graphics, computer aided drafting, and sustainable construction and materials. High-quality color photographs of detail installations and finishes are still found in the "Design" and "Profile" sections, but are rarely discussed as such.

Hubbard and Kimball[4]

An Introduction to the Study of Landscape Design, first published in 1917 by Henry Vincent Hubbard and Theodora Kimball, was a seminal, comprehensive introduction to, and textbook in, landscape design. Chapter 10, "The Design of Structures in Relation to Landscape," included such topics as walls and fences, pools and basins, roads and paths, and their materials, as well as illustration of the variety of expressions in layout. The instructions in the appendix concerning drawings and construction direct "the location and general form of such constructions as are planned—roads, walks, walls, buildings, planting beds and so on" to be shown on the topographic map with supporting cross sections.

Country Life Magazine

The documentation of gardens, houses, and surrounding landscape environments of the "country estate" or "country place" era, roughly between 1900 and 1930, was noted as an early influence on designers, even though they had rejected the "Beaux Arts." Of particular interest and use was the high quality of black-and-white photographs present in each edition, which rendered the material and tactile qualities of the landscape forms with a clearly defined view and infinite attention to detail.

Civilian Conservation Corps (CCC)

Created by an act of Congress, March 31, 1933, the CCC implemented work projects that were carried out under the jurisdiction of the Department of Agriculture. These included the development of recreational and hiking trails, campgrounds, and bridges, with detail designs and construction related to local materials and vernacular detail forms. A number of these detail practices were published as handbooks or guides. For example, the *Portfolio of Park Structures and Facilities* was published in 1934 by the United States Department of the Interior and the State Park Emergency Conservation Work. This was the work of Dorothy Waugh of the State Park Emergency Conservation Work, who prepared the drawings and text. This publication includes a survey of landscape detail forms and elements and a final section of standard scaled blueprint drawings of campground detail forms, including seats, tables, fireplaces, shelters, and cabins. Another notable handbook, *Camp Stoves and Fireplaces,* was published by the Forest Service in 1936, based on the work carried out by the CCC in the national forests; its author was A. D. Taylor, consulting landscape architect for the Forest Service. The book included drawings similar to those that appeared in *Landscape Architecture* magazine.

The designers noted the significance of these documents mainly as an attempt to bring together a series of standard detail elements that could be replicated or adapted in project work.

55

Process Architecture

When these journals were first published in the 1970s, they repeatedly featured the documentation of landscape detail through editions with specific landscape themes or through the monographs of individual landscape designers or offices. The photographs made available to designers for the first time, in a large format, detail elements of both familiar and little-known work. As technical sources for landscape detail these publications had limited use, but as a pictorial guide with color photographs, they became, and still are, a common source for detail imagery in the profession. Examples of note include "Plazas of Southern Europe" (16), "Landscape Design in Japan — Current Issues and Some Ideas" (46), "The Art and Mechanics of Landscape" (117), and monographs on the work of Lawrence Halprin (4), Dan Kiley (33), and, more recently, Peter Walker and William Johnston and Partners (118), EDAW (120), Jones and Jones (126), and Hargreaves Associates (127).

Although this selection represents only a minor amount of published sources or material on landscape detail, they indicate the nature of the subject material, extracted from the general body of landscape design history and practice. In addition, they illustrate the way in which designers have discovered, within design periods and styles that hold little formal interest for them, a wealth of detail information and inspiration. Finally, this material emphasizes the need for a study of the subject of landscape detail. Such a work could focus on the last 100 years, or bridge the gap between landscape history and landscape design.

In continuing the examination of professional concerns that inform detail design, irrespective of project type, size, or location, let us return to the subject of detail itself and review the types and classes of landscape detail that are commonly found and used in practice.

5. TYPES AND CLASSES OF LANDSCAPE DETAIL

The detail types of current landscape design projects may be grouped in the following categories:

- Standard
    Required Details
    Recommended Details

- Nonstandard
    Customized Details
    Vernacular Details
    Singular Details

The first category includes those details that are prototypical: standard detail types that are either required or recommended. The second category is concerned with details where an original and sometimes distinctive aesthetic expression has been developed, either by adapting standard details or starting from other sources. These are the nonstandard detail types, which include customized, vernacular, and singular details.

Standard Details

This is the class of details that, because of their nature, are *repetitively* used or have achieved, over time, a general consensus as to their success in application and performance. This has resulted in their acceptance as the landscape details required or approved by regulatory agencies and review boards or recommended by manufacturers and suppliers. They are used in repetitive or extended detail elements such as sidewalks, road curbs, or any detail elements that are duplicated throughout a site or a project type, such as signage and seating, tree grates and brick pavers, scored concrete sidewalks and stone curbs (see Figure 2.7).

Standard details are blamed for encouraging a lack of aesthetic and artistic merit in design projects, as well as a visual monotony in the built landscape resulting from a restricted choice and range of materials and detail solutions.

This view is, however, wrong, for standard details are essentially neutral, they are neither right nor wrong. It is their use or misuse by the designer and the context in which they are used that is more likely to blame.

When a standard detail and a nonstandard landscape detail are under review as alternatives, it is likely that the scrutiny and performance levels expected will be more exacting for the latter than for the former. Therefore, the custom is often to select standard details over the nonstandard for this reason alone. An example is the use of gravel-paved surfaces in public parks in this country. This type of surface has a long tradition of use in other coun-

Figure 2.7
Standard detail—granite curb and scored concrete paving surface.

tries, and the current technology, construction methods, and materials for gravel walks are well understood and documented. They provide benefits to the growth of tree roots, drainage, and the aesthetic properties of a granular pedestrian surface. There are however, few instances in which the installation of a gravel surface has not been accompanied by an arduous process to convince the necessary authorities of its performance capabilities and the reliability of future maintenance. Standard surfaces of asphalt and concrete often win out. Certain standard details, however, are also of the highest order—aesthetically, technically, conceptually, spatially, and experientially.

Standard details developed in design offices are the result of many years of research, development, and refinement and have reached a point where their application in projects is carried out in such an efficient manner by the use of standard detail files that they form the basis of much of contemporary detail practice.

Standard details fall into two subcategories: *required* standard details and *recommended* standard details.

Required Standard Details

Required standard details include all details that are required by codes, regulations, or by-laws enacted by federal or state legislation or local controls, such as the following:

- *City parks and street departments.* The City of New York Department of Parks and Recreation, for example, is known for the development and use of a wide range of landscape elements through standard detail forms. These include many site details related to specialized park and sports equipment and public playgrounds, as well as benches, tree plantings, and boundary fence details. Some date from the 1940s, the Robert Moses era of planning and development in that city. They are replicated across project location and type as programs dictate, thus ensuring a consistent detail language and maintenance requirements. In addition, this approach establishes a practice of using repetitive and sound detail forms that have undergone repeated evaluation and analysis of field performance.

- *State highway and transportation standards.* A series of "design guides" were published by the American Association of State Highway Officials (AASHO), which include the topics of safe rest areas, roadway lighting, and protective screening of overpass structures. In 1973 it also published *A Policy on Design of Urban Highways and Arterial Streets,* which contains many aspects of landscape detail design related to highways and streets. Chapter H, "Elements," includes illustrations and descriptions of, for example, curbs, slopes, drainage, fencing, guardrail protection, and detail sketch profile drawings with dimensions of a typical highway barrier, mountable curbs, and high-visibility curbs.

Recommended Standard Details

The primary source of information and guidance on the use of particular materials and detailing practices is contained within a range of standards published by manufacturing companies and trade organizations. Criteria for fabrication tolerances, storage, handling, and installation of materials are included. Typical details are also included that identify design factors, detail types, notes, and dimensions. In addition, products or materials that can be used to solve difficult design problems, unusual applications of the products, unique construction techniques, and specific design excellence achieved by their use are also identified (see Figure 2.8).

Among these resources are the Concrete Paver Institute and the Indiana Limestone Institute of America (ILI). The publication issued by ILI, the *Indiana Limestone Handbook,* contains general information on limestone, recommended standards and practices, product use with typical details of steps, platforms, wall copings, balustrades, and balusters, information on ashlar stone veneer, documentation of case histories, and cleaning and maintenance definitions.

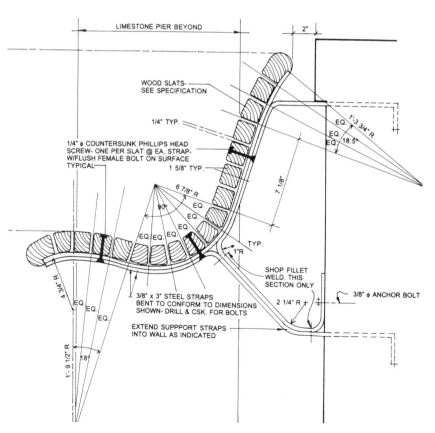

Figure 2.8
Manufacturers' information. Timber bench and fixings. Drawn by Sara Peschel for the author.

59

Nonstandard Details

Customized Details

Customized details can be an alternative to standard details and the use of a manufacturer's standard range of in-stock products, such as lengths of metal fencing, light poles, paving bricks, or shaped stone. Details are produced in a "custom" or customized fashion for a particular condition, on a project-by-project basis, as needed by individual designers and clients. The information is transmitted to the manufacturer by models, drawings or sketches, or digital or computer software. This information can be stored and reused or altered on subsequent work by the designer. A raw material, such as wood, metal, stone, or concrete, can be manipulated, formed, turned, or cut according to certain spatial requirements. Although this form of manufacture is normally associated with projects with more extensive budgets, it should not be considered to be a luxury. It has enhanced the ability of designers to work with manufacturers and suppliers in developing their lines of products. This type of customized details should not, however, be confused with "hand-crafted" details that serve to customize every element and every part of the design and manufacturing process. Customized detail relies on there being a standard inventory of material in a warehouse that can provide replacement parts as needed and, at the same time, the ability to manipulate standard material through the manufacturing or production processes.

Vernacular Details

Vernacular details constitute the range of ordinary details commonly found in the built landscape that are not the result of professional designers or practices, as well as builders working in familiar idioms and with a knowledge of locally available materials, regional weather patterns, and parochial customs and values (see Figure 2.9).

These details therefore account for most of what are termed *vernacular* or *regional* detail variations, found throughout the country.

Figure 2.9
Generic detail—New England. Brick pavement and crosswalk with granite bollard.

Examples include the full range of idiomatic detail elements such as pathways, roads, walls, fences, markers, and steps in varying historic periods, aesthetic styles, and idioms and in a range of local materials.

Although vernacular details are most closely associated with rural or provincial built landscapes, they are also found in particular periods of settlement and expansion associated with large and powerful urban institutions, including banks, manufacturing companies, and colleges.

Vernacular details are particularly noticeable in a historic landscape or in a region or district that has a very clear and identifiable "character" throughout its landscape detail. These include the New England landscapes of gray and rounded stone walls and white-painted plain wood architecture, and the thick, saturated-color stucco enclosures and warm red-tiled paving of New Mexico. However, such details are also clearly identifiable within the acutely urban landscapes of Manhattan in the 1920s, such as found at the outdoor spaces of Rockefeller Center. Many vernacular details are appropriated into a designed landscape. If repeated and reused out of context or out of scale, over time they become caricatures of their originals and subsequently lose both their integrity and original meaning.

Many examples of this condition are found in retail and entertainment centers across the country, as well as on new recreational waterfronts where details of working marine environments are replicated in contemporary materials and finishes as "nautical site furniture" (see Figure 2.10). If used correctly, with due attention to place, materials, scale, and workmanship, such a detail becomes, in turn, an "iconographic" detail in the built landscape—that is, a symbolic detail form or forms that bear the meaning of an entire work of landscape design or the place where the project is carried out.

Figure 2.10
Details of caricature—the marine waterfront edge, London Docklands.
Courtesy of Hanna/Olin Ltd.

Figure 2.11
Singular detail—pathway
and molded detail
transitions. Dumbarton
Oaks, Washington, D.C.

Singular Details

Singular, or "one-off," details make up the very small number of unique and idiosyncratic details that are individual to one project or client. They differ from custom-designed and vernacular details in that their source of inspiration, or starting point for the designer, is derived from an aesthetic or cultural idea that is separate or external from the site location or context.

Such details are most closely associated with commissioned artwork, sculpture, or specific site installations. Because of their intimate association with one project or client, they are rarely reproduced by the designer in the original form. They may, however, be one of a series of individual pieces of work carried out over a range of projects or locations. Examples include the detail used in the gardens and outdoor spaces at Dumbarton Oaks in Georgetown, Washington, D.C., indicated in Figure 2. 11. This was undertaken for the original owners, Robert Woods and Mildred Bliss, under the design direction of landscape architect Beatrix Farrand in the 1920s. In this case, the detail entailed the site-specific stone carving of step transitions and embellishment.

Examples of standard and nonstandard details, as outlined in this section, are also likely to appear in the landscape architecture registration examination. Here the subject of landscape detail forms and the detail design process are presented in a format that allows an individual's success or lack of success in addressing detail concerns to be graded. The detail design process is therefore reduced to the rapid selection and placement of standard drawn detail forms within a restricted palette of materials and finishes.

6. DETAIL DESIGN AND AESTHETICS

The topics related to design and aesthetics in landscape detail that are likely to arise as issues during the detail process are as follows:

• Detail Material

• Detail Structure

• Detail Form

• Detail Language

• Detail Expression

The outcome of the landscape detail process is often viewed as a result of constant interaction and resolution among these areas. In fact, all five areas of detail design exert a particular control over the final detail element. Although these terms are part of basic design teaching and studio and are familiar to all design students, their application and use in detail design is briefly described here.

Detail Material

The concerns about materials as they are applied to landscape detail arise from two issues, availability and compatibility. Extreme care is to be taken in the initial decision on the range of material sources and the selection of particular textures, whether refined or rough, for example, or where changes take place within a single group of materials or between materials of similar types. Suitable care must be taken where excessive amounts of time are required to make materials work together, while addressing the issues of finishes and finishing.

Detail Structure

Materials are brought together in landscape detail through the consideration of detail *structure*. Among the most significant in the making of detail parts are the ongoing issues of support and assembly. The feasibility of approaches to structure are tested against the concerns for the appropriate selection and strength of materials and the integrity of fabrication, fixings, and maintenance. Site handling techniques and installation practices are developed from the concerns arising from ongoing site coordination and supervision.

Detail Form

Form in landscape detail is a result of material and structure having been brought to the surface plane. Initial concerns are focused on achieving the correct proportion of the detail elements and all their parts—for example, surface thickness and the dimensions of widths and heights of site elements. Further considerations of detail form cover such issues as their order and scale in relationship to adjacent detail forms—for example, through a selection of contrasting materials. Finally, the objective of achieving a balance of details across an entire built landscape is realized through the hierarchy of the detail parts. Major and minor detail forms are used to reveal and accent spatial and programmatic relationships. For example, primary and secondary pathways are resolved with attention to the amount of detail resolution or intensity of landscape detail to denote importance.

Detail Language

The evolution of detail form and the consistent appearance of the detail parts result from the repeated use of a clear detail *language* throughout the entirety of a project. Central to the clarity of the detail language are the repetition of forms, the selection of particular detail themes and motifs, their application at varying scales, and a strict concern for the issues of detail interpretation. For example, the use of a detail language based on certain appropriate historical precedents allows the development of a potentially rich detail vocabulary. The selection and use of this detail language establishes or continues the overall character of the built landscape and leads to the articulation of each part in a rational and consistent manner. However, as pointed out in Chapter 1, the development of a more contemporary detail language based on aesthetic principles that may challenge conventional wisdom will still remain an evolutionary, rather than a revolutionary, process.

Detail Expression

A detail language is made apparent and realized through the *expression* of the landscape detail. This concerns the tone or weighting given to each of the detail parts in relation to each other and to the context in which they occur. The detail parts can be muted and quiet, whereby each detail recedes into the general background of a built form. In contrast, the parts can be visually loud and advancing, drawing attention to certain detail conditions—surfaces, junctions, and joints—through the selection and juxtaposition of materials and forms. How the detail expression of a built landscape is articulated is as much concerned with establishing the mood and "feel" of a space as with determining the character of the individual parts. In addition, the concerns of establishing and developing a personal detail expression are realized through the repeated use of individual detail forms and languages.

7. DESIGN SERVICES

Design services are described in the American Institute of Architects (AIA) document B163. Included is their relationship to the phases of the landscape design process.

LANDSCAPE DESIGN SERVICES	LANDSCAPE DESIGN PROCESS *(AIA Document B163)*
a. Predesign	Inception
b. Site analysis*	Conceptual design
c. Schematic design	Schematic design
d. Design development	Detail design
e. Construction documents	Documentation
f. Bidding and negotiations	
g. Contract administration	Implementation
h. Postconstruction	Maintenance and postoccupancy evaluation

Forms part of the schematic design phase.

Although it is most likely that details and detailing are realized within the conceptual, schematic design, and design or detail development phases, there are instances in which problems or issues of a detail design nature will form part of other phases of the process.

• *Predesign/inception.* In the preparation of the program issues and scope, and of the timetable, phasing, and initial economic concerns, specific detail issues—for example, those concerned with the restoration of existing details forms—may arise.

• *Site analysis/conceptual design.* Specialized details may be part of the initial design concepts or may be part of the program elements. Investigations of site conditions require analysis and documentation of existing detail conditions and the recording of elements proposed to be saved or enhanced and new ones to be sited.

• *Schematic design.* This phase is the critical time in the design process for the establishment and formation of the detail language of the project and the evolution of the precise expression of the detail parts.

• *Design/detail development.* As the name suggests, this phase completes the development of the overall project design, as well as the group of detail forms and their assembly, into an entire body of site detail work.

• *Construction documents.* In recording the detail execution and site implementation in drawings and written specifications, the finished qualities and performance that are required in the detail forms are described.

• *Bidding and negotiations.* Changes or alternates to detail installations, assemblies, and landscape materials and finishes are reviewed with reference to comparative costs and overall project budgets.

• *Contract administration/implementation.* The execution of the detail design is observed on-site. Changes to landscape detail forms, arising from inaccurate information on site conditions or issues of craft, workmanship, and quality of materials, are noted.

• *Postconstruction/maintenance and postoccupancy evaluation.* This phase includes review and alteration of detail forms that have weathered badly or are required to be changed because of inadequate detail performance, variation to codes and legal requirements, or part of regular maintenance.

8. LIABILITY AND INSURANCE

The various types and classes of landscape detail all have one thing in common: the liability for their design performance ultimately lies with the designer, where they have been installed according to the contract documents. The issue of insurance to cover liability claims against site detail construction and design is of importance to practitioners.

This is one part of a professional relationship that links design (and the ability to practice design) with detail design practices and techniques, and the ability to carry out the original intent of a design idea.

Increasing costs of liability insurance for detail design malpractice and injury directly connect detail design procedures in landscape design with the ability to innovate and take calculated risks. Failure may lead to lengthy lawsuits, substantial legal costs, and disruption to office work. Examples of detail and detail design issues that give rise to liability lawsuits include the omission or failure of particular installations and detail assemblies in the public realm, such as paving, roads, and walls, or the collapse or break-up of landscape materials, as indicated in Figure 2.12.

Unlike engineering or architecture, in which liability may arise from the structural collapse of bridges, roofs, or floors, internal fires, or gas inhalation, built landscapes are rarely the cause of accidental death or serious injury.

Figure 2.12
Detail failure. Broken paving surface with standing water.

66

Major natural events such as forest fires, earthquakes, floods, and mud slides commonly lead to the secondary failure of built landscapes. Minor accidents that occur in outdoor spaces include tripping over misarranged steps, breaking an ankle in a fall because of an unexpected or unaccounted-for displacement of paving, and bruising or injury resulting from the collapse of detail installations of walls, seating, and minor structures.

Figure 2.13
Stepped public terrace,
Parque Industriale,
Barcelona, Spain.

The Perception of Public Safety and Danger

Of greater concern is the perception of physical safety from minor accidents in public outdoor spaces. In addition, the responsibility for public safety and social behavior is not that of the visiting individual or group, but of the designer, the client or owner, and the public municipality. Peter Shepheard, landscape architect and former dean of the Graduate School of Fine Arts at the University of Pennsylvania, has observed that on his travels to outdoor spaces of various kinds in other countries, the following is true: The measure of perceived public safety is in direct proportion to the lack of provision of safety measures.[5]

A collective responsibility is in operation. This is a concern very closely related to landscape detail and the detail design of outdoor space. For example, as illustrated in Figure 2.13, users of a new urban park in Barcelona are required to be alert to the extreme changes of grade, steps, and unprotected overlooks as they circulate and inhabit the spaces.

Another example is the complete absence of protective barriers and railings along the numerous canal edges of Amsterdam, Holland, and the walkways, streets, and footpaths that adjoin them, as shown in Figure 2.14.

Although an occasional car must be hoisted out of the water, the local pedestrian and biking population have developed a perception of safety based on known danger. This can be summarized as "If you are not alert at the water's edge, you may fall in," which results in responsible individual public behavior. Of significance is that the detail qualities and aesthetic properties of the Amsterdam canals result, in part, from this lack of additional and supporting detail elements.

Figure 2.14
Water edge transition,
Amsterdam Canal. Courtesy
of Alistair McIntosh.

Figure 2.15
Water edge coping.
Lechmere Canal Park,
Cambridge, Massachusetts.

In recent years, concerns about waterside safety and a number of incidents of unsupervised children drowning in public spaces in the United States has caused a review of the safety standard details of water edge barriers and railings.

This has resulted in the evolution of these barriers into details of the lowest common denominator, in an attempt to address all possible detail conditions of barriers and restricting access to the water, at the same time excluding access to dry land from the water's edge. Such barriers act as landscape details of restriction and exclusion.

There have been instances when water-edge barrier details have been allowed to remain less complex or even absent altogether. For instance, at Lechmere Canal Park, Carol R. Johnston and Associates, landscape architects, have recently created a finely drawn, clear, and durable built water edge by treating the detail design of the gravel pathway of this commercial complex with the marina and canal as an elongated flush curb. Completely absent are railings, fences, and barriers. Small metal bollards provide mooring points for pleasure boats (see Figure 2.15).

The issues covered within liability insurance are mostly identified as "trivial," owing to human error or mistake, and are settled out of court. However, they add another dimension to the subject of detail concerns, as not just a design and technical matter but as interconnected with landscape professional practice and dedication to the health, safety, and welfare of the public.

9. PROFESSIONAL LANDSCAPE ARCHITECTURE REGISTRATION EXAMINATION

Individuals who practice as landscape architects or use the title Landscape Architect complete the Landscape Architect Registration Examination (LARE) prepared by the Council of Landscape Architectural Registration Boards (CLARB).[6] Two sections of this examination address landscape detail form and the processes of landscape detail: Section 5, "Integration of Technical and Design Requirements," and Section 7, "Implementation of Design Through the Construction Process."

The following is a summary of the purposes and key points of two sections of the overall examination. What is important to recognize here are the concerns of the examination body regarding detail design in landscape architecture and how those concerns are demonstrated through the structure of the questions and the criteria by which detail design is to be judged.

Section 5 — Integration of Technical and Design Requirements

This section of the test, which calls for a drawn answer, examines the "ability to prepare design development details given program requirements, physiological conditions and a design plan." Two subdivisions under this heading outline specific requirements:

• "Ability to design and implement miscellaneous site improvements (pools, fountains, walls, site furniture, play equipment, signs, etc.), to meet requirements."

• "Knowledge of typical construction details and material assemblies, including fasteners, finishes, etc." This includes "Connecting materials using standard construction practices in an economical and safe manner" and "Developing a design development detail using specified materials and finishes."

Section 7 — Implementation of Design Through the Construction Process

This multichoice written test section examines the "knowledge of Construction Processes, Materials and Methods of Construction, Supporting Systems, and Construction Documents." Two subdivisions under this heading outline specific requirements of this section in regard to detail and detailing.

• Materials and Methods of Construction: "Knowledge of typical construction details and material assemblies, including fasteners, finishes, etc."

• Construction Documents: "Ability to determine appropriate scale, level of detail, and organization of information on a base sheet."

The purpose of preparing these details is to "show an understanding of structural detailing *principles* through shape, materials, finishes, critical dimensions, fasteners and finishes" and to prepare detail drawings to "explain the design *character* to laymen."

All detail materials are selected from a list of materials; in addition, detail forms are selected from a catalog sheet of drawn examples that are also made available to all candidates. It is evident in reviewing published sample solutions to these detail problems that the understanding of detail context and site concerns in this particular examination is based on the following factors:

• Selection of external architectural materials

• Response to soil type and footings

• Construction practices in connections and junctions

• Correct use of labeling and notes

Points are awarded and deducted according to the correct or incorrect selection of detail forms and materials. The role of landscape detail design within the activities and practices examined by this method is one of standard detail forms. Each of the detail conditions responds to a prior set of design decisions. In this way landscape detail forms are viewed as the outcome of the prior decisions and appear at the end of the entire design process. Thus, through this method of examination, the role of detail design is reduced to a minor part of the landscape design process.

10. SUMMARY

We return to the questions identified at the beginning of the chapter, to be considered by the designer:

• *How are the landscape detail concerns, once they have been established, to be weighed or judged one against another, and which are found to be more important than others?*

Of interest to the designer here is how the general concerns of professional practice, liability, and standard detail forms direct aesthetic and design decisions related to those of detail design. This is further discussed in Chapter 4, "Constructing Detail."

• *Do these concerns change over time?*

As with other aspects of detail design, periodic alterations will occur to change concerns about and around the subject of landscape detail form. The issues of control or planning for detail change are further discussed in Chapter 5.

• *Finally, and most important for designers, how can these issues be reconciled during the detail design process?*

The answer requires an understanding of the different approaches to detail design that are presently used by designers. This is the subject of the next chapter in Part One, "Approaches and Themes."

11. DEFINITIONS OF TERMS

Key terms and phrases discussed in this chapter are defined below:

Detail considerations: broad range of detail concerns, including spatial, contextual, technological, and aesthetic issues.

Standard details: details that, because of their nature, are repetitively used or have achieved over time a general consensus as to their success in application and performance.

Nonstandard details: details in which an original and sometimes distinctive aesthetic expression has been developed, either by adapting standard details or starting from other sources.

Customized details: details produced in a "custom" fashion, for a particular condition, on a project-by-project basis, as needed by individual designers and clients.

Vernacular details: details commonly found in the built landscape, based on familiar idioms and with a knowledge of locally available materials, regional weather patterns, and local customs and values.

Singular details: one-off details in which the source of inspiration is derived from an aesthetic or cultural source that is separate or external from the site location or context.

12. CLASSROOM EXERCISES

These exercises form a series of assignments to be carried out as part of a design studio or within the structure of a course on landscape technology or design in detail.

Assignment 2: Landscape Detail Concerns

1. Select two historic or contemporary built landscape projects. These should consist of one example of a similar landscape type from different time periods *or* locations (for example, parks from the nineteenth and twentieth centuries or from different parts of the country), or two examples of different landscape types from the same time period. Research the back-

ground of each project and the range of detail concerns that were addressed in the project by the designer(s) involved.

By comparing the two precedents, determine either the changes or similarities in the detail concerns that designers address over time or between locations and project types. Are certain detail concerns related only to specific landscape types? What are the contemporary detail concerns of different landscapes?

2. Visit a designed landscape project in your locale that is currently under construction in the field (after obtaining official permission to access the site). Inspect the range of detail forms being executed; determine which are standard and which are nonstandard.

Of what type are the detail forms? Are they recommended or required, custom or singular, made on-site or brought to the site? The intention is to examine the percentage of each type present in a single project.

3. Perform a review of the detail issues of detail design and liability, using the precedent examples selected for Assignment 2, Exercise 1. What landscape details were executed as a result of the detail concerns for professional liability, as opposed to other concerns? In particular, examine older built landscapes where alterations have been made over time.

How are these concerns realized on-site through detail design? What forms of public safety are covered, and which areas and types of detail design are the focus of this detail attention? The purpose is to examine the basic conditions, related to practice and aesthetic issues, under which detail design is carried out, irrespective of project type, size, or location.

13. REFERENCES AND SOURCES

Section 2. Detail Considerations

1. Gaston Bachelard, *The Poetics of Space* (Boston: Beacon Press, 1992), Chapter 7, "Miniature," 155.

Section 3. Detail Concerns

2. See, particularly, a translation of Giorgio Vasari's (1511–1574) technical treatise on architecture, sculpture, and painting in Louisa S. Maclehose (ed.), *Vasari on Technique* (London: Dover Publications, 1907, reprinted 1960).

3. See Adolphe Alphand, *Les Promenades de Paris* (Paris: J. Rothschild, 1867–73. Reprint, Princeton: Princeton Architectural Press, 1984.)

4. See Henry Vincent Hubbard and Theodora Kimball, *An Introduction to the Study of Landscape Design* (New York: Macmillan Company, 1917; reprinted 1924).

5. In discussion with the author, 1985.

6. See Council of Landscape Architectural Boards, *Understanding the LARE* (Landscape Architectural Registration Examination), pp. 61–70, 79–82, C104–113.

14. FURTHER READING

The following is a brief selection of references that contain aspects of landscape detail and the detail design process for a range of historical landscapes.

Beveridge, Charles E., and Paul Rocheleau. *Frederick Law Olmsted: Designing the American landscape.* New York: Rizzoli, 1995. Details from Central Park, Prospect Park, Boston Fens.

Olmsted, Frederick Law. *Forty years of landscape architecture: Central Park.* Reprint. Ed. Frederick Law Olmsted Jr. and Theodora Kimball. Cambridge: MIT Press, 1973. Chapters on design, construction, and costs. Roads, walks, rides, boundaries, and entrances. Includes notes on detail materials.

Tishler, William H., ed. *American landscape architecture: Designers and places.* Washington: Landscape Architecture Foundation, 1989.

CHAPTER 3

APPROACHES AND THEMES

THE KEY QUESTION ADDRESSED in this chapter is how to proceed in detail design—where and how does one start? It introduces design approaches and themes that are used by the designer in the landscape detail process. The most important, and at the same time one of the most difficult aspects of landscape detail as an art form is the ability to bridge the gap between an idea in detail design and the realization of that idea. To adequately transfer a conceptual sketch or a vague series of roughly drawn images and diagrams requires a broad range of design techniques and tools. The prospect is made more difficult for the student or young designer by an initial lack of trust in his or her own design process, as well as an incomplete understanding of the specific procedures that will allow detail forms to be fluidly created.

1. INTRODUCTION

A designer, during the course of work on a design project, will restore, reinterpret, or replicate numerous existing landscape detail forms. A designer may also combine and assemble existing landscape detail forms to create hybrids or, in certain cases, be required to invent new landscape detail forms from scratch. The designer uses, at various times in these detail operations, three aspects of the detail design process; these are concerned with detail *approaches,* detail *themes,* and detail *categories,* which are introduced and covered in this chapter as follows:

1. *Detail approaches.* Three approaches to developing landscape detail are outlined. Derived from the processes of design and design development that are most commonly used in landscape practice, the purpose is to examine the generic ways in which landscape detail forms are arrived at, and the methods open to designers in starting a piece of detail design work. More commonly, these approaches are combined and used together in the duration of a project.

2. *Detail themes.* Design techniques that support the various approaches are described, foremost among which is the use of landscape detail themes. These and, more important, their variations over time are described as underlying subjects or points of view that are expanded upon in detail design. Examples range from ideas of nature and time, the medium of landscape architecture itself—earth, water, and plants—to more tangential subjects such as cultural or scientific ideas (chaos theory, fractals) or other artistic activities, particularly the forms and structure of painting and music. It will not have escaped the reader's attention that the use of thematic variations is central to both classical music and the more contemporary musical forms.

The purpose is to illustrate how generic detail approaches and the categories of details are brought together through an integrative and underlying point of view by the designer. These themes are at the same time both personal and universal—personal because they arise from individual choice and interest and universal because the themes are concerned with ideas and issues that are timeless and ubiquitous.

3. *Detail categories.* How the detail parts of a project are broken down in the three detail approaches will be introduced through a description of the categories of landscape detail. These are the general areas of surfaces, transitions, and boundaries within a landscape design proposal where the focus and location of detail design work occurs. In previous literature these have been described and organized as either discrete elements such as curbs, steps, and fences, or as separate assemblies: paving, walls (freestanding or retaining), and stairways.

The purpose is to avoid looking at the detail elements and assemblies as isolated parts and to concentrate on their relationship to the design principles of site organization and the particular types of detail work that are being carried out through the project.

We now return to the example of an individual approach to the detail design process that introduced the opening section of this book entitled "To the Reader." It focused primarily on the author's initial exposure to the workings of an experienced practitioner who developed the conceptual design and detail ideas simultaneously at the beginning of every project. Two questions arise that are significant in introducing the range of detail approaches and the resultant themes and categories of detail elements.

- Is it possible to conceive of the form and expression of a built landscape simultaneously at this range of scales?

- What are the ways in which designers are able to find or give aesthetic meaning through appropriately scaled details, at the same time conceiving of the entire design project?

In short, how does any approach to landscape detail alter or establish a different sensibility between the parts and the whole? In answering these questions, it is necessary to first address the range of work associated with landscape detail design, a topic that is intrinsically tied to the types of detail design and detail forms, as well as the processes of conceiving and making built landscapes.

2. RANGE OF DETAIL WORK

In Chapter 1 a series of detail characteristics were identified and listed, derived from examples of detail forms that addressed the movement of water over a landscape surface. These include the following detail characteristics.

Detail Characteristics

- *Precision*
    The expression of site
    The expression of design ideas
    Hierarchy of detail language

- *Scale*
    Multiple scales
    Spatial continuity
    Visual continuity

- *Execution*
    Materials and their assembly
    Ability to accommodate changes
    Restraint

A wider range of landscape detail subjects and detail practices will now be examined and illustrated. These are necessary in determining a broader range of landscape detail approaches and themes. A more comprehensive set of detail conditions are also needed to continue to demonstrate the multiple types and forms of landscape detail that exist in the built environment. They represent a more extensive selection of the detail forms that the author has found useful in identifying certain detail approaches and themes, rather than in demonstrating "successful" or "less than successful" detail forms. The selection was based on the following seven criteria:

- Location

- Climatic conditions

- Project type

- Range of materials

77

- Age or time period

- Detail language

- Detail form

Location

Examples of landscape detail subjects and detail practices from North American cities are selected because of their richness of detail and range of types of open space. Examples from European capital cities are also included to illustrate landscape detail subjects and detail practices that developed during earlier periods of inhabitation and growth and have been the source of inspiration for stylistic movements and influences in the development of landscape architecture.

These choices are presented to show that many good examples can be found in countries and regions other than one's own and that quality and artfulness in landscape detail design transcends culture, time, and location.

It is left to the individual designers to reinterpret this vast resource of detail subjects and practices through the focus of their own areas of interest. Although many types of outdoor space that contain detail interest are to be found in rural and suburban locations, the intention here is to focus on urban conditions. Many types of landscape design and detail work are to be found in conjunction with transportation systems, highways, airports, waterfronts, and ferry terminals. These, however, entail many specific requirements that must be addressed, and that make them the focus of specialized detail research and use. The sites of outdoor urban space are more constantly occupied, and are, as a result, robust, developed to withstand more traffic and use. In addition, they have been consistently altered and rebuilt over time and thus are of more use for study. This does not suggest that details worthy of study are found exclusively in urban settings; it is a matter of the author's bias in this regard.

Climate

A range of climatic and microclimatic conditions are presented, representing aspects of the extremes and changes in temperature and weather patterns in the country and their influence on detail design.

Project Type

Detail subjects and practices from both public and private landscapes are featured. Detail quality can be brought equally to bear in a public outdoor space to be used by individuals and groups freely, as in a more restricted and controlled outdoor environment related to an individual family, institution, or corporation. It is worth noting that many of the historical spaces that we look to as models of landscape form and detail were conceived first as places for private activities and uses, then became public space.

Range of Materials

The range and type of materials is determined by their applications, ranging from the functional and economic to a more lavish use of natural and man-made materials. The variety of applications is demonstrated by both mass-produced industrialized production and handcrafted manual work. As indicated, these materials range from inexpensive to expensive, from cost-effective to costly. The intention is to indicate that although cost and budgets are important in influencing the quality and choice of materials and the over-all appearance of a project, they are not the determining factor in the execution of quality detail forms, nor do they guarantee the desired results. Some of the worst excesses and mistakes in detail design have been made when extravagant budgets have allowed a reckless use of inappropriate materials, finishes, junctions, and details. Rather, the most humble of materials used in a skillful manner can produce the most sublime of results.

Age or Time Period

The detail subjects and practices have been selected from a variety of time periods, ranging from the eighteenth and nineteenth centuries to the 1990s. No attempt is made to relate longevity with quality in detail forms, but the criteria of age and durability are important in determining the suitability of the choice of detail. It should be noted that there are cases in which it is difficult to determine whether the original detail forms still exist or have been altered by successive changes of use, ownership, or period. Adaptability over time is taken into account in determining the ability of the detailing to react to change of function, use, or application.

Language

Several types of detail languages are demonstrated arising from an extension of architectural principles of the surrounding context or buildings to individual, idiosyncratic, and personal detail forms reflecting aesthetic, artistic, religious, social, or cultural ideas.

Form

Different scales and types of details are considered in terms of their overall form. Considerations include, as well as their initial functions and purpose, the following forms of landscape detail:

- Standard and nonstandard

- Individual and massed

- Repetitive and single

- Off-the-shelf and made-in-place

- Continuous and episodic

• Unifying and separating

• Composite and whole

Landscape Types

Examples of landscape detail subjects are taken from three major outdoor spaces or landscape types found in urban locations:

• The park

• The square

• The street

No attempt has been made to be comprehensive in describing the scope of projects that a landscape architect might tackle within the profession. It is to be noted that common characteristics that can be identified in these three urban spaces can also be found in spaces of other types. It should also be noted that there are no private gardens covered here. These have been documented more comprehensively elsewhere,[1] and their use, size, and ownership type present a more eclectic range of spatial forms; in addition, they are likely to be more focused on plant material and detailed botanical displays and effects than the spaces discussed here.

The Park

An outdoor space that is closely associated with the development of built space and contemporary design expression in landscape architecture is the public park. Parks and park landscapes are composed of a variety of types of outdoor space, large and small, hard and soft, with a variety of detail uses in multiple or singular built forms and styles. They range in size from the regional park to the "pocket park," which is the size of a small urban lot. Landscape elements include pathways, roads, and paths for pedestrian and bicycle traffic, water bodies and landforms, active recreational facilities and modest supporting site structures. Many parks now show the effects of construction and the use of landscape detail forms over a number of historical periods and need constant cycles of maintenance and repair. One of the remarkable things about public landscapes like parks is the existence of consistent and comprehensive landscape detail forms. They are able to absorb changes of style and taste and to accommodate the juxtaposition of landscape detail forms of differing periods.

Parks also afford the designer great scope in the choice of detail forms— allowing a scale of size and repetition of elements that is rare. For the most part, parks were established and detail work carried out by public agencies and groups or partnerships of public and private institutions. As pressure of use on these spaces increases in the coming years, along with the need to replace or regenerate parks created in the nineteenth century, an understanding of the possibilities and choices in landscape detail design will become increasingly essential. It will be important, in terms of the detail design of a park, to focus on both the character of the ground surface and transitions and the materials, living and inert, as the main unifying detail elements. In addition, the *singular* forms and detail design of each park include detail elements that are associated with it alone, as well as a vast number of *repetitive* detail elements used throughout that are also found in other parks.

The Square

A square is a single, bounded urban or semiurban space, usually surrounded by buildings and forming part of the fabric of the city. Squares are mainly composed of hard, durable inert materials, paved or built with granular materials or grass panels. They are important places for social activities, ranging from civic functions and state gatherings to memorial services and celebrations of historic events. They may also be related to places of entertainment, theater, opera, music, or sport. Squares are currently seen as an extension of pedestrian areas in the city, even though many of them are used for parking, vehicular traffic movement, or sites for building. They exhibit a range of stylistic variations in detail form, offering a wide scope of historic and contemporary examples.

Of significance, in terms of the detail design of the square or plaza, is a focus on the nature and extent of the ground surface as the main unifying detail element.

In addition, the *singular* form and detail design of each space includes unique detail elements that are associated with it alone, as well as the identifiable materials and patterns that are developed there.

The Street

As the main method of direct pedestrian circulation and space in the city, streets, including sidewalks, pavement surfaces, curbs, roads, and street furniture, have traditionally been the focus of much energy by designers.

Detail forms such as paving surfaces, lighting, graphics, banners, planting, bollards, kiosks, artwork, and other landscape elements considered singly or in groups are now the signature, or identifying visual factors, in describing the location or context of particular streets or pedestrian ways.

As motivated by the regeneration of downtown retail areas, the "pedestrianization" of shopping streets and suburban malls, and the designation of historic towns and tourist destinations, streets have become important open spaces. They have been identified as significant places for the designer to develop specialized detail forms, fixtures, and site furniture. However, spaces of these types are few in number. More common in the urban landscape are streets with sidewalks. These also include the detail requirements for drainage, lighting, and accommodation of street tree planting, parking areas, and the adjacent cartway or roadway. There are also configurations of this simple arrangement in which the balance of pavement to roadway is reworked and reversed. The focus of detail design here is the attention to the entire grouping of the detail forms, their compatibility and balance, and the relationship of parts and materials. In addition, the linear nature of the landscape detail forms along the length of the street means that each part is developed as a member of a *repetitive* system of detail forms, unified by material, shape, and proportion.

Other Civic Spaces

There are two other significant outdoor spaces that form part of, or contain aspects of, the three previous landscape types but are still seen as individual forms in their own right. These are waterfront spaces and parking areas.

Waterfront

Waterfronts vary from natural river and lake fronts to hard urban maritime edges, built up over years of fishing, trade, and industrialization and still developing.

Of particular interest here is the water edge that was continuously occupied as an industrial working environment, was abandoned, and is now undergoing incremental reuse and alteration for public recreation, commercial retail activity, and/or housing.

In this case, the detail issues of new programmed uses and types of space, for example, walkways, promenades, ferry terminals, marinas, and boat docks, are required to be balanced against the historic character of existing in-place landscape materials and found site artifacts and structures, many in disrepair or requiring part or complete removal. This situation calls for new detail forms to be developed that are *adapted* from, or replace, existing detail forms or *reinterpret* existing historic detail elements.

Parking Areas

Although parking areas may appear at first to be a simpler form of landscape space, their importance in the contemporary built environment is based on their sheer quantity and the total area of ground surface covered by this land use. Their importance in terms of the subject of detail design rests on the variety and inventiveness of the resultant detail parts, based on such a limited type and palette of detail forms.

Parking details are reworked through *repetitive* detail forms. Some also aspire to using repetitive forms to create a *singular* detail language—for example, those attached and related to commercial retail, hotel, and entertainment centers.

This detail language is still realized through the repetition of identifiable motifs and the consistency of detail forms, materials, and finishes. The central detail component consists of the horizontal plane of the ground surface and the methods employed to direct and manipulate the movement of water and traffic circulation.

Further Landscape Detail Subjects and Detail Practices

In Chapter 1, eight landscape detail forms were described for the *movement of water over a built landscape surface.* The list that follows describes six other detail conditions arising from a range of detail subjects and practices found in the urban locations of parks, squares, streets, waterfronts, and parking areas. The intention of this list is to illustrate a selection of generic detail conditions, each of which will produce a range of specific detail responses, according to project location, type, and detail language and expression.

Detail Subjects

• *Overlaying materials.* Placing, layering, and overlapping horizontal and vertical detail surfaces, facings, and their supporting base materials. Examples are found in the landscape detail forms of paving surfaces and subbases in squares, streets, and parking areas where different circulation routes and movement paths are connected and overlaid together, as illustrated in Figure 3.1. Another detail form includes enclosures and boundaries where thin facings and veneers are supported by backings and supporting structures.

Figure 3.1
Overlaying materials. Driveway surfaces, Beacon Hill, Boston.

83

- *Turning corners.* The movement of horizontal and vertical surfaces changing direction produces detail concerns related to coursing, indentations, and the articulation of materials. Examples are found in streets, squares and, to a lesser extent, parks, where paths, boundaries, walls, and curbs are angled with joints and seams to produce a series of smooth transitions, as shown in Figure 3.2.

- *Shaping profiles.* Linking surface changes from landform to water and all other forms of detail transitions, thresholds, and bridges in the built landscape; in addition, the formation of detail openings, enclosures, and screens where shaping profiles helps in articulating surface changes. Examples are landscape detail forms arising in changes of surface level in parks (as shown in Figure 3.3) and waterfront edges.

Detail Practices

- *The placement of elements on a landscape surface.* The focus of individual or grouped detail forms on a ground plane, including methods of centering, realignment, and composition.

Figure 3.2
Turning corners. Curb edge,
London Docklands.

Figure 3.3
Shaping profiles. Raised
lawn coping, London
Docklands.

- *The concealment or expression of detail joints.* Detail junctions and treatments indicate the fixing, bringing together, and juxtaposition of landscape materials. This involves recessive or advancing detail forms. These are related both to detail organization and disclosure of the overall means of assembly, including gaps and reveals.

- *The support of detail edges.* Considerations of detail structures, including the issues of depth, strength, and balance, related to boundaries and openings, as well as the framing and outline of the horizontal ground plane.

3. APPROACHES

The process of detail development in a project involves the complete understanding and visualization of the final built landscape form. One of the important issues that must be addressed early in this process is the information that is to be generated. The skill of the designer lies in determining the following:

- What landscape detail forms have to be developed, and what do not? The total scope of detail forms has to be understood as an integral part of the evolution of the entire project. However, precise detail design study is especially needed when the detail forms are complex in their arrangement or assembly, or the quality of certain detail materials and finishes requires them to be more closely described.

- If there are areas where there are likely to be detail design problems, how can they be identified and addressed? This is particularly important when unknown or experimental materials or techniques of construction are being used for the first time.

- What are the detail parts that can be left to the discretion of others—for example, the contractor, the craftsperson, the specialized fabricator? What is significant to ask here is, Under what conditions can the development of landscape detail forms be left to those other than the designer?

The designer establishes the detail type that is most appropriate in relation to the qualities of the site and the client's requirements, and within the opportunities and limitations afforded by the budget, project site, local codes, material choice, manufacturing limits, and abilities of construction workers in the field. Landscape detail forms result from the following detail activities:

- The designer discriminating early in the detail process between the different forms of details and reviewing them as changes occur to the project scope, form, and budget

- The selection and portrayal of the detail parts and their components and assemblies, including descriptions of materials and finishes

- The consideration of material dimensions required by engineering and codes, including structural integrity and economy of component parts

- Tackling both typical and nontypical details in a systematic way

During the landscape design process, there are six subjects for detail investigation, derived from a range of sources:

1. The site location and context

2. What the designer has been asked to do

3. What the designer brings to the project in terms of individual ideas and experience

4. Evolution of conceptual detail ideas

5. The development of detail form

6. The expression of that detail form

Let us now examine three general approaches to detail design that utilize the results of these detail design investigations. In the first, *concept to detail,* the progression from the general conceptual design ideas to the detail forms is sequential, following the six subjects for detail investigation previously identified, leading from broad principles of design and spatial organization to specific solutions to detail forms. The second, *detail to implementation,* starts initially with the development of detail form, then reverses the process, leading to a final resolution of the project in terms of design and detail. The third, the *integrated* approach, combines the first and second, whereby concerns of overall site design and detail design, concept to implementation, are considered together at the beginning of the process.

> Detailing, in fact, obeys the same principles observed in spatial organization. The great lessons of the past are there, the high tradition of craftsmanship, perfect adherence to purpose and context, strict observance of functionality, and the unmistakable penchant for an organism that must evolve naturally. The individual parts take shape slowly, each pursuing its specific role, initially schematic in concept, gaining in complexity as it continues to evolve into a new form. At this stage, the processes of articulating, connecting, and interlocking must combine harmonically to produce a precisely machined, perfectly efficient and near organic whole.
>
> BIANCA ALBERTINI and SANDRO BAGNOLI,
> *Carlo Scarpa: Architecture in Details.* 1988

Detail Approach A — Concept to Detail

The concept-to-detail approach (A) is the most commonly understood method of developing or evolving design work, starting from a general or generic overall design concept and developing through a series of steps a more resolved understanding of the spatial relationships, materials, structure, forms, and dimensional organization and coordination. This involves a gradual shift in scale (from large to small), clarification of spatial order and hierarchy, determination of the shape and density of materials and form, as well as written descriptions in the form of preliminary specifications and notes.

Landscape detail is therefore seen as the *outcome* or *resolution* of the entire design process, occurring at the end of the phase of design development.

There are instances in certain projects in which the design process can be carried on during the implementation phase on-site. In such cases, changes to detail design owing to site conditions, inaccuracies in original surveys and documentation, or instructions to alter original design proposals for aesthetic, economic, or programmatic reasons are required. Here the details form part of a reevaluation or redesign process that may involve total redesign or alterations at various stages in the process. The relationship between the landscape design proposal and its detail is one in which the detail serves as a part or fragment of the larger whole and represents supporting aspects of the conceptual idea or ideas. The landscape detail form reinforces this notion through its identification in size and scale as a secondary role.

Detail Approach B — Detail to Completion

In Detail Approach B the landscape details become the initial components of the project, leading eventually to completed built design work. There are two alternatives for this detail approach. The first starts with a set of *design concepts* that are resolved at the detail scale and then developed, moving in size and resolution, from the part to the whole. The second alternative starts at the beginning with a set of existing and fully resolved *detail ideas* or *detail forms,* then applies them to a specific landscape design condition.

Alternative 1

The first alternative requires as its starting point a single design idea or set of ideas that have been conceived at the detail scale. The conventional process outlined in Detail Approach A is therefore reversed. Instead of approaching landscape design development from the whole to the part, or from landscape concept to detail, it starts at an intimate scale of a single or group of conceptual detail ideas and landscape detail forms. It then moves and develops to a larger scale, from the part to the whole. This approach proposes that the basic nature of a design idea is found within a fragment of the whole landscape, and that the detail forms become generators for the entire project. This approach has two potential methods for evolving and developing the rest of the design project:

- The detail forms establish *centers* or points of *detail focus* within a larger and less differentiated quantity of design material. These centers act to articulate a design hierarchy for the project design and to articulate areas of design and detail importance with an inherent value.

- Through their early establishment, the detail form or forms create a physical, visual, and conceptual *order* that is continued throughout the design process in multiple permutations and interpretations.

From this starting point these detail forms or detail parts are assembled or reconfigured in various ways according to site, program, or design aesthetics. What is significant here is the way these details support the evolution of the total project, the relationship between the individual parts and the whole, and the relationship between the parts, how they are configured, and the strategy of their assembly; these become the main conceptual idea of the project.

Alternative Two

The second alternative is the application of an initial set of detail ideas to a series of landscape conditions. Instead of developing details at the end of the landscape design process as the conclusion and outcome of all site and program issues, it starts by designing the landscape details first as abstract detail pieces. These landscape details become the generators for the project, with a focus first on their structural and material properties and fabrication and then their ability as fragments of a larger landscape to originate or seed other new parts, or to be broken down and systematically repeated over a larger area.

Some of issues at stake here are the means by which the detail ideas can be expanded. Here questions arise regarding the initial size of the abstract detail parts to the final size of the landscape project.

What are the limits and boundaries of expansion and scale change? Can landscape details be conceived at the scale of a single boundary element or barrier—for example, as a fence post or rails—and then expanded to encompass larger features across a whole site? Finally, this alternative raises the question for the designer, What if the landscape details are the determinants for a design project and there are many versions of the final design form and expression?

One example of this is the "kit of parts" technique, whereby the initial problem is solved by a group of individual detail parts or elements that are either selected as *standard, off-the-shelf,* or *customized.* Their scale, materials, and spatial relationships are considered from the point of view of establishing a clear but flexible detail language that can be developed not only over one location or site, but with repetitive use and local variation. Examples of this detail approach occur in the many forms of institutional work, such as corporate headquarters, campuses, hospitals, and city projects or work concerned with transportation agencies in which recognition of identity is central and ongoing work is performed over long periods of time under different consultants and leaderships. The necessary skill lies in the correct weighting and coordination of the detail elements so as to maintain both individual design freedom and a consistent detail language over time.

Detail Approach C—Integrated

The third and final approach combines both Approaches A and B to create a multiscaled and interconnected process.

Here, considerations of design at the detail scale and the larger site are addressed simultaneously.

The ultimate goal in developing the general and the detail design together is to create an unified and integrated design proposal. An example is illustrated at the beginning of the introductory section to this book. This was based on the author's early experience in practice, watching the inception of a project where considerations of both detail design and overall site design were studied at the outset. The isolation of detail design forms at this stage focuses on the conceptual making and fabrication of the detail parts, as well as the detail language and references such detail forms establish beyond their own scale. The future enlargement and reduction in scale raises issues regarding the detail design in relation to the overall conceptual site design. Do alterations to the site design change the detail form, and vice versa?

The observation and recognition of the forms of landscape detail surfaces, transitions, junctions, and joints at the beginning of the conceptual design phase relies on an understanding of the following aspects of detail design:

- What the designer has been asked to do. The initial conceptual design elements, plan, section, and detail forms reflect the first understanding of the program and the design and detail requirements of the project type. This includes the *early selection* of the necessary landscape detail forms in relation to the appropriate scope and range of the project.

- What the designer brings to the project in terms of individual ideas and experience. This is related to the group of *detail themes* that the designer recalls and works with in every project and constitutes the main focus of design and detail attention. The sources of these themes are as varied as the themes themselves, such as artistic and aesthetic preoccupations or interests in cultural and social topics. Included in these design themes are also individual and personal issues regarding the medium of design and landscape. Part of the designer's ongoing training involves building up and storing these themes for future use in design projects.

Present within each of the three detail approaches are certain detail design ideas that the designer returns to, time and time again. These are the *themes* that were identified earlier. These remain independent of project type or scale and are to be found in detail design as much as larger design concerns. In fact, this book argues that most of the central themes in landscape design and landscape architecture are discovered and resolved at the landscape detail level.

4. THEMES

What are the thematic ideas that are present in landscape detail? In addition, how do these themes relate to a search for individual expression in detail design and the need to develop a personal constructional detail language? This section introduces the role of detail themes in landscape detail. It considers the place of individual expression and a detail language in the work of a designer and reviews examples of four of the most commonly found themes in detail design work.

The recognition and evolution of individual detail themes by the designer is one of the main struggles of individual artistic expression in landscape architecture. The results, when fully realized, appear as suggestive and significant detail forms in the landscape, representing design ideas and narratives and demonstrating the ways in which they were conceived and the values of the people who made them.

Although a number of publications have attempted to address the origins of conceptual design ideas, it is clear that there are as many potential sources of ideas as there are projects and designers.

Many ideas come from the medium itself, with concern for the varied natural forms found in the world, the influences of site, place, and context, and the various types of human behavior—how people work, play games, and inhabit and use outdoor social space. Design sources in landscape architecture encompass all of these. The most familiar things are, in the end, the most useful.

Cutting across the range of ideas in landscape design, *detail themes* prove meaningful in bringing together work from different designers, periods, or locations. They can allow us to examine critically each landscape designer's work by concentrating on detail matters that are gathered together through various scales, operations, and assemblies, and their placement and nuances within the larger amount of material. Themes, and particularly their variations, that are worked out in different ways over time are more lasting and important in the understanding of the evolution of detail practices.

Themes are used by designers either singly or in combinations. They illustrate aspects of the aesthetic and spatial character of landscape detail: the properties of harmony, accent, tone and texture, the honest expression of materials, respect for craft and craftsmanship, and the unity of design versus the issues of fragmentation. Four aspects of the nature of detail themes are introduced here, *language, expression, hierarchy,* and recurring *detail motifs.*

Detail Language

Detail language is concerned with the way the overall thematic and conceptual ideas of the initial landscape design proposal are organized, conceived, and structured. It is concerned with the motivation underlying formal and material choices and is consistent across scales of work.

A detail language is personal to the designer in terms of the repetition of certain shapes, lines, configurations of materials and finishes, and ideas that are continuously repeated in various forms and locations. A detail language is a consistent part of a designer's working practice. Details can be appropri-

Figure 3.4
Detail language. Metal
bridge and walking surface,
Bamboo Garden, Parc de la
Villette, Paris.

ated into a language. An example is the consistent use of certain geometries and shapes, or the repeated use of classical or contemporary detail forms, objects, or industrial materials, as illustrated in Figure 3. 4.

Detail Expression

Detail expression is concerned with how a detail language is individually handled and is closely tied to thematic ideas. It concerns the original intent of the project; what qualities is it intended to portray—somber, restrained, reticent, or confrontational? or exuberant, playful, or celebratory? All depend on program, type, and location.

Detail Hierarchy

There are occasions when a designer must be conscious of the variation and variety of aesthetic, artistic, cultural, and material values present and must determine their hierarchy, choosing which to emphasize. Here the articulation of the landscape detail is one of weighting or structuring the parts of the landscape according to the importance of the detail forms. To articulate means to differentiate according to a clear set of values or rules. The aim here is not to combine or separate the detail elements that concern us, but to single out each of them without discriminating against any of them.

Detail Motifs

Motifs are recurrent thematic figures or elements. A designer's repetition of detail themes and their subsequent identification and development lead to certain features that are closely identified with an office, an individual designer, or a style. They include the following:

- Motifs concerning the detail order and ordering of landscape elements

- Motifs in regard to the fragmentation of landscape elements

- Motifs concerning the layering of natural and man-made materials—for example, earth, concrete, stone, and wood and their deformation and manipulation through natural forces and design processes

- Motifs concerning the appearance of natural forms and the role of nature in their making

- Motifs in regard to craft and craftsmanship

What are the subjects of landscape detail? Are they separate from the subjects of study in landscape design, or do they have their own range of issues and ideas? As outlined in Chapter 1, landscape detail forms are the outcome, development, and resolution of initial conceptual detail design ideas. It is therefore reasonable to expect many of the conceptual ideas with which designers work at the critical stages of a landscape project to be the same as those dealt with at the detail scale. However, landscape detail design has issues that are particularly relevant at this scale and that are consistently worked out at this level. These include the following three, which appear consistently within landscape architectural detail design as major topics: ideas of *order,* ideas of *construction,* and ideas of *time, durability,* and *material change.*

Ideas of Order

Many of the subjects or ideas in site design and landscape architecture are concerned with detail ordering or structuring. These derive from the need to control or provide frameworks by which a site can be organized and developed from the detail scale onward. A common example is the utilization of surface patterns or the structure of circulation routes and pathways. Related to this ordering is the role of detail hierarchy and the emphasis of this hierarchy through detail forms and material uses.

Ideas of Construction

Landscape detail concerns the elements of the built landscape as to how they are organized and how they fit with and relate to each other during the design process, as well as the pragmatic concerns of the completed built form. Landscape detail forms are concerned with the interaction of structure and materials, the integration of ideas of proportion, assembly, and fabrication, and the organization of detail site assemblies and fabrication.

Ideas of Time, Materials, and Change

Time alters a built landscape by the direct effect it has on the landscape, not on the conceptual ideas behind the landscape. We can attempt to reverse change through regular maintenance and reconstruction, thus producing a static piece of work. This, however, is also a form of change, creating a built landscape space at different phases of its design evolution and development. Ideas that attempt to register change can do so by deliberately proposing detail forms that will fail or will have a restricted or limited life. The built landscapes of international events—for example, Olympic arenas—and their supporting gathering spaces and developments produce the landscape details of public outdoor spaces with a three- to five-week life, all placed within an infrastructure and other built forms that have a more permanent life. Ideas about change come from the selection and juxtaposition of materials, the methods of working the materials and their assembly, and the relationship and sequence of joints and junctions in those materials.

All these ideas are present individually or collectively in many of the detail themes of detail design work. Let us now review examples of four of the most commonly found themes in detail design work; these are as follows:

• *Continuous* or *Discontinuous*

• *Recessive* or *Active*

Theme A—Continuous

Continuous detail forms are concerned with the unity of detail language, expression, and hierarchy and are the most commonly found in the built landscape.

The scope of detail work covers a range of landscape elements and conditions. The detail design process may be carried out over a long period or in phases. In addition, the need to establish a unified detail language over the whole project requires careful consideration of all the parts and their relationship to each other in terms of detail character, scale, material, and expression. Continuous detail forms aim to add, progressively, each detail condition, one after another, with the shapes, profiles, and forms repeated or revised as each detail is developed. There is a distinct connection between all the parts and the central ideas of the whole. As the horizontal and vertical surfaces join, the surface finishes move from rough to fine in a controlled manner, according to the evolutionary process.

Consider the example of grounds and approach to the United States Capitol in Washington, D.C., by the office of Frederick Law Olmsted. This plan unites pathways, open lawn areas, and circulation up to and around the Capi-

Figure 3.5
Continuous detail. United States Capitol Grounds, Washington, D.C. (1874–1891). Office of Frederick Law Olmsted.

tol Building by adding, progressively, material, weight, and finish to the details as the sequence unfolds. Starting as small round stone buttons in the grass, these elements rise slowly to become seating and retaining walls, as illustrated in Figure 3.5, light bases, and, finally, pavilion structures, while changing in texture, quality of finished surface, and applied iconographical markings (grasses and plants of the United States). This is a set piece in which every part plays a role.

Theme B — Discontinuous

In opposition to the unity of continuous detail, themes of the *discontinuous* or *episodic detail* attempt by deliberate contrast to fragment parts of the landscape and address each of them on their own terms, irrespective of adjoining elements, conditions, and detail expression.

This theme, which dominates the design detail process, corresponds to the idea of contrast in design. Contrast in detail produces an immediate and obvious effect; it is an element of variety, it distracts and diverts visual attention, programmatic concerns, spatial focus, and experiential character, as illustrated in Figure 3.6 with the varying detail forms, materials, and elements of a modern wall.

Figure 3.6
Discontinuous detail.
Glazed tile and precast
concrete walls and bench,
Moll de la Fuesta,
Barcelona, Spain.

Theme C — Recessive

The *recessive* nature of new detail forms appears as a theme in working with many built landscapes of historical significance. Here the intention of the detail design work is to reduce the impact of new detail forms on an existing environment or context, to make the work "go away" visually and spatially, and to create a built landscape that is complete and consistent.

The theme of recessive detail is also used where the designer intends to create the built landscape as a background or setting for other built forms. Here, a careful manipulation of materials, shapes, and junctions takes place, with thoughtful consideration of the transitions between different detail elements, pathways, walls, and planting, as shown in Figure 3. 7, and between the built landscape and its surrounding environment.

Theme D — Active

In contrast to the previous recessive theme, the *active* theme is applied in the detail design process where each detail form is proposed to be dynamic, visually abrupt, and distinct from its surroundings and other detail forms. *Additive* procedures bring each detail part into sharp focus. This consists of either the juxtaposition or applying together multiple detail forms that are stylisti-

Figure 3.7
Recessive detail. Retaining
wall, pathways, and canopy
trees, River Seine, Paris,
France.

Figure 3.8
Active detail. Parc de la
Villette, Paris, France.

cally different or are of different materials, particularly those that appear at first antithetical and to clash in terms of their finished textures, colors, and scales. This also results in built work that is innovative and progressive, continuing to demonstrate the creative potential of detail design as shown in Figure 3. 8. *Subtractive* procedures produce similar results, but in a different way. Through a reductive process of removing excessive detail material and forms, the programmatic, spatial, and experiential character of the built landscape space becomes enriched through elimination and abstraction.

5. CATEGORIES

The traditional identification of general categories for landscape construction details is based on the following:

• Their location within the project

• Where the need for clarification of the design intent is needed

• Where there is variation from standard construction practices

For example, Gary Robinette, ASLA, in *Landscape Architectural Site Construction Details*[2] identifies such locations as follows:

a. Any place that is critical in the design should be detailed carefully.

b. Any place where there is an ambiguity or question in the possible method of construction...

c. Anywhere there is a joining of material...

d. Any point or any area which is constructed, joined or detailed in a manner which is different from standard accepted practice.

e. Any situation on a plan that is repeated or replicated a number of times...

Overview of Detail Categories

The detail approaches described in the previous section are applied in an infinite number of locations and conditions during the evolution of a project. In order to address the vast range of types and forms of external landscape details, three detail *categories* in which landscape details are *located* spatially have been devised: *surfaces* (the horizontal ground plane), *transitions* (changes in the horizontal ground plane) and *boundaries* (the vertical or overhead plane).

Although these categories cannot possibly cover every detail that is likely to occur during the normal range of a project, they describe or break down the built landscape into a series of spatial planes. These categories rarely exist on their own, but are part of a spatial understanding of the landscape. Therefore, there are landscape details that have aspects of all three categories in their structuring order and form. A pergola, for example, consists of a horizontal ground plane and overhead planes and may be partly bounded by side screens, trellises, or walls. It may include additional planting details, as well as lighting, irrigation, and seating elements.

1. *Surfaces: The horizontal ground plane.* The category most closely associated with landscape architecture design through the manipulation of the ground plane, or the placing of one material on another. The details of pedestrian paving, pathways, and roadways are formed in materials of earth, asphalt, stone, concrete, gravel, and brick.

2. *Transitions: Changes in the horizontal ground plane.* Modulations to the horizontal surface in the form of steps, stairs, curbs, ramps, and sloped planes.

3. *Boundaries: The vertical or overhead plane or enclosures.* Detail transitions that form temporary or permanent edges, barriers, and enclosures. These

include vertical and horizontal boundaries in the form of opaque or perforated walls, fences, railings, screens, pergolas, and trellises.

Professional Detail Practice

Everyday detail design practices are in constant use within professional landscape offices. As outlined earlier, they consist of approaches that repeat a series of rules of thumb that have been compiled from project experience within an office over a long period and have, in the opinion of the principals and senior staff in that office, stood the test of time. They have typically resulted in completed and occupied projects that have required little or no alterations or corrective work to change design or installation faults. In addition, they were carried out within the economic, legislative, and aesthetic constraints present at the time. One of the issues in practice that determines the success or failure of the application of rules of thumb is the ability to recover the detail information and apply it in any new project situation. This is an ongoing issue of document storage, project management, and record keeping. Another thing to consider is the turnover of project personnel who have worked on earlier projects. They may have left the office, taking this information with them, or they may have moved into different roles within the office that do not allow them to participate in design development work.

In recent times there have been a number of detail "special cases" related to changes within the structure of landscape practice. There are alterations to legal aspects of the physical environment and outdoor space and a shift in the type of projects available to be carried out by landscape architects and their design collaborators and colleagues. These projects include work arising from the Americans with Disabilities Act of 1990 (ADA),[3] air rights development and building landscapes over roof structures,[4] and special detail practices that enhance, support, and extend emerging ideas in land reclamation and applied ecological restoration design.[5]

The range of professional landscape office types and configurations is diverse, and so are the levels of experience and depth of knowledge in detail design work. However, there are a number of categories of landscape office that can be based on the offices' approaches and techniques of landscape detailing and detail design development. Bruce Sharky outlines four generic areas of practice under the heading of "Forms of Professional Practice": *public, private, academic,* and *nontraditional.*[6]

• *Public and private.* The most common types of practice that make up the landscape profession are the public practice and the private practice. The private office varies in size from the single practitioner working at home, to the large corporate landscape architecture office, including landscape departments as part of larger architecture and engineering firms. The public office ranges from one consisting of a sole landscape practitioner to a medium-sized design and planning office or cluster of medium-sized offices that form a larger regional or national organization. The approach to detail design can vary as much as the size and scale of operation. Operations range from local, small-scale design and construction projects with ample opportunity to be involved in day-to-day detail practices and decisions, to large-scale overseas multidisciplinary projects in which the detail design phase may be removed from the initial conceptual and planning design team. All office types require the use of a range of techniques, including innovative conceptual detail design and the selection of office detail standards from a variety of in-house manuals, handbooks, standards, and government or local agency guidelines.

• *Academic.* Of all the forms of practice, the academic practice is likely to be the most diverse in terms of type and scale of work, office size, organization, and range of activities that are carried out. The split between teaching full- or part-time and the daily rigors of a practice are such that a single practitioner may be absent for long periods of time or that the office work may be shared by two academics or an academic and his or her full-time business partner. The academic may be the person responsible for the technology curriculum of a local design school, and many of the exercises and detail practices given in these classes are drawn from practice. In a small, local office with student help or recent graduates, much of the burden for detail development may typically rest on the recent graduates. There are likely to be detail examples derived from local construction practices including their own, as well as from other local or national offices, in the form of construction documentation sets (blueprints), specifications, and photographic documentation. The collective memory of a seasoned landscape practitioner will be invaluable. If the academic is a recent graduate or younger, much of the time may be spent on competitions or speculative work and the opportunity to build will be slight.

• *Nontraditional.* Sharky defines nontraditional practices as "institutional, non-profit, and service organizations,...construction and green industry, ...and emerging forms and specialty areas of practice." It is likely, therefore, that these types of detail design practices will adjust and edit the existing detail practices from the profession or adopt a detail process closer to design/build. This is where design and implementation are closely interrelated through the physical execution of detail design on-site.

A prospective entry-level landscape designer or young practitioner should observe the range and scope of various practices. It is important to determine how involved each office type is in the design development phases of work and what a practitioner is likely to encounter on a daily basis if he or she joins a practice of a particular type.

6. TYPES OF DETAIL WORK

Types of detail work can be described as detail *restoration and renovation* and detail *editing*, where the sources of landscape detail form are clearly derived from site sources. Detail *innovation* arises when landscape detail forms are not derived from identifiable site or project sources.

Restoration and Renovation

Detail forms can arise from renovation, restoration, or addition within an acknowledged historic landscape or grouping of significant open spaces and building structures.

Work in this area includes the identification and recording of existing landscape details from one or more historical periods and the preservation, restoration, or adaptation of those details, as shown in Figure 3.9. Examples range from sites identified on the National Historic Register and National Park Service sites to local and community landmarks. This type of detail work may involve research into extinct or little used construction processes, materials and elements that are no longer available or are difficult to obtain, and the development of details that reconcile contemporary approaches and current technologies with the historic patterns of detailing that are required. It is worth noting that the term *historical* as used in landscape design does not always refer to the nineteenth century or earlier. Many projects or places dating in the twentieth century until as recently as the 1960s, although having no official listing or registration as significant places, fall within this category. Examples include the work from the Works Progress Administration (WPA) and the Civilian Conservation Corps (CCC), as well as more recent work in the urban plazas of the 1960s and 1970s that are recently undergoing renovation or, more likely, complete replacement.

Detail Editing

In current landscape work, it is unusual to encounter a site composed of elements of a single time period. More likely, a collection of fragments or disparate periods is the norm, with jarring or conflicting juxtapositions of detailing periods and styles and, in some cases, overlapping or incongruous materials or assemblies brought together in seemingly random ways. The qualities of these spaces result in part from this condition.

The addition of new landscape work adds yet another layer, or part, to this mixture, as shown in Figure 3.10. The work of the designer and the detailing scope may involve the selection or discrimination between different detailing approaches, which are developed into a composite approach. This process of editing the detailing parts results in a complex mix of old and new, various historical periods, and a range of technologies and assemblies. The development of a detail language is dependent on a process of precise selection and careful weaving together of eclectic elements to form a new series of forms and structures.

Figure 3.9
Detail restoration and
renovation. Ramp and step,
New York Public Library,
New York. Courtesy of
Hanna/Olin Ltd.

Figure 3.10
Detail editing. Rainwater
channel edge.

Detail Innovation

The final detail condition involves the creation or invention of landscape detail by the designer. This occurs when the requirements are to develop a singular group of details that do not use either the extension of an existing vocabulary or the piecing together of a number of existing detail languages as shown in Figure 3.11. This is, in short, the area of detail design innovation.

Figure 3.11
Detail innovation. Parc
Guell, Barcelona, Spain.

7. SUMMARY

It is difficult to separate the subject of landscape detail from landscape design or, specifically, the landscape design process. Designers spend an inordinate amount of time refining and developing the individual form and expression of landscape detail. This has enabled their work to be of a consistently high quality, regardless of project type, program, budget, location, or materials. The following statements regarding the conception and evolution of landscape detail summarize Part One, "Fundamentals":

1. *It is as important to detail well as it is to design and build well.* We cannot design well if the way we detail is not considered an active part of how we organize and achieve the original design intentions. It is in this idea, the interrelation of design and construction processes, where the potential and, ultimately, the form, beauty, and significance of future built landscape space lies. It addresses a concern for the relationship in landscape architecture between landscape and detail, how things are conceived in design, and how they are finally executed on-site.

2. *The care and attention with which details and detail forms are shaped, articulated, and made is part of the meaning of landscape detail.* How the designer conceives and ultimately develops details, either through shaping on paper with sketches and drawings or with models or mock-ups, is of primary importance to the final interpretations. Meaning can be found not only through the final detail (whether as traditional, symbolic, or figurative motifs or associations), but also in the "mechanics" of how an artifact was brought into being, not only by hand tool on-site or industrial machine, but as a design activity. In short, in the fashioning of a detail the designer is attributing meaning to each part through design choices, whether they are made deliberately or not. In addition, and more important, detail design is not only the means by which built landscapes are achieved, but also one of the central design concerns of the field.

3. *Research of the medium of detail design for artistic and poetic expression requires sustained effort, rather than isolated investigations.* Efficient detail design study may be better achieved by focusing on a more limited palette of materials and deepening their artistic possibilities, rather than broadening the selection of materials while working superficially with all of them. Examples include infinite variations of stone, brick, plants, and wood in which the detail palette arises from the regional and local limitations of raw materials.

4. *No detail is small.* The idea of landscape detail is not confined to the final resolution of all previously agreed-upon design issues; rather it is the con-

105

tinuous testing and designing of scale relationships throughout a project. No detail is small refers to the notion of giving equal emphasis to the whole and the parts. The activities of enlargement and reduction therefore remain a significant aspect of the entire landscape design process.

8. DEFINITIONS OF TERMS

Key terms and phrases discussed in this chapter are defined below.

Detail approaches: design and detail development processes that are most commonly used in landscape detail practice.

Detail categories: general areas within a landscape design proposal where the focus and location of detail design work occurs; these include detail surfaces, transitions, and boundaries.

Detail themes: underlying subjects or points of view and their variations that are expanded upon in detail design.

Detail motifs: recurrent thematic figures or elements in detail themes.

Detail hierarchy: ordering or structuring the detail parts of the landscape according to the weighting of importance and location of each detail.

Detail innovation: creation or invention of landscape detail by the designer.

Detail editing: selection or discrimination between different detail approaches, which are developed into a composite approach.

Detail restoration: identification and recording of existing landscape detail from one or more historical periods and the preservation, rehabilitation, or adaptation of those details.

9. CLASSROOM EXERCISES

These exercises form part of a series of assignments to be carried out within the structure of a course on landscape construction, or landscape technology and detail, or as part of a design studio.

Assignment 3: Landscape Detail Approaches and Themes

1. Identify a set of detail forms in a contemporary built landscape that has been recently documented in a landscape design monograph or magazine article.

What are the detail approaches that have been used in developing the detail elements? Use the definitions given in this chapter. Why was this approach used? Was it based on the project type, the designer, or the context of the project? The aim is to examine, first, why there is no single method of tackling detail design and, second, how the aesthetic intent and integrity of the conceptual detail ideas have been safeguarded through the particular approach that was taken.

2. Locate and develop a landscape detail form that adds to, or modifies, an existing detail condition in a local built landscape. The approach is to be based on *one* of the following approaches. The detail form can either be an existing detail element that is required to be extended or increased in size with the use of a similar set of detail forms, *or* an existing detail element that is to be modified with the use of a new set of detail forms.

   The intention is for designers to become familiar with the variation of existing detail forms. Which detail approach is appropriate in these cases? How does the detail approach protect the integrity of the existing detail form?

3. Locate and carry out a series of short detail exercises for a single landscape element — for example, a bridge, seating area, or building entrance — in your locale. Using a "freestyle" approach to generating detail form, execute three alternate detail themes for the same landscape element.

   Compare and contrast the results, in terms of their ability to generate original detail forms, and their relationship to the selection of landscape materials. Are certain themes more appropriate to particular types of detail work? How does the use of these detail themes enable the evolution of different landscape detail forms?

10. REFERENCES AND SOURCES

Section 2. Range of Detail Work

1. The range of books on public and residential garden design and detail is extensive. See, for example:

   Christopher Thacker, *The History of Gardens* (Berkeley: University of California Press, 1979).

   Dorothee Imbert, *The Modernist Garden in France* (New Haven: Yale University Press, 1993).

   Monique Mosser and Georges Teyssot, *The Architecture of Western Gardens* (Cambridge: MIT Press, 1991).

Section 5. Categories

2. See Gary O. Robinette, *Landscape Architectural Site Construction Details* (Reston, Va.: Environmental Design Press, 1976).

3. See, for example, *Accessible Design Handbook: The ADA Troubleshooter Guide and Workbook* (Norwalk, Conn.: Cash Callahan and Company, 1991).

4. See, for example, John Simmonds, *Roof Gardens* (New York: McGraw Hill, 1997). See also *Landscape Design Magazine* (September 1992) (issue on roof structures and air rights).

5. See *Ecological Design and Planning,* ed. George F. Thompson and Frederick Steiner (New York: John Wiley & Sons, 1997).

6. From Bruce Sharkey, *Ready, Steady, Practice* (New York: John Wiley & Sons, 1994).

11. FURTHER READING

Hubbard, Henry Vincent, and Theodora Kimball. *An Introduction to the Study of Landscape Design.* New York: Macmillan Company, 1917.

Woodward, Graham. "Federation Design." *Landscape Design* (October 1990): 35–37.

PART 2

PRACTICES

Much but by no means all world-making consists of taking apart and putting together, often conjointly: on the one hand, of dividing wholes into parts and partitioning kinds into sub-species, analyzing complexes into component features, drawing distinctions; on the other hand, of composing wholes and kinds out of parts and members and subclasses, combining features into complexes, and making connections.

NELSON GOODMAN,
Ways of World-Making, 1978

In Part Two, Chapters 4 to 6, an introduction to the working methods of landscape detail will review significant detail practices that shape an initial concept into a final built detail form. The detail categories of surfaces, transitions, and boundaries in Chapter 4 embody ideas of making connections and *constructing detail* as a design activity. These ideas are first established in the tectonics, the "putting together," the production of landscape details at the detail design stage. In addition, issues of detail quality and craftsmanship are reviewed. In Chapter 5, the issues of *detail durability* are covered and the influence of site and climate on landscape detail is explored through the concerns of time, materials, and weathering. Finally, Chapter 6 describes the *research* of detail and documentation of detail precedents in the field. Designers are advised on outstanding areas of detail research still to be carried out.

CHAPTER 4

CONSTRUCTING DETAIL

THIS CHAPTER CONCERNS the broad range of topics under the heading of landscape detail "construction." It should be noted that the term *detail construction* refers here to the creation and structuring of physical detail forms in the design process rather than, as it is more commonly used, their final implementation on site by others. Aspects of detail construction during the design process are applied to the three categories of landscape detail forms previously identified in Chapter 3: *surfaces, transitions,* and *boundaries.* The conditions are reviewed under which these detail categories are "taken apart and put together"—the process of shaping them into landscape detail forms. This chapter also examines the terms *techne* and *tectonics* and their meaning and application in landscape detail design and contemporary built work in landscape architecture. This examination focuses on the translation of detail ideas in landscape architecture into physical reality. Student readers will gain an understanding of the roles of tectonics, materials, structure, and assembly in the making of landscape detail form. In particular, the focus will be on the issues and ideas of craft and craftsmanship in current detail making and, thereby, the possibilities open to designers in the future.

1. INTRODUCTION

Acts of Detail Construction

Among the central foundations of landscape design is the translation of conceptual ideas into built work. This is one of the reasons that students still enter the professional landscape design field and practitioners continue to remain in it. Theirs is the passion for making and expressing physical form through design and the joy of finally seeing the results of their design work executed as appropriately scaled and crafted spaces.

Let us now consider the methods by which conceptual landscape ideas are translated into built work, the materials that are considered and selected, the ways in which they are put together, and the skill and craft associated with such activity. In this regard, we will examine three related topics:

• The nature of *tectonics*

• Detail making and construction

• The ideas and issues of detail craft, quality, and craftsmanship

First, it should be recognized that a significant aspect of the art of landscape detail is its making and construction, and the uses and meanings we attach to this activity.

For the designer, part of the skill in developing the varied range of landscape detail forms within a project lies not only in the formulation of the initial concept, but in understanding how the idea is "made visible" — physically shaped through detail design. In short, the designer must be adept in the landscape detail practices of construction.

Landscape architect Dan Kiley considers the process of actual site building and knowledge of the building industry to be central to this process and a key to detail design. "If you know how to build, details just roll off your fingers," he states emphatically,[1] suggesting an organic process of detail development and design. Although he is referring to his own long experience and exposure to the practices of site implementation, this philosophy has been translated into a reliable set of office detail practices that are now carried out by others in his office.

This is not the case, however, with most design students and entry-level practitioners. It should be emphasized that the lack of practical skills and experience of implementation in the field should not hold back a designer from fully developing his or her understanding and skills in this area of detail design. There are many designers who lack this practical experience in their initial training, who are still able to develop a deep appreciation for "making" in detail design and to translate it into their daily work. This they achieve through an understanding of landscape tectonics and the use of tectonic ideas in the conceptual development of landscape detail.

Landscape Tectonics

The relationship between landscape detail design and tectonics has been seen largely in terms of rationalizing the functional parts of detail form, such as the description of a pedestrian brick surface with its prepared subbase and bedding layer.

Making an idea visible within the existing landscape in this way is termed *techne*, a word derived from the Greek that characterizes the detail practice of construction as both an artistic and pragmatic one. We refer to the "tectonic approach" taken by the designer during the process of design development and detail design. We can also refer to the "landscape tectonics" of a particular project. Recent studies in architecture[2] have continued to acknowledge the central role of tectonics in the comprehension and development of architectural structure and building form. In landscape architecture, however, tectonics has had little bearing on design and detail thinking to date.

The tectonics of landscape detail determine how the detail idea is made visible and the necessary forces that establish and mold its eventual physical form.

Landscape tectonics is derived from a spatial and physical ordering brought to a particular landscape condition. It allows the designer to conceive of the detail design in terms of "taking apart and putting together" the detail parts, an ordering and structuring of the detail parts conceptually, while at the same time developing a language of construction that is both expressive and functional.

An example of landscape tectonics made visible in detail design is illustrated in Figure 4.1 through this set of external stone steps of Shaker construction. The tectonic approach here is one of *stacking* material—in this case, setting blocks on a stepped base. In this example each block can be seen and identified as both an individual stone tread, square in section, and part of a stairway assembly of solid treads and risers. This detail form served a daily practical purpose as a mounting platform for people alighting to carriages. The stability and support of the landscape form, built from a durable local stone, is clearly demonstrated by the three individual stair blocks resting on the base, each with its complementary ledge. The connection between the two is indicated by a thin jointing line that traces the outline of the platform and the stairway profile. The stone is plainly cut, with little articulation to the faces, edges, or joints. The changes in stone pieces are neither accentuated nor hidden. In fact, the

Figure 4.1
Landscape tectonics.
Mounting steps, Fruitlands,
Massachusetts. Courtesy of
Gary Hilderbrand.

112

structure can be considered monolithic in its overall final detail form. The thin metal rail and post added to the whole assembly not only provide support, guiding the pedestrian up and down, but contrasts the mass of the solid stairs with a delicate, thin extrusion shaped to the movement of the human hand and arm during the process of mounting and dismounting.

What is demonstrated here is not only the idea of stacking blocks to make a set of stairs, but also the means by which it was articulated, the size of block, the single sections of stone, and the way in which it was all finally put together—each stone lifted individually into place on its respective ledge. The means by which the platform was originally conceived and made are evident in the final detail form.

The landscape detail form at Fruitlands displays a complete and harmonious built element. It is self-contained, but part of a larger site detail language based on the reduction and elimination of redundant material and a striving toward simplicity and economy of means. In addition, a usefulness and concern for durability is manifest in all aspects of this three-dimensional form.

There are other, more contemporary examples found today in the public realm. Consider the stone bench in Los Angeles shown in Figure 4.2, which combines a base support and pedestrian seating surface. The detail form reinterprets a piece of interior furniture for an external location. The means the designer chose were the separation and assembly of the detail parts and the selection and manipulation of the material to be used. The tectonic approach here is one of *layering* horizontal surfaces, one upon another, the upper surface resting and pinned onto a lower base. The upper stone surface is laid like a cushion on top of a solid block of a similar stone.

Figure 4.2
Landscape tectonics. Contemporary bench, Wilshire Boulevard, Los Angeles, California.

The means of support becomes, quite literally, one solid mass of stone—polished granite in this case—shaped and molded to human scale and use. However, the upper surface and base are separated into two distinct parts by the recessing and articulation of the top from the base. This piece of street furniture, its parts having been created from the same material with similar finishes, is able to exhibit at the same time both a single detail form—the final bench—and the two detail parts—the seat and the base. Thus, the assembly of the detail form, the tectonic approach, is clearly evident, describing the initial conceptual idea (the reinterpretation of a piece of interior furniture) and the means by which it was expressed (the stone base and pillow) and then carried out (a stone cap laid on top of a stone base). This bench falls within a category of detail form that attempts the reinterpretation of one material through another. This particular detail transformation is based on a tectonic approach of layering horizontal surfaces that focuses on detail reduction with enrichment. The use of a single refined material and the shaping of the seat's surface reveals a contemporary concern for uniting function and human comfort with sculptural detail form.

Summary of Landscape Tectonics

Synonymous with landscape tectonics are concerns for the following:

• Structural support, stability, and the mechanics of jointing

• The assembly of the detail parts and how they are to brought together or separated

• Material selection

Detail Making and Construction

We now explore how the elements of the built landscape are organized and how they fit and relate to each other, both during the detail design process and in the completed detail form. We also address the evolution of a construction language for the project that is used within the detail design process. This language is finally executed on-site through the engineering and installation techniques of landscape construction. We are concerned here with the development of a design sensibility as to how landscape detail design determines and is determined by "construction" as a design activity, rather than the actual techniques of assembly and implementation.

A spatial and dimensional organization of materials, structural relationships, and forms is developed on paper, with the use of the conventions of drawn sketches, sections, and plans, or in rough or crafted models. Through this early development of a detail vocabulary, a shaping and modulation of landscape details by the designer becomes itself a mode of construction, and the forms that arise during this process are found embodied and reflected in the final design. From this process, significant questions now arise related to the influences and effects on landscape detail of construction as a design activity:

- How are landscape details forms "made" in the studio as opposed to on-site?

- What are the issues to be considered during this process?

- How is the "constructability" of a detail, its ability to be physically made, related to the development of detail form and its final detail expression?

When finally considering detail implementation, the designer is confronted with an array of materials to be joined together, both natural and manufactured, and a variety of fixings, glues, mortars, bolts, wires, strips of metal, and coatings that function to bring them together physically. When the designer first addresses tectonics and the issues of detail resolution, there is usually less concern for the specifics of hardware and the precise descriptions of their materials than for the "fit" of a series of detail parts.

How these detail parts go together starts with the designer's understanding of their shaping from an original parent material, whether a block of stone at the quarry, a mix of cement, aggregate, and water with the shaping and articulation of supporting form work, or raw lumber from a sawmill. The parent material is molded, cut, or shaped like a sculptor's clay into a more precise and accurate form. The designer is also required to understand the variety of means by which the range of pre-made or manufactured landscape elements are assembled together. During the detail design process, there are two general means to achieve detail "fit," *reduction* and *combination.*

Reduction

Individual detail forms are shaped and reduced from a singular, much larger mass of landscape material, as indicated in Figure 4.3.

Grading earth, chiseling and chipping stone, pouring concrete into molds and form work, even planing and sawing wood, are means of reduction, a taking apart of a larger dense body of material to create a more refined and articulated detail element. Attention is given to how this is to be achieved, the nature of the finished surfaces (for example, the exposed textures and coloring of the initial natural and man-made materials), and the levels of craft and craftsmanship that are required.

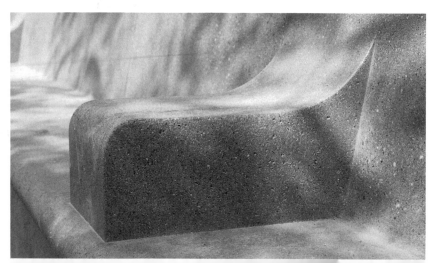

Figure 4.3
Landscape detail form (shaped). Courtesy of Frank Kluber.

115

Combination

Individual landscape detail forms are derived from the combination of shaped or pre-made elements to make more complex landscape detail assemblies.

Landscape elements are organized and arranged in the example of a fence assembly (Figure 4.4) through a series of ordering principles. These are concerned with the hierarchy of detail forms. For example, in the selection of detail forms and the means by which the landscape detail elements are combined, the contrast between their materials, and the characteristics of the finishes. Considerations include the contrast between the lightness of painted timber and the heaviness of vertical stone posts, their visual sequence—for example, the repetitive pattern of horizontal and vertical members of the detail barrier—and, again, the levels of craft and craftsmanship that are required. Figure 4.4 also illustrates the structural order between the thinner

Figure 4.4
Boundary, landscape detail form (small parts).

timber members and the heavy vertical stone posts. The more durable stone posts fixed into the ground support and elevate the lighter, more vulnerable material away from the ground. In these two ways — by reduction and shaping from a larger landscape element or by the addition of smaller detail parts — the detail design process takes apart and puts together the infinite variety of landscape detail forms.

Craft and Quality

> Utility does not permit unsoundness or frailty, for between use and beauty there is a close relationship. Utility demands faithfulness in objects; it does not condone human self-indulgence. In creating an object intended for practical use, the maker does not push himself to the foreground or even, for that matter, to the surface. With such objects, self-assertion and error — if present at all — are reduced to a minimum. This may be one reason why useful goods are beautiful.
>
> Muneyoshi Yanagi (1889–1961),
> *The Unknown Craftsman: A Japanese Insight into Beauty* (1989)

We continue by examining briefly the issues of craft and quality as they relate to landscape detail design, aspects of which are present in both previous examples of reduction and combination.

Although ongoing changes in professional, business, and construction trades and site work will continue to influence detail design, the constants that will influence and drive landscape detail forward within the design discipline are *the issues of quality in detail design* and the continuing need *to explore the poetics of detail as an expression of civic ideals and individual aesthetic needs.* Closely related to detail quality are the issues of workmanship, craft, and craftsmanship applied to landscape detail.

Detail workmanship is the art, skill, and technique of detail work and the products of such labor. It should be noted that no mention is made in the definition of detail workmanship of the resulting quality of the work, or whether it results from good or bad workmanship. Craft, on the other hand, concerns the application of art, skill, and technique *and* is closely related to manual dexterity and a close attention to finished quality in a detail form.

The term *craft* is often used in relation to detail traditions that result from accumulated knowledge and experience — for example, the craft of stream bank reconstruction, whereby traditional detail techniques of "wattling," in which woven structures of plant materials are used, or the laying of brick pathways on sand beddings, following the experienced judgments of hand and eye.

Craftsmanship relies on both craft and tradition in a combination of skill and accumulated experience.

In *The Nature and Art of Workmanship*, educator and designer David Pye further distinguishes *craftsmanship*, where the quality of the result is not predetermined, but depends on the judgment, dexterity, and care which the maker exercises as he works, from *workmanship of certainty*, where the result of each operation done during production is predetermined.[3]

Of significance here is the perception that craftsmanship in the built landscape is more closely associated with former days with their radically different social and professional foundations. Craftsmanship has become an entity, separated from us in time, reflecting differing values through the use of tools, techniques, and labor that today appear time-consuming and archaic.

Landscape craftsmanship has also become, by association, synonymous with luxurious use of materials and economic excesses. It is true that a great amount of genuinely outstanding detail work has in the past been commissioned by rich and powerful churches, governments, and private institutions, but what is its relevance today for designers?

Contemporary Craftsmanship?

The construction of landscapes today (as well as every other type of built form in the environment) very clearly reveals how the issues of quality and craftsmanship are understood by the public. Historic sites containing examples of nineteenth- and early-twentieth-century landscapes in the form of gardens, parks, and natural and cultural preserves become tourist destinations, displaying the commissioned landscape detail work of both local and imported craftsmen and artists. These are visited by crowds of sightseers, and the detail qualities of wrought metal gates, fine woodwork, carved stone ornament, and mature plant installations are admired, photographed, and commented on. Returning to the environments where they shop, eat, and recreate, and the communities in which they live and are educated, people are starkly reminded of the contrast between the detailed visual beauty of one setting and the indifferent detail qualities of the other.

It is neither desirable, useful, nor practical to hanker after the products of a long vanished era such as the fine metal screen railing shown in Figure 4.5. Theme parks and the entertainment and tourist businesses have tried unsuccessfully for many years to replicate the physical fabric and detail of other times and places. Working from within our own historical period, it appears that only careful detail restoration techniques or very small amounts of faithful copying can approximate the same level and qualities of detail craftsmanship.

True craft and craftsmanship are therefore commonly attributed to a very limited group of items that are hand-worked and expensive, carried out by a few highly skilled professionals apprenticed and trained in their respective fields, such as cabinetmakers, blacksmiths, and stonemasons. A question arises,

however, as to the applicability of this type of craftsmanship to current and future detail design. Is this the only form of craftsmanship that exists now, or is there a more contemporary form of detail craftsmanship that is more universal, using commonly available materials, applicable to a larger group of works and rooted within the detail design process? In short, can the ideas of "craft" be part of the initial detail considerations of tectonics, materials, and structure and their evolution into built detail form?

In Figure 4.6, a type of contemporary craftsmanship is demonstrated that is concerned with tectonics; through issues of structural support and stability, how the landscape detail parts are to be brought together within the detail design process, the selection and use of materials.

The detail element is the combination of a pedestrian stairway, a retaining wall, and a drainage runnel on the campus of a company headquarters. Addressing the initial site concerns of grade transition, slope establishment, and surface drainage, the detail language of the element illustrates a transition in the landscape between a highly precise work of contemporary architecture and a remnant of a vernacular agricultural landscape, a physical and aesthetic gradient from inside to outside. The three detail forms of the landscape element, the stairs — the wall, and the drainage runnel — were conceived as

Figure 4.5
Landscape detail form, historic.

119

Figure 4.6
Results of contemporary craftsmanship. Wall, stair, and runnel. Pitney Bowes Headquarters, Stanford, Connecticut (early 1980s). Courtesy of Hanna/Olin Ltd.

singular, identifiable but integrated. Solidly formed, with the necessary battered wall faces, subfoundations, washes to horizontal surfaces, and joint connections, the three forms are unified by a collective material, stone, worked in three separate ways: (1) as rough stones in a length of a random laid fieldstone wall, (2) as a set of refined steps with contrasting scarified and polished stone faces and gravel landings, and (3) a short, recessed irregular stone channel. What elevates this set of detail forms above conventional detail design are the craftsmanship and detail balance established across the entire landscape element during the detail design evolution and, in particular, the transitions in the stone finish from fine to rough. Here the runnel, which collects modest amounts of moisture from the wall and steps, was crafted in the conceptual detail stage as an oversized joint, preventing the troublesome junction of irregular fieldstones and shaped stone blocks. It displays aspects of the detail form of the edge transition in the Montmartre Steps reviewed in Chapter 1. However, this element is firmly placed in its location and time by virtue of the detail scale, material, and expression. In this way, craft and tectonics, landscape detail pragmatics and poetics, unite to create a form that demonstrates and expands on the initial conceptual idea of a material gradient, expressed in final physical form.

In the small public outdoor room shown in Figure 4.7, just off a busy city street, the craft involved in working with more ubiquitous and humble materials is illustrated. It also demonstrates that a level of detailed attention and craftsmanship can be brought to the most modest of landscape detail forms, resulting in a richness, consistency, and wholeness of the detail parts.

Poured-on-site concrete is used to produce paving surfaces, benches, steps, shallow pools, and a fountain. The form-work and mix produces a roughly textured finish consistently across all detail parts. Set into the horizontal paving surface in random fashion are irregular sections of a local stone, a schist speckled with mica. Although producing an irregular visual rhythm and coarse texture to the overall walking surface, this stone, where placed in the pools, creates a more dominant configuration, reflecting and adjusting to sunlight and splashing water. Here the concrete surface becomes a thickened joint between the elongated slabs of stone. What makes the craftsmanship integral to the detail design is the studied attention given across all the detail parts, where vertical and horizontal concrete and schist are brought together. It is worth noting that this site is also populated with the more currently recognizable and understood forms of "craft" and "craftsmanship." Here and there are placed small cast-bronze objects representing animals found in the surrounding regional landscape. In addition, entrance gates devised in scrolling metalwork, overlaid with more animals and insects,

Figure 4.7
Results of contemporary craftsmanship. Chestnut Street Pocket Park, Center City, Philadelphia, Pennsylvania (late 1970s).

121

formed part of the art program. While their level of skill and artistry in execution is undeniable and their general placement and use are handled with care, they continue through their alliance with the "art" program to perpetuate the notion that "craft" is to be associated with the studio or workshop "art object" rather than as part of a broader consideration of the landscape detail forms.

Summary

Craft and craftsmanship in current landscape detail are concerned with the following:

- Manipulation of dimension, scale, and proportions of the detail form

- The choice of certain detail properties in materials that are selected, including, for example, their density, textures, and finishes

- The placement and weighting of the landscape detail form within both a larger amount of material and hierarchy of detail forms

- The final harmony and balance of the detail form

Combining the concerns of *landscape tectonics* and *detail craft and craftsmanship,* the following issues are addressed:

1. Mechanical support

2. Dimension, scale, and proportion

3. Selection of materials and their properties

4. Assembly, placement, and weighting of the landscape detail parts

5. Harmony and balance of the detail form

In the following sections covering the detail conditions of surfaces, transitions, and boundaries, craft and craftsmanship are discussed further in relation to the initial issues of detail making and the nature of detail tectonics. Surfaces, transitions, and boundaries are initially shaped, composed, "taken apart and put together," in the design office during the process of detail design. It is at this time, in parallel with the issues of detail making and construction, that tectonics and craft are brought together by the designer in a manner that is complementary and additive.

Important in this regard is the relationship between the separate "conditions" of surface, transition, and boundaries, their basic structure and order, and how they are addressed during the detail design process when they are finally reconnected and brought together through a common detail language and expression. Let us now continue by examining the first in the categories of landscape detail identified in the previous chapter, that of *surfaces.*

2. SURFACES

The main surface of a built landscape that first merits the attention of the designer is the ground plane, or ground surface, which is manipulated to mark, contain, and support human activities. A range of landscape detail forms are developed that address the issues of detail making and landscape "craft" — the choice of certain detail properties, including density, color, and the wearing capacity of finishes. Although the selection of surface finishes applied to the ground, whether paving brick, stone, gravel, asphalt, or earth, is important, along with the various techniques of finished site implementation, these have been described more comprehensively elsewhere. In Part One of the bibliography, a number of basic textbooks are referenced that can guide the reader through different techniques and applications. Among these, the following titles take the reader through the scope and range of surface finishes: Carpenter's *Handbook of Landscape Architectural Construction,* 1976; Nelischer's *Handbook of Landscape Architectural Construction,* 1985; and Weinberg and Coyle's *Materials for Landscape Construction,* 1992.

Surfaces for Pedestrian Movement and Orientation

Chapter 1 focused on detail examples of the movement of *water* over the surface of the ground plane. Here the primary focus is on aspects of the ground plane surface for the circulation and orientation of pedestrians, particularly those surfaces with durable finishes. For the designer, a number of other significant activities must be accounted for through detail design: vehicular movement and parking, active recreation, and the siting of utilities including the detail requirements of the movement of surface water and drainage mentioned earlier. In addition, surfaces include a wide variety of finished treatments — bare earth, grass, gravel, asphalt, and unit and monolithic paved surfaces of all types and materials. In focusing exclusively on the movement of people on foot and its relationship to the detail design of the ground surface, the intention is to demonstrate a further aspect of the detail design process, specifically, the precise nature of "constructing" detail form. In particular, we will examine the relationship of the making of the ground plane surface to initial detail ideas about pedestrian movement. We will also review its influence on both the evolution of the specific detail form and aesthetic considerations related to overall conceptual design proposals about the ground surface.

> The value of defined pedestrian circulation routes lies not so much in greater safety to pedestrians and less in speeding up continuity of flow of traffic attainable, but chiefly in the freedom from distraction and the greater comfort of people who come to the town for its enjoyment.[4]
>
> Frederick Law Olmsted

The terms "freedom from distraction" and "greater comfort" described by Olmsted a century ago are rarely applied today to the issues of pedestrian movement, however appropriate they may still be. They suggest a more leisurely form of circulation, one that is closer to a gentle stroll, a promenade in a pastoral scenic park, taken with the luxury of available time and redolent of a certain social status. The physical action of walking slowly, however, has not changed much over time. "Strolling and relaxing has been shown to be the most popular use of public outdoor space."[5] It is certainly taken seriously by designers as a major activity and program use in outdoor spaces, while at the same time the physical presence and form of pathways and trails continues to shrink, whittled away in terms of their spatial dimensions, scale, and quality.

The advent of rollerblading and recreational jogging and running, along with the growing use of skateboards and bicycles, makes many a public circulation route less a "freedom from distraction" and more an obstacle course, as Figure 4.8 indicates for this 8-foot-wide asphalt recreation path during a typical weekend. Of more use to us now, in starting to examine the detail design process for surface movement, is the following simple definition from

Figure 4.8
"Freedom from distraction."
Recreation path, Stowe,
Vermont.

124

Peter Shepheard regarding the nature of the pedestrian surface and its relationship to the ground plane.

> The primary purpose of paving is simply to make bare earth fit for walking on.[6]

Although the use of paving is mainly a functional response to the movement of foot traffic, there are two areas of detail design regarding pedestrian surfaces that are related to the conception of the entire surface covering and to the specifics of the making of the surface itself. These are broadly concerned with the patterning or marking of the proposed built surface itself, and the breaking up and dividing of the built surface area by junctions and seams. The following sections examine the ground plane and the nature of the paving covering in two ways: first, and with more focused attention, the *surfaces and patterns* that are used, and, second, more briefly, the *surfaces and joints* that form part of the initial tectonic considerations of the paving surface. A number of issues are considered:

• The relationship of surface and pattern and the completed face of the ground plane is examined. The surface is thought of as an external skin or covering and is formed and constructed with multiple variations and proportions of applied distinct exterior forms.

• The relationship of surface and joints on the exterior face of the ground covering is recognized. The surface is broken up with seams that are introduced according to two scales: first, at the size of the surface material and, second, based on the size of the joints of expansion and their tolerances.

Surface and Pattern

At the entrances to parks, on the surrounds of fountains, along streets, walkways, and plazas, one may find paving surfaces constructed with inlays, shapes, lines, emblems, and integrated materials. These are laid into the pattern of the built surface and are related to the detail design of the space in which they are located. Their sources of detail construction are derived from the following:

• The unit size and dimensions of the surface material itself

• The layout and geometry of the surface in question

Both may be created from bands or blocks of contrasting materials and color or more complex and figural representations of flat decorative images and symbols. These are to be considered in contrast to applied treatments that often embellish paving surfaces, such as plastic laminate markings, rubber strippings, and brushed or sprayed coats of paint.

How are patterns and figures applied to a ground surface? Are they specific to certain types of construction and materials, and do they always have to be geometric in nature? The patterns and figures are devices that are used in evolving the detail form of ground surfaces. They establish the following elements:

• Direction and lines of pedestrian and vehicular movement

• Reduction or enhancement of scale

• Manipulation of the dimensions and proportions of the materials used

They achieve these ends through the use of contrasting colors, textures, finishes, sizes, shapes, and material selections in the proposed built surface.

The Nature of Pattern

All surface materials have pattern, whether it is part of the designer's original detail intent or not. Patterns are derived from the jointing and placement of the unit parts—whether blocks, bricks, tiles, or slabs—or the irregular texture of whole surface areas of a homogeneous or granular material like gravel. Many of the general coverings used today are more monolithic, composed of a single material, such as concrete or asphalt, which has little variation in its final appearance. In these cases short vertical edges that restrain and define the overall area appear and are "read" on the surface as a coarser form of patterning.

In the detail design of paving surfaces, pattern can be made to be conspicuous or almost invisible, to stand out or recede. Pattern itself is neither good nor bad. Like other formal detail devices it can be used by the designer appropriately or not—to greater effect, or to the detriment of a project. If pattern is overused, it produces visual clutter and unnecessary complexity; if too little is used, it goes almost unnoticed. Patterns organize and frame movement and activity on a ground surface. They also provide visual clues to edges and boundaries and can define the extent and ownership of an outdoor space. When used in a restrained and deliberate manner, detail patterns establish landscape detail forms that are aesthetically rich and whose detail precedents derive from a long history of inventive construction.

Forms of Pattern

There are four generic types of patterned forms in constructed ground surfaces, designated by the terms *fields, carpets, runners,* and *figures.* The metaphor of a fabric or woven material is useful here in alluding to a wide range of thin coverings of an infinite array of designs and textures. The detail construction can therefore be thought of as a weaving, each layer adding to the pattern, texture, support, and integrity of the whole. This image contrasts with the conception of more substantial constructed ground planes as solid stratums as, for example, in a the thick accumulation of soil or rock, the pouring of deep concrete cores and slabs, or the uncovering of sections of ledge and bedrock. The following paragraphs summarize each of the patterned detail forms.

Field

The field is the most common type of patterned form found in the constructed landscape, an expansive area with a generally uniform finish and surface. The covering can therefore be perceived as a single piece of fabric laid out over the ground surface and pulled tight. All the irregularities—the swelling and pitching of the ground conditions—are smoothed and shown in the resulting surface skin (see Figure 4.9).

The use of an equalizing intensity of pattern, color, and/or density unifies a space, forming its edges and boundaries and masking the very localized differences that are to be found. Like a fabric covering, a field is also infinitely expandable in all surface directions and can accommodate all forms of edge conditions by being "trimmed" or accurately cut, just as fabric is cut with scissors. Thus, all obstructions or junctions with objects on the ground plane or boundaries, whether buildings, streets, or other landscape detail elements, can be cleanly resolved.

Figure 4.9
Field detail image.

127

Figure 4.10
Carpet detail image.

Carpet

Used alone or in conjunction with surface fields, the carpet form is applied to smaller, more concentrated areas of a ground plane where the desire is to have a focus at a particular point, an entrance, or a gathering place, or any combination of these, as shown in the stone "carpet" in Figure 4.10. Such concentration is achieved by one of three methods:

• *Contrast* in intensity and variation of the detail carpet finish in relation to a larger base or underlying background field

• *Overlap* and *folding* of a number of carpet areas within a larger background area

• *Placement* and relationship of built form sitting on top of the carpet area

Contrast. The analogy of a woven textured rug thrown down on top of a wooden strip floor is useful to visualize the detail design possibilities. Here the choice of material properties, whether of density, hardness, reflectivity, or color; the orchestration of scale, dimension, and geometry; and the placement of the new surface on the old must be clearly considered to achieve maximum impact. The carpet form relies on the built surface in order to be designed as a series of coverings for an existing simpler base.

Overlap and Folding. Combinations of carpets can be piled together, overlapping and obscuring each other, to highlight areas of greater intensity; or a lone square or rectangle within a vast and calmer background can powerfully focus attention.

Placement. A carpets can also be used as a boundary "mat" or ground definition for a built object—a building or smaller site element. Here the object or form is placed on the carpet. The relationship to the edges of the surface can denote the feeling of solidity and strength by centering, axial orientation, or movement, or even uncertainty and tension through misplaced, twisted, or skewed alignments.

Runner. A variation of the carpet is used to denote directionality and movement. Narrow strips of patterned or plain surface are laid out between points to orient pedestrians and lead movement in a particular sequence. Like a carpet, a runner relies on a base condition and the use of contrasting surface finishes, colors, and textures to achieve its effect (see Figure 4.11).

A runner is most effective used in groups of varying dimensions, widths, and lengths to produce a hierarchy of circulation; the closer you move to the destination, the larger and more active the pattern becomes. The more important the destination, the wider the path and its surface runner.

Figure 4.11
Runner detail image.

129

Figures

Figures are found within surface patterns and are used to provide cultural symbols, emblems, and other images and to form a potential location for expressions of cultural site art or contextual design.

Inlaid elements and mosaic forms have historically been used in public and private outdoor spaces to denote ownership or boundaries and to govern the use and control of space. Their subject matter ranges from realistic depictions of insignia, crests, and signs to more abstract forms. Nonnostalgic uses of these precedents have been explored in contemporary built landscapes, ranging from the development of geometric symbols and shapes in such locations as public plazas related to international sporting events—for example, the Olympic games—to more overtly commercial appropriations of regional, cultural, or artistic forms in promenades, walkways, and streets—for example, the Ramblas in Barcelona, illustrated in Figure 4.12, with its maritime-inspired swirling wave tiles and insets of vibrant colored forms inspired by the work of painter Joan Miró, a native of Barcelona.

The types of ground coverings previously described—fields, carpets, runners, and figures—establish a broad group of devices and forms of surfaces that can be placed on the ground. However, there are possibilities in the combinations of these types to develop the forms further, as in the following examples:

- By overlaying and overlapping different pattern forms to create more forceful, larger, and bolder surface combinations.

- By conceptually "ripping," "tearing," and "cutting" the top patterned surfaces to reveal the other surfaces below. This form of surface relies on a strategy of excavation and uncovering rather than the application of new layers.

Further Aspects of Detail Patterns

A number of issues in the development and use of patterns should be noted here:

- The perception of the ground surface from the *viewpoint of a pedestrian* or a person seated in a moving vehicle

- The *simultaneous construction* of all the detail parts of the pattern, and their eventual wearing and weathering

- The introduction of *breaks and fractures* in the surface to accommodate changes in surface conditions during and after implementation

The Pedestrian's Viewpoint

The ability to comprehend the flat horizontal surface is greatly diminished from the pedestrian's viewpoint because of the angle from which it is actually

Figure 4.12
Figure detail image. The
Ramblas, Barcelona.

viewed on-site, whether the person is walking through the space or sitting. The design and detail development of paving patterns is usually derived initially in plan. Yet elements on a drawing board translated onto a site depend on being recognized and understood from a point in the air located directly above the center of the space. This is rarely feasible, apart from dense urban situations where it is sometimes possible to view outdoor plazas and streets from adjoining tall buildings.

Simultaneous Construction

The implementation of all landscape detail parts at the same time implies that there will be even and incremental changes brought to the material surface and the pattern. This is rarely accomplished, owing to the hierarchy of circulation routes and their rates of use and the selection of differing materials.

Breaks and Fractures

Related to the issue of material changes over various periods of time, the whole surface as a built detail construction must be established as separate and discrete parts or zones. These are related to changes brought about by thermal movement, site working procedures, and material changes.

We now consider briefly the issues raised by breaks and fractures in the surfaces of the ground plane and their effect on the qualities, expression, and constructability of landscape detail forms.

Surfaces and Joints

There are two types of joints found in detail surfaces such as shown in the paving in Figure 4. 13.

Figure 4.13
Joints and seams in detail surfaces.

132

Natural Joints

These are derived from the size of a single unit of the surface material, such as a small tile, for example, 6 inches square, a block or slab 1- to 2-feet square, or even larger monolithic areas. Considered to be the "natural" joints or junctions between the surface material, these seams are the normal surface pattern of the material.

Thermal Expansion and Tolerances

These are derived from the extent and placement of joints required for thermal expansion and the tolerances related to movement of materials or substructure. These produce a noticeable geometric framework or grid over the surface area, in many cases following their own logic rather than that of the proposed finished surface. Commonly found in monolithic surface areas as a method of breaking down larger sections into panels or where there is a connection with other surface materials, such a grid is also present in smaller unit surfaces. In form and appearance it represents a "mechanical joint."

The subject of detail joints and jointing is rarely considered at the outset of detail design. However, there are noticeable benefits to be gained through an early introduction of natural and mechanical joints in the conceptual detail ideas of a project. One benefit is an understanding of how the final detail surface will be influenced and altered by their placement, geometries, and pattern. This avoids problems of coordination and unsuitable placements as well as conflicts of pattern and jointing. Second, it continues to introduce the nature of tectonics at the early stages of conceptual detail development.

Figure 4.14
Conceptual idea. Detail joints in landscape surface, Plaza, University of Pennsylvania, Philadelphia. Courtesy of Hanna/Olin Ltd.

Of more lasting importance is the concept of jointing and the breaking down of the detail surface *as the initial detail idea.*

This leads, in turn, to considerations of detail scale, proportion, and material selection based on the concerns in the breaking down of the built surface according to the requirements of movement, climate, exposure, and use. Consider, for example, Figure 4.14, which illustrates an urban campus plaza paved in a durable stone surface and located over a concrete substructure. Here the organization of the joint is the origin and structure of the surface pattern. Small thin strips of granite, off-cuts (flitches) from the processing and sawing of stone sections in the quarry workshop, establish the main framework of the plaza surface. Loosely fitted with butted edges, the strips both mark and function as the joint, the contrasting larger bluestone pieces fitting into this structure as an in-fill pattern. In this way this seam not only performs as a joint in the plaza structure, but is also the origin of the detail idea and its subsequent form.

Summary

Surfaces in landscape detail design act in following ways:

- Surfaces establish the orientation and separation between different hierarchies and degrees of movement and circulation.

- Through the designer's selection of certain material properties, surfaces guide the pedestrian so as to make progress as smooth and agreeable as possible. These material properties include density, toughness, color, reflectivity, and continuity or discontinuity of coverage and scale.

- The art of surfaces' detail forms lies in the placement of detail devices such as patterns and figures and the precise arrangement of detail joints and seams within a larger measure of material. This placement is also concerned with the repetition and variation of thematic ideas about the ground surface and its coverings and the nuances of folding, laying out, and overlapping surface materials and forms.

3. TRANSITIONS

Transitions locate and establish detail connections between adjacent surfaces in the built landscape. Transitions also occur as changes in the ground plane and boundaries in the vertical plane. These include the range of landscape detail forms associated with steps and stairways, ramped surfaces, and curbs, individually or in their varying combinations, as well as boundary walls and enclosures. When surfaces come together, they are the focus of the designer's considerable studied attention, and the resultant detail transitions demonstrate a range of both poetic and pragmatic concerns and the embodiment of detail ideas concerning aesthetics and implementation.

Detail transitions prepare materials to meet each other, and they form and articulate these detail connections. The scales at which detail transitions operate may vary from the simple juxtaposition of two individual materials, for example, metal to wood (a circular steel handrail to a timber deck) or stone to concrete (a dressed granite curb to a sidewalk) to larger and more complex differences between separate horizontal or vertical levels in the landscape. These include waterside edges, sloped earthworks, retaining walls, and overhead enclosed structures, pergolas, trellises, and canopies.

Movement, a significant aspect of detail transitions in the landscape, is examined here during the development of landscape detail form. In addition, the issues of transitions and *boundaries* are briefly reviewed.

- *Transition and Movement.* As with detail surfaces, we are concerned with movement rather than circulation. It has been the subject of considerable research and study: scientific and physiological study, and the research of spatial and material issues.
  - *Scientific.* The study of the expenditure of human energy through the motions of, for example, a pedestrian moving up and down a stairway. This results in the consideration of efficiency of movement in detail transitions and its influence on design and dimensional standards.[7]
  - *Physiological.* The study of the pedestrian's passage and journey. This results in consideration of movement in the ascent, descent, and negotiating of transitions and the related issues of comfort and safety.[8]
  - *Spatial and material.* The detail issues arising from the human "markings" of movement. These include the issues of passage and erosion, the sculptural and artistic possibilities of landscape materials, and their accommodation of pedestrian pathways.

- *Transition and Boundaries.* Boundaries and other forms of vertical transition faces and edges are examined as physical barriers as well as forms of detail connections. In addition, they become the focus of deliberate attention in the conceptual ideas and evolution of landscape detail form.

Transitions and Movement

The image of the Montmartre Steps on the cover and as described in Chapter 1 exemplifies the detail characteristics of an urban transition. This transition constitutes a remarkable urban detail because of its particular scale and length, the purposes of movement, and the materials selected and used. When viewed for the first time, it is seen as simply what it is—a flight of steps, and a very long and exacting one at that. It moves the pedestrian from point A to B in the most efficient and direct manner. What later comes to mind is the circumstance it describes and responds to in the landscape—an extreme change of elevation on the hillside of Montmartre. Pedestrians climb up or down the steps in order to negotiate a significant change in the ground plane. Like the surfaces of pathways and sidewalks, the steps prepare the bare ground surface to accommodate the movement of foot traffic and to connect one part of the urban landscape to another.

Detail Forms

A common use of the term *transitions* is therefore applied to the range of detail elements that form methods of ascent and descent. These elements are developed for the use of pedestrians but also for vehicular servicing and access. They include pedestrian *steps and stairways, ramped surfaces* in the many forms found in the built environment, and *curbs,* as well as any or all of these in numerous combinations and design expressions.

Steps and Stairways

Steps and stairways, such as those at Vaux le Vicomte, France, shown in Figure 4.15, constitute one the most important classes of detail elements in the built environment, one that requires the full experience, skill, and understanding of landscape detail forms to be conceived and developed correctly. The steps and risers that describe the means by which the ground surface is covered, as well as the accompanying detail elements of railings, handrails, side walls, barriers, drains, and lighting fixtures, along with adjoining surface grading, planting, and detail construction, must be considered as part of one detail assembly.

Figure 4.15
Steps and stairway, Vaux le Vicomte, France.

136

With the use of the individual detail parts, steps and stairways can be invested with inventive and individual detail characteristics that elevate a simple passage into a landscape form with an intricate spatial and constructional language. These characteristics may include changes of scale, manipulation of proportion and dimensions, and the juxtaposition of materials, textures, and finishes. The range of forms of steps and stairways is as follows:

- Individual groups of straight aligned steps

- Flared and tapered steps

- Continuous or broken stairways with landings

Ramped Surfaces

Ramped surfaces include a range of pitched slopes with and without steps and risers, which vary according to their context and the conditions in which they occur (see Figure 4.16). They are used for pedestrian, vehicular, and service movement as transitions between inside and outside and upper and lower parts of the built landscape. Such surfaces include the following:

- Straight ramps

- Broken or interrupted ramps

- Universal access ramps

Figure 4.16
Ramped surfaces, Exchange Square, Broadgate Development, London.

137

Curbs

Curbs consist of a range of short transitions between road and pedestrian movement areas or between movement areas and adjacent raised elements such as planters or lawn, which use single-step forms or derivations of such forms. In addition, they frame or restrain surface edges. On roadway edges they act as transitions to warn of a change of use and speed of traffic, to direct water toward drainage inlets, and to provide structural support for pathways and walkways, such as shown in Figure 4.17. Curbs include the following types:

Figure 4.17
Detail curb, St. Andrew Square, Edinburgh, Scotland.

- Raised pavement curbs

- Dropped curbs

- Pathway flush curbs

Combinations

When steps, stairways, ramped surfaces, and curbs are used in combination, a range of more complex transitional forms are developed, which include *perrons* and *curb ramps*.

Perrons. A perron is a sequence of ramped sloped sections with intermediate short step risers between 2 and 4 inches in height. This ramp form is able to accommodate both pedestrian and vehicular access up and down its length (see Figure 4. 18). A perron can be thought of as a set of extremely elongated steps, which is primarily a form of pedestrian passage. It can on occasion allow vehicles to park temporarily or have access for deliveries. The plastic nature and manipulation of the ground plane allows the formation of a series of levels and modest platforms, located from side to side as extensions of the steps. Figure 4.19 illustrates the detail design potential of manipulating perrons in combination with the stepped transitions and surfaces of minor urban spaces.

Figure 4.18
Perrons, "Olana," Hudson, New York.

▲ Figure 4.19
Perrons, Paris.

▶ Figure 4.20
Curb ramp, Denver.
Courtesy of Hanna/Olin Ltd.

Curb Ramps. In a curb ramp, a minor form of a ramped sidewalk, surfaces and curb edges are cut, twisted, shaped, and flattened to slope down to meet the grade of the roadway (see Figure 4. 20). The resultant curb ramp cuts into the pathway surface and produces two "flares" that tilt the path surface downward. In response to the requirements of universal accessibility, the detail forms developed for this combination of short ramped transitions are recognized as a significant detail element of the current built landscape. Today's detail design issues are now related to the evolution and refinement of this form of transition.

Transitions and Boundaries

The term *boundaries* is applied to the range of detail transitions that form temporary or permanent edges, barriers, and enclosures. The landscape detail elements associated with transitions and boundaries are developed in the following ways:

- Landscape detail elements are formed by junctions between separate detail forms, elements, materials, or spaces, which include vertical and horizontal boundaries. These boundaries structure and frame the connection between adjacent landscape elements.

  These include opaque or perforated walls, fences, and framed openings, as well as overhead transitions such as pergolas and trellises.

- Landscape detail elements are formed by vertical surfaces that enclose or contain outdoor spaces.

  These surfaces include barriers or obstructions that simultaneously include and exclude, permitting the establishment of security, privacy, and shelter. The range of landscape detail elements related to these boundaries comprises solid walls, fences, railings, and screens.

Two detail concerns related to boundary elements and their detail development and construction are the nature of *boundaries and profiles,* and the detail design issues of *boundaries and turning corners.*

Boundaries and Profiles

In establishing boundaries and profiles, we are concerned with the detail shaping of the surfaces and edges of solid landscape materials. This includes sawing, molding, and cutting to contour, form, and articulate reveals and the boundary limits of landscape detail elements. Figure 4. 21 illustrates a typical detail profile for a pool edge, the transition between earth and water, and displays all the reveals and articulated edges that shape and cast light and shadows and hide changes of line and jointing.

The dictionary definition of the word *profile* is derived from *pro,* meaning "forward," and *filare,* meaning to spin thread or draw a line.[9] Although its normal usage is associated with describing the human personality, another meaning more useful to detail and construction is the description or action

141

Figure 4.21
Detail profile. Courtesy of
Hanna/Olin Ltd.

of making an edge or line—quite literally, drawing a line forward as in a drawing on a drafting table. This is similar to the method of tracing the edges or profile of a detail element, such as a piece of a stone retaining wall or a seat section. Through this pencil or ink line, the means by which it is constructed, the template outline to cut, score, or pour, the profile is also formed. The two-dimensional marks on paper start to construct a profile, an edge, which will be realized on-site as a three-dimensional form.

The articulation of profiles in detail design, whether for landscape elements such as boundary walls, steps, or curb edges, is a design activity, rendered and made visible in the office or studio through repetitive drawing and study.

Boundaries and Turning Corners

Of all the profiles under consideration the most complex and most necessary in dealing with boundaries and transitions is the detail condition related to the turning of corners, both in the vertical and in the horizontal plane.

A situation to be avoided is the placement of a vertical joint exactly at a corner turn. This presents visual, aesthetic, and tectonic issues regarding the instability of the detail assembly and final detail character that results. In Figure 4.22 the use of a special detail form, a cornerstone, takes the stone wall around the corner without requiring any joints to be located directly on the corner. The hooker stone, which is shaped to "hook" around the corner, is reversed or flipped at each course to allow the alignment of joints to be structurally and visually consistent with the adjacent coursing. Although the action of extending a vertical boundary wall along a length is a simple matter of repetition and extrusion of detail forms, the angling or reversing of direction of a vertical surface requires detail considerations of the placement and form of corner detail elements and materials. The beginning, ending, and turning of these detail elements require the greatest consideration.

Figure 4.22
Turning corners. Courtesy of
Hanna/Olin Ltd.

142

Summary

Transitions in landscape detail design act in the following ways:

• Transitions prepare detail surfaces to meet each other. A transition may occur where surfaces meet or at some physical distance to where a connection takes place. This activity is a central part of the development of the detail expression of a project. It focuses on the methods of working with material textures and coverings and the placement of contrasting or supporting detail elements and finishes.

• Transitions articulate detail overlaps and changes of level. These attend to the nature of alignments and juxtapositions of detail elements and materials in the built landscape either by drawing attention to them (making them visible) or by deliberately obscuring or hiding them (making them invisible). This develops an important part of the detail language of the project and sets up a method of addressing all the junctions and joints of detail elements in a manner that is consistent across an entire project site.

• Transitions establish how horizontal and vertical detail shifts of materials and detail elements are to be resolved and achieved on-site.

4. FUTURE TRENDS

Has landscape detail a future? As long as landscapes are designed and built, details in many shapes, sizes, and forms will continue to be developed and implemented. It is not the future of details themselves that we can be concerned with, nor the idea of landscape detail as part of the design process. Rather, we must be concerned with shifts in the way that details are developed, the processes of detail design as they are carried out in practice, and who may carry them out. The following questions arise:

• How will future detail practices change?

• What will be the outcome in terms of new and emerging detail practices?

• How will that affect which group of professionals will execute detail design?

Finally, in the future, what are the issues and concerns that the designer will face when considering landscape detail? The preceding chapters noted the ability of landscape detail to alter and adapt to a wide range of aesthetic, design and site circumstances. The transformation of landscape details will occur, responding to the wide range of changes previously outlined. However other alterations, external to the design professions and construction industries, will also occur, which will have an effect on the future nature and performance of landscape detail. These include:

- Processes and techniques of manufacture and construction will change in response to diminishing natural resources.

- New classes of composite and synthetic products will be introduced into the marketplace as changes occur in the supply and quantities of raw industrial products and natural materials, and as changes occur in legislation governing built environments, especially those concerned with children, elderly people, and those who are physically challenged.

- Changes in detail design will be brought about by the concerns for sustainable design and design attitudes in responding to local and world ecologies and resources.

- Alterations to on-site working methods and project management will bring about changes in the drawing office regarding documentation and processing through computer aided design[10] and timing of the phases of design work, and the role of the landscape architect in project management may shift considerably.

There are many unknowns, particularly in regard to the range, scope, and types of work landscape architects will be involved with and who will be responsible for designing and implementing work in, for instance, the public realm of cities. Will multidisciplinary projects produce experts in distinct areas, such as paving, drainage systems, and planting installation, and will that affect the detail development of these areas? It is noticeable that specialist consultancies in urban street tree planting, soil manufacture, and unit paving surfaces have already arisen, along with proprietary products, detail forms, and specifications. What will distinguish all future detail work, no matter how it is influenced by these and other changes, are the ongoing issues of detail and design quality.

Arising from these issues there follow two areas of interest to design students and young professionals:

- How will instruction in landscape detail change within the curriculum of design schools?

- Will the implementation section of examinations for professional licensure that cover landscape detail and detail processes alter over time, and how?

Two areas of landscape design practice that have an effect on landscape detail have already shown signs of changing:

- New *types of work* carried out by landscape architects

- Emerging landscape *materials and processes*[11]

New Types and Scope of Work
A range of new and emerging project types, as well as some that have been

renewed, will again involve landscape architects. Designers, including landscape architects, already work in many of these specialized sectors with great success:

• Landfill, mining, and quarry reclamation

• Wastewater treatment plants and environments

• Urban waterfront regeneration

• Restoration of historic landscapes

• Redesign of structured plaza decks in urban centers

• Golf course planning and design

• Ecotourism centers

• Zoo habitat exhibits and theme park environments

Arising from this work are a series of landscape details derived from conventional practice that have been elaborated and altered to fit. Other detail practices and materials have been imported from the engineering and design fields. These include the vast range of architectural, theater, and film set design detail that are now part of the work of outdoor and enclosed landscapes and habitat environments within contemporary zoo design.

The following section explores aspects of the new types of landscape detail work used in exhibition design and the range of new and emerging technologies, materials, and processes a designer is able to work with.

New Types of Detail Work: Emerging Technologies, Materials, and Processes

This section was prepared by Sally Coyle, landscape architect, and Quentin Caron, habitat and exhibit designer,[12] based on their extensive research, detail design documentation, and field work in this area of built landscape work.

Overview

Exhibit technologies fall into two main categories: on-site technologies, usually involving one or more types of concrete applications, and fabrication technologies, whereby products of varying materials are fabricated off-site. Most concrete used in exhibit design and development is applied to a steel armature through a pressurized pump. This allows for further shaping of the concrete as it is applied, known as the technique of "carving."

Emerging site technologies and detail design have found ready acceptance among clients requiring emulation of local, distant, or exotic environments. Zoos, aquariums, and resorts have applied site technologies and detail design for many years, but recently a much more varied use of detail forms, materials, and processes has begun to appear. In zoos and aquariums these are referred to as "living exhibits," either terrestrial or aquatic.

Natural materials must be moved from their original location so that they can be used for building. The necessity of picking up, transporting, and then placing the material on-site not only restricts its size but, in turn, limits the designer's ability to freely utilize appropriate utilities—for example, lighting, water, and special effects. More workable and "plastic" materials, such as concrete and fiberglass, are restricted only by the imagination and skill of those involved. An entire geological feature of any domestic or exotic environment can be carried out in design detail: large trees may be used as part of the design; water may flow, trickle, gush, splash, or pool; fog can conceal, sound can entice; and light can enhance. The elements of these built environments can also act as structural armatures. Environments employing such technologies are, in fact, hyper-realistic sculptures used to safely and securely control the environment while providing the dramatic setting imagined by the designer.

What are the types of technologies that can emulate natural settings? There are two main technologies: hand carving (positive) and casting. Both can be used in what the industry has divided into construction, typically referring to on-site built environments, and elements and fabrication, which refers to environments and elements built off-site. The structural requirements of each varies by size and material. The range of materials used in these technologies is constantly expanding, but the most common materials are concrete, fiberglass reinforced concrete (FRC), rubber, fiberglass, and epoxy. Typically, a formation is produced by the following method:

1. Laying out the formation

2. Constructing an armature

3. Applying a structural coat over the armature

4. Applying a texture coat of material

5. Adding a mural

6. Applying any special effects

All this is done while containing or disguising any infrastructure required by the scope of the project.

How much detail, specification, or description is enough to produce results? Just as with sculpture, the success or failure of the built environment rests in the awareness and skill of the artist and craftsperson in enlarging and enhancing the design. A collaboration is desirable, because the artist must interpret and realize the designer's and client's requirements through the use of scale models and numerous site visits. Various technologies and materials are borrowed from the fine arts, traditional building construction, landscape detail design, set design, animal management, and related fields such as zoology, botany, and biology, such as shown in the sequence of implementation in Figure 4.23. These ele-

Figure 4.23
Exhibit design detail.

(a) Typical structure showing
steel rebar, lathe, and
spacers prior to application
of structural concrete layer.

(b) Spraying texture coat of
cement over structural coat.
Exhibit at Aquario di
Genova, Larson Design.

(c) Final carved appearance.
Exhibit at Aquario di
Genova, Larson Design.
Courtesy of Quentin Caron.

ments, used for the masking of infrastructure or the production of special effects, include utilities, lights, fiber optics, irrigation, sensors, sound, security, pumps, water filtration equipment, and robotics.

Structure

When is steel or other reinforcement necessary? Unless a form is providing a supplementary purpose, such as soil retention, or is undercut, most forms of rock work are shaped arches and columns, which need only support themselves. If the form is submerged, a waterproofed steel or plastic structure or a waterproof cement coating is used. Armatures are coated with a minimum of 2 inches on every side; therefore, to be accurate the armature must be from 4 to 6 inches smaller than the finished form.

- *Armature.* Armatures are most often bent steel reinforcing bars either welded or tied. Smaller sizes are the most flexible, and to reduce wastage only enough material is used in many formations to produce the requested strength and aesthetics. These formations are often hollow, so the armature is backed by either plastic or metal lathe, burlap, plastic, or another backing that will stop the concrete during application; and a chicken wire outer layer is required to stop any "sluffing" of the cement.

- *Pumped Concrete.* Most concrete used in exhibit construction is applied to a structural armature with the use of a pump. This allows flexibility in shaping or carving the concrete as it is applied and dries. Several types of concrete can be used during the process in order to attain a balance of structural integrity and detail variety: shotcrete, Gunite, and plaster.
  - *Shotcrete.* Concrete that is mixed at a plant, delivered by truck, pumped using a shotcrete pump wet through a hose, then blasted onto a structure using air. Shotcrete is typically an "aggregate mix" consisting of pea gravel, sand, portland cement, and water, but may also contain additives for coloring, accelerating drying, waterproofing, or retarding drying. Custom mixes with more, less, or replacement additives are common, depending on the requirements of the project. For instance, leaching of fish-toxic additives may need to be contained in a pool containing fish, and therefore require alternative non-toxic additives.
  - *Gunite.* Concrete that is mixed and pumped dry through a hose by a Gunite pump. Water is then added at the nozzle as the mix is blown onto an armature. Gunite is a "mortar mix" consisting of sand, portland cement, and water and is typically used for the structure of most swimming pools.
  - *Plaster.* A mortar mix concrete consisting of sand, portland cement, and water applied with a plaster pump, a smaller version of a shotcrete pump used for greater control. Its applications include the final texture coat for artificial geology or effects, and as a highly variable additional coat of concrete, averaging 1½ inches thick, applied over shotcrete or Gunite detail textures.

Materials

• *Cast (Fabricated) Concrete.* The level of detail obtainable from a cast taken from a well-built mold of a natural feature is exceptional. Landscape elements at the scale of plants, fungi, corals, and small boulders are resolved at a very fine grain. When the item to be cast is larger than conventional casts, difficulties arise. In applying casts to create geological formations, great care must be taken by those connecting the panels to avoid a visual patchwork. It is easier to create geological continuity by positive carving than by relying on a textured cast.

How is a cast made? A mold is made by applying layers of a flexible membrane—for example, silicone or urethane rubber—to the object and allowing it to dry. A solid layer called the mother mold is then applied over the mold in one or more parts, which when dry will support the flexible mold material without allowing it to be distorted. Then the mold is sprayed or filled by other means with a thin solid layer of fiberglass reinforced concrete, epoxy, or fiberglass.

When is it appropriate to use cast rock? When the feature is "in the face" of the viewer, the importance of the texture increases, and for some types of rock or botanical displays only a cast can accomplish the desired effect. When used in overhangs and caves, casts can be structurally filled from above and the cast can be left with very little additional carving work.

Special Effects

The use of planters is the primary means of incorporating vegetation into large exhibit areas of carved or fabricated rock work. Three factors must be considered when designing and constructing planters: soil mix, drainage, and irrigation.

Soil mixes are required to be specified for interior use rather than exterior use. Because most planters do not have the soil capacity for water retention and tend to dry out quickly, irrigation is required to ensure the viability of plants. Moreover, because of need for irrigation and the limited soil capacity, planters can also stay moist; therefore proper drainage is the most important factor in plant sustainability.

New Applications

• *Erosion Control.* Shotcrete is frequently used for erosion control in extreme conditions such as steep highway cuts. This technology may be expanded upon aesthetically and environmentally by integrating and incorporating areas of vegetation. Cuts can be minimized by "soil nailing," using Gunite to stabilize steeper banks and protect existing trees during construction.

• *Bank Vegetation/Revegetation.* Gunite embankments can be designed to allow long-term phase-in of vegetation of steep slopes. Concrete embankments may be successfully combined with bioengineering technologies for wetland creation and riparian edge stabilization/creation.

In addition, the following areas of detail design and development of site materials and processes have evolved out of the specific requirements of this type of landscape detail work.

New Types of Detail Work

- Artificial Rock Work
  - Used in conjunction with natural rock and cast concrete.
  - On-site construction includes the use of Gunite and shotcrete.
  - Fabrication construction includes fiberglass reinforced concrete (FRC), glass fiber-reinforced concrete (GFRC), fiberglass with urethane and silicone molds.

- Pools and Ponds
  - These include the use of fiber-optic lighting.

- Special Detail Effects
  - Epoxy simulations include artificial vines and trees and climate simulations including rain, fog, and thunderstorms.

- New Technologies
  - These include erosion control, bank creation, and stabilization for new or rejuvenated wetlands.

5. DEFINITION OF TERMS

Key terms and phrases discussed in this chapter are defined below.

Construction: creation and structuring of physical detail forms in the design process.

Techne: making a detail idea "visible" within the existing landscape.

Tectonics: how the detail idea is made visible, and the necessary forces that establish and mold its eventual physical form.

Workmanship: art, skill, and technique of detail work and the products of such labor.

Craft: application of art, skill, and technique, *and* the source of manual dexterity and close attention to finished quality in a detail form.

Craftmanship: craft and tradition together in a combination of skill and accumulated experience.

Surface: built ground plane constructed for human activities.

Pattern: detail device to organize and frame movement and activity on surfaces.

Figures: symbols or decorative images added or laid into the pattern of a surface material, usually related to the geometry and layout of the surface.

Field: a large, expansive patterned area with uniform finish and surface; a base paving material.

Carpets: concentrated surface areas achieved by their contrast to a larger field.

Runners: narrow strips of patterned or plain surface laid out between points; used to denote directionality and movement.

Natural joints: juxtaposition of single units of a horizontal material that are perceived as the normal surface pattern.

Mechanical joints: extent and placement of joints required for thermal expansion and the tolerances related to movement of materials or substructure.

Transitions: locate and establish detail connections between adjacent surfaces in the built landscape.

Boundaries: detail transitions that form temporary or permanent edges, barriers, and enclosures.

6. CLASSROOM EXERCISES

These exercises form part of a series of assignments to be carried out within the structure of a course on landscape construction or landscape technology and detail, or as part of a design studio.

Assignment 4A: Landscape Detail Surfaces, Transitions, and Boundaries

1. Build a scale model, in card and colored paper, of a pattern in paving derived from a color photograph of a historical example. Make sure that there is a high contrast in the colored papers chosen to represent the different areas of paving. View the model both from above and obliquely, placing your eye close to the horizontal plane. Use a modelscope if available.

   Record your impressions of the changes that occur perceptually between the two, for a variety of pattern and figure types. Do any study at both viewing angles.

151

2. Locate three stair transitions in your locale that are accessible for the purposes of this study. First walk up and down the stairs about five times each to determine and compare the ease of movement, energy expended, and general comfort level across the selected examples. Measure and record on-site the riser and tread dimensions of each stair condition and note their relationships. In addition, record their width and general condition of materials and installation.

Is there a relationship between the ease of movement and the details of steps and risers? What is it? Does the wearing and weathering of the stairs indicate excessive pedestrian use? Is the movement straight up and down, or do pedestrians cross the stairs diagonally?

3. Locate, measure, and record photographically a series of sloped landscape surfaces that start at 1% and then increase as follows: 2%, 3%, 5%, 6%, 8.33%, 10%, 20%, 25%, 45%. The surfaces can be grass or paved.

The intention is to for the designer to become familiar with the range of sloped transitions usually found in the built landscape through a variety of media. Analyze these conditions and the surface treatments for each.

Assignment 4B: Future Forms of Landscape Detail

4. Conduct research on any new detail materials that are in use locally or that are the by-products of local industries or manufacturing processes. They may consist of new applications for existing products or new products developed from the recycling and reuse of existing materials, including by-products and waste. Propose other detail materials that are not currently being considered but could be developed from existing local industries and manufacturing.

Document through photographs and drawings the use of these detail materials in built landscapes. What are the implications for landscape detail forms? What new criteria do they impose in terms of detail design and installation methods and techniques? What is the expected life span of these new detail materials?

5. Investigate the traditions in contemporary detail craftsmanship in your locale. Consult trade directories, Yellow Pages, and chambers of commerce listings to discover local makers of fine woodwork, metalwork, craftspersons in stone, brick, terra-cotta, clay, metal, precast concrete, and contractors or builders who specialize in execution of such details.

Visit these makers at their workshops, studios, or on-site. What are the specific regional detail characteristics? Document them in photos and sketches or visit examples in the surrounding built environment. Integrate examples of detail craftsmanship into studio projects sited locally.

6. Review new types of emerging landscape work or projects that require landscape design services. Design magazines and newspapers as well as professional sources, including publications of the national or regional chapters of the American Society of Landscape Architects, should be consulted.

What are the detail implications of this work? How will the current forms of landscape detail have to adapt to these changing circumstances? Identify a range of these types of work and suggest a suitable approach for developing landscape details.

7. REFERENCES AND SOURCES

Section 1. Introduction

1. In conversation with the author; see interview with Dan Kiley in Chapter 7.

2. For example, see Keneth Frampton, *Studies in Tectonic Culture: The Poetics of Construction in Nineteenth and Twentieth Century Architecture* (Cambridge: MIT Press, 1995); see also Cecil O. Elliott, *Technics and Architecture: The Development of Materials and Systems for Buildings* (Cambridge: MIT Press, 1992).

3. David Pye, *The Nature and Art of Workmanship* (New York: Van Nostrand Reinhold, 1972).

Section 2. Surfaces

4. Frederick Law Olmsted, quoted in Charles W. Eliot, "The Influence of the Automobile on the Design of Park Roads," *Landscape Architecture* 2, no. 13 (Oct. 1922–July 1923): 27–37.

5. From Elizabeth Barlow Rogers et al., *Rebuilding Central Park: A Management and Restoration Plan* (Cambridge: MIT Press, 1987). See "A Park for the People," pp. 23–29, and "Circulation: Drives, Paths and Bridle Trail," pp. 33–39.

6. From *Landscape Development Plan Report*, p. 89, Center for Environmental Design, Graduate School of Fine Arts, University of Pennsylvania, 1977. Prepared by faculty members under the leadership of Peter Shepheard, director.

Section 3. Transitions

7. See James M. Fitch, "The Dimensions of Stairs," *Scientific American* (Oct. 1974): 82–90.

8. See John Templer, *The Staircase: Studies of Hazards, Falls, and Safer Design.* (Cambridge: MIT Press, 1992), Chapter 5, "Behavior on Stairs," pp. 81–89.

9. See *The American Heritage Dictionary of the English Language* (Boston: Houghton Mifflin, 1971).

Section 4. Future Trends

10. See, for example, the new role of digital media in landscape detail documentation in James L. Snipes, A. Paul James, and John Mack Roberts, "Digital Details," *Landscape Architecture* 86, no. 8 (Aug. 1996). These authors raise the issues of standard versus nonstandard details and the uses of "libraries" of proven and documented detail types.

11. See Kim Sorvig, "Brave New Landscape," *Landscape Architecture* 82, no. 7 (July 1992): 75–77, for a survey of new materials and their uses in landscape design.

    See Daniel Winterbottom, "Plastic Lumber," *Landscape Architecture* (January 1985): 34–36, for a discussion of recycled plastics found in packaging and industrial waste.

    See Joyce Gagnon, "Glass: Landscape Applications," *Landscape Architecture* 85, no. 6 (June 1995): 25–27. Covers use of recycled glass products in landscape architecture; includes resources guide and suppliers.

    See also Robert Holden, "Please Walk on the Glass," *Architects Journal* 206, no. 12 (Oct. 2, 1997): 46–47.

12. The designer represents the office of Rampantly Creative, Habitat, Exhibit Designers of Scituate, Massachusetts.

8. FURTHER READING

A number of articles about surfaces, transitions, and boundaries have appeared in professional magazines. The following selection is from different time periods that represent the range of topics covered.

Surfaces

Bafile, Mano. "Design in Pavement, Examples from Italy." *Landscape Architecture* 6, no. 1 (Spring 1939): 10–15.

Bartels, Elizabeth. "Cobbles and Other Stones." *Landscape Architecture* (March 1992): 84–87.

Campbell, Craig. "Custom Precast Paving." *Landscape Architecture* (June 1993): 84–85.

Howcroft, Heidi. "The Techniques of Sett Laying." *Landscape Design* (Sept. 1988): 46–49.

Sipes, James L., and John M. Roberts. "Grass Paving Systems." *Landscape Architecture* 84, no. 6 (June 1994): 31–33.

Smith, David R. "Interlocking Concrete Pavers." *Landscape Architecture* (Aug. 1991): 72–74.

Sorvig, Kim. "The Path Less Traveled." *Landscape Architecture* 84, no. 12 (Dec. 1994): 30–33.

Transitions and Boundaries

Hansen, Richard. "Limestone and Granite: Texture and Finish." *Landscape Architecture* (Oct. 1992): 114–117.

Jewell, Linda L. "Granite Curbing." *Landscape Architecture* (Jan. 1981): 97–100.

Jewell, Linda L. "Curb Ramps at Intersections." *Landscape Architecture* (Nov. 1982): 87–89.

Olmsted, Frederick L. "Notes upon the Sizes of Steps Required for Comfort." *Landscape Architecture* 1, no. 2 (Jan. 1911): 84–90.

Olmsted, Frederick L. "Some Further Notes on Steps." *Landscape Architecture* 2, no. 18 (Oct. 1927–Jan. 1928): 125–129.

CHAPTER 5

DETAIL DURABILITY

THIS CHAPTER CONCERNS the viability of landscape details as built elements over time. It considers questions of durability raised during the detail phase of a project, the levels of performance to be expected from landscape detail forms, and how attitudes toward postoccupancy and maintenance influence the final outcome of detail design. Climate and its effects on materials and changes to landscape details are reviewed. A summary of failures in landscape detail and their likely causes are listed, as well as steps to promote durability in future detail forms. Throughout, weathering is emphasized as a potential source of detail design invention for designers, rather than an exacting condition of a context and site to be addressed and overcome. Students will gain a greater appreciation for the longer view of detail and an understanding of the ability of built landscapes and their detail to change or modify while maintaining their basic integrity. This chapter also introduces time as a central concern for the designer to consider at any point in the development of landscape detail design ideas and forms.

1. INTRODUCTION

Durability is concerned with the soundness, constancy, and permanence of landscape details as design elements and built forms over set periods of time. These periods may last for a single day, in the case of temporary site installations or artwork, or as long as periods with yet unknown endpoints, assumed to be far in the future—for example, for permanent landscapes. Landscape details, because of their scale, physical exposure, quantity, and sensitivity, act as prime indicators in this regard, a litmus test of physical denigration, markers in the changes brought upon, and to, the built environment. Landscape architect Martha Schwartz has stated, however, that "all landscapes [meaning designed landscapes] are temporary, even the ones which we now consider permanent, like the pyramids in Egypt." [1] In a sense, this statement is true: all landscapes, all human-built landscapes, will over a period of time be reduced to dust. Although this appears obvious, it is not particularly useful in the designer's considerations of landscape detail.

Schwartz's statement comes from a particular view of design informed by rapid cultural and physical change, rather than the notion of permanence within a sense of historical continuity. This view, associated with the late twentieth century, is concerned with the veneration of contemporary materials and conditions as a facet of modern design [they are temporary because we and our culture are temporary] and has been embraced by some designers. This stands counter to the more traditional viewpoint based on adapting and building on what has gone before, literally and figuratively.

Today it is not uncommon that a relatively short period of time passes between the completion of a built outdoor space and its rapid deterioration. Design failures are most clearly visible in the built landscape detail, such as indicated in Figure 5.1. Broken pavements and steps, flooded plazas, dead or dying trees, and collections of twisted and damaged site furniture indicate that despite the best efforts of the designers, these "permanent" landscapes may have an expected life of only 20 to 30 years, some even less.

In Boston, Massachusetts, Copley Square, one of the major civic open spaces in the city, continues to be the focus of renewed design activity. National design competitions were held in 1966 and 1984, and reconstruction work from winning schemes was carried out and completed in 1969 and 1989, respectively. In both cases the failure of earlier schemes was attributed not only to the changing role, purpose, and formation of open space as a public amenity, but also to the execution of the physical elements of the designs and the breakdown of elements of construction and detail.

Figure 5.1
Detail failure of public stairs.

157

▲ Figure 5.2
Failure of landscape detail surface. Station Plaza, Barcelona.

▶ Figure 5.3
Failure of landscape detail surfaces and transitions. Station Plaza, Barcelona.

In Barcelona, Spain, the extensive redevelopment of urban public open spaces, parks, streets, and plazas in the 1980s won international recognition from the design community. However, following the failure of detail surfaces, transitions, and elements (see Figures 5.2 and 5.3), the first wave of reconstruction and rebuilding of these spaces is under way just 10 years after their initial completion.

These examples offer an extreme view of the condition of current landscape implementation and detail practices. There are, however, serious issues that clients such as educational institutions, corporations, public agencies, governments, and town officials are now facing in the commissioning, execution, maintenance, and upkeep of the streets, parks, squares, gardens, and campuses for which they are responsible, namely:

• Is the expected life of current built landscape projects and landscape details to be no more than 10 to 15 years?

• Beyond the cost of regular maintenance, will large expenditures of money, materials, and labor still be required to counter failure in construction practices and detailing?

• Who is responsible for this failure: the designers, educators, and the design programs they oversee, the manufacturers, the builders, the construction industry, or the clients themselves?

It is also apparent from the restoration and redesign work under way that there is a great danger of simply repeating these earlier landscape detail forms. Landscape architecture has long considered the matters of durability, climate, and weathering a subject for detail study only in relationship to maintenance issues.

With a need to take a responsible attitude to future resources and expenditure on materials, it is more reasonable now that designers in landscape architecture comprehend and act according to how their details will perform over time. It is also important that they understand the role climate plays in the modification of detail work and that they be informed about the appropriate design responses to the actions of weathering so as to use appropriately robust and durable landscape detail forms. At the outset of any design project the following issues arise:

- The desired performance of any particular detail

- The durability of that detail

- The factors that will influence and affect performance and durability while the detail is being developed, under construction, and finally completed and used on the site

From these issues three questions arise:

1. What are the ways in which details are modified, and what are the probable causes?

2. Why do certain details deteriorate and fail, and what can be learned from these failures in order to produce successful details in the future?

3. Is longevity in detail design a worthwhile goal for the designer?

To answer these questions it is necessary to discuss the issues surrounding endurance or impermanence in landscape detail and what constitutes the nature of performance in landscape detail. We will continue to review how details change, and the reasons for those changes, and then examine the types and forms of weathering and the issues of failure as they apply to landscape detail. A concluding section entitled "Anticipating Change Through Detail Design" summarizes the key points in answer to the previous questions.

2. HOW AND WHY DETAILS CHANGE

Some may suppose that landscape details, like cars, telephones, or household appliances, become a problem only when they fail to work or perform as they were intended. If this were true, then the issues of durability and change in landscape detail would be quite a simple matter of performance—that is, a designer would merely need to understand the way a landscape detail is

159

expected to function over time. The original detail would be matched against an expected life span, given a small number of constraints: the use and misuse of the detail, any physical damage, and the replacement or advance of component parts and associated technology. In considering landscape detail, however, there are three significant factors, related to the detail medium, exposure on-site, and the nature of detail form, that ensure that this model of performance and maintenance is not relevant to designers:

- *Character of the landscape medium.* Materials will alter and change, irrespective of use or operation, because of their organic nature and character. Such materials range from larger earth forms and water bodies to plants and natural wood, clay, and stone products. This wide variety makes their performance more difficult to codify and finally specify.

- *Exposure to natural forces and weathering.* Landscape elements are especially vulnerable because of their placement and use in exposed, harsh outdoor conditions—for example, in marine edges or in heavily trafficked urban streets, sidewalks, and parks. Even in unexposed situations landscape detail forms are open to changes brought about by constant weathering.

- *Life span of projects.* Many landscape design projects form temporary installations or are part of larger phased proposals. The implication is that they are expected to have a limited life span, and they are designed accordingly. Examples include temporary outdoor sculpture areas, detail forms associated with occasional episodic public gatherings and concerts, and seasonal sports and cultural events, including garden displays and expositions.

Genuine permanence in any work of landscape detail, however desirable from the viewpoint of a client, owner, or designer, is, with rare exception, unobtainable. Built landscapes are irreversibly transformed over time. Materials acquire markings and abrasions, surfaces are worn, plants grow to maturity and die; landscape detail forms are, in turn, removed, replaced, altered, added to, recycled, or discarded by successive users and owners.

It can be said, quite simply, that details undergo forms of change, and not always in ways that the designer can control, may desire, or have ever considered at the outset of a project. This may be the inevitable result of one of the following effects:

- *Wear and tear.* There are general changes brought about by daily use and normal climatic conditions. These are differentiated from the more specialized forms of wear and tear as a result of vandalism or deliberate misuse.

- *Extreme patterns of weather.* Occasional severe storm events can cause total and permanent alterations to the physical form and structure of landscape detail forms and materials.

- *Poor design.* The failure of particular detail elements may be the result of poor detail practices. Examples include the misuse of installations and site assemblies and the selection of inappropriate materials. Such situations can be made worse by additional wear and tear or when detail elements are subjected to severe storm events.

- *Professional negligence.* Detail design negligence in the lack of anticipation or understanding of the first three events may also affect the life span of a project.

The subject is a complex one; however, it is most similar in practice to the tasks associated with maintenance and the postoccupancy evaluation of built work, a professional service that is not always carried out by the original designer. Two related areas of professional practice come to bear on this matter:

- *Health, safety, and welfare.* One of the designer's roles as a licensed professional is to ensure that all reasonable steps are taken during the detail design process and implementation to protect the health, safety, and welfare of the public users of any space. Responsibility therefore lies with the designer to use reasonable judgment in determining whether an element of detail design has the potential to endanger those engaged in the normal patterns of use expected in a public outdoor space. The selection of materials, the form and nature of a surface, and the dimensions and spatial character of a transition must all be considered. What constitutes "reasonable" is itself open to interpretation.

- *Liability insurance.* Liability insurance plays a significant part in the need for designers to ensure that all reasonable professional care is taken during the detail design of projects. They must ensure prevention of accidents to the public caused by slipping, tripping, collapse of landscape elements, or flooding as a direct result of design detail failure. Such failure can occur through the malfunction of landscape drainage, circulation, or structural landscape systems. The designer must be concerned about the use of new or untested materials or assemblies and the reliance on standard details or tried-and-true detail solutions. The different responsibilities for detail design work must be more clearly articulated. Otherwise, blame for detail design failure is often assigned to either the execution of the original idea or its site application and use.

In all, there are as many categories of change that occur to landscape detail forms as occur to details in architecture or civil or structural engineering. The types of changes most commonly encountered in landscape detail design are described in the following paragraphs.

How Details Alter: Types of Changes

The types of changes to details fall into four categories: *material* changes, *structural* changes, *mechanical* changes, and *aesthetic* and *environmental* changes.

Material Changes

Material changes include all *cosmetic* changes to material surfaces and textures, such as cracking, flaking, splitting, blistering, discoloration, indentations, scrapes and abrasions, and the breakdown of applications and coatings (see Figure 5.4). Such changes are particularly important when treatments to timber, stone, and concrete are used to extend their longevity or to protect them against aggressive environments. Particularly vulnerable in this regard are the range of finishes on surfaces in a ground plane including paints, stains, and spray applications or dusted-on powders, for example, on colored concrete pathways.

Material changes also include all internal and external changes to the *composition* of the materials themselves, such as oxidation, corrosion, rot, chemical instability of concrete, plastics, and metals, and damage from insect and wildlife attack, as well as dimensional alterations caused by material creep and shrinkage. Such changes are particularly noteworthy where the integrity of the final material itself is important for visual, tactile, and continuity purposes. Here, the designer must be concerned with the juxtaposition of detail materials on-site that would lead to the eventual breakdown of their composition—an example is the combining of two metals such as copper and zinc and the resulting electrolytic action.

The gradual *wearing away* of the integrity of natural and manufactured materials by the actions of repetitive human use or weather is another

Figure 5.4
Material change. Erosion and decomposition of vertical marine wall surface.

162

instance of material change. It is particularly important to be aware of this type of change when using living plants, as sudden and significant alterations to their form, appearance, and health can result in aggressive growth and development or outright death. Less drastic is the erosion that occurs to natural materials such as timber and stone, particularly softer limestone and sandstone, and deposition to natural and man-made materials such as brickwork, concrete surfaces, and boundary wall elements.

Structural Changes

Structural changes are *comprehensive* alterations to the *stability* and *support* of detail forms. They include the deformation, deflection, or slippage of detail elements, with results ranging from initial fatigue to total collapse. Examples include simple cases of movement and expansion of unstable horizontal deck surfaces and pedestrian detail elements, such as shown in Figure 5.5, where joints crack and open, vertical boundaries such as fences, walls, and railings with inadequate foundations, detail members, and mechanical fixings, as well as the breakdown of more complex structures—for example, pergolas, trellises, bridges, and small pavilions.

Structural changes also include *progressive* alterations to the *stability* and *support* of detail forms. Modest and incremental changes over time can result finally in comprehensive alterations; these include most forms of weathering involving patterns of wetting and drying and heating and cooling in locations with normal exposure. Examples include small and often inconspicuous forms of moisture buildup, leading to movement and buckling from the actions of freezing and thawing in traditional paving systems, or the shifting and degradation of fixing anchoring systems of elevated roof deck surfaces,

Figure 5.5
Structural change.
Expansion joint in bench seat.

163

Figure 5.6
Mechanical change.
Balustrade, Shelburne,
Vermont.

balustrade edge walls as shown in Figure 5.6, and veneered step transitions and facings to boundary and retaining walls.

Mechanical

Mechanical changes produce modifications to the *operation* and *performance* of detail forms. These include the influence of drainage, moisture control, and soil stabilization—for example, in the failure of drainage systems to efficiently direct water away from wall bases leading to soil slippage and foundation collapse.

Aesthetic and Environmental

Aesthetic and environmental changes are alterations to the original *design* and *artistic intentions* of the project through its detail forms. These include all manner of transformations, additions, and redesigns owing to programmatic, user, or regulatory requirements (such as shown in Figure 5.7), including shifts in patterns of use, manipulations in appearance (in materials, finishes, and textures), or those brought about by stylistic concerns or the needs of detail language or expression.

There may also be modifications to the *immediate* surrounding site context. These include microclimate changes of temperature and exposure resulting from alterations to detail mass, orientation, and type.

Transformations to the *larger* design context are further instances of such change. These include detail forms that are associated with inappropriate or outdated design strategies or have been altered because of new insights into our understanding of environmental and natural systems—for example, in the preservation of natural resources, uses of energy, concerns for air and water quality, issues of sustainable design, and the health and future of habitats and built environments.

Figure 5.7 Aesthetic change. Addition of universal accessibility ramp.

How Details Alter: Summary

The detail design process is concerned with aspects of each of these four categories. Whereas material, structural, and mechanical changes are central to the initial detail processes, aesthetic and environmental changes in a project are less predictable (see Table 5.1).

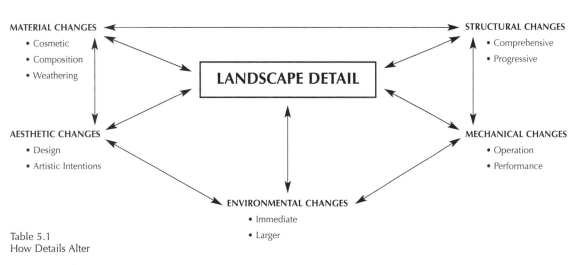

Table 5.1
How Details Alter

165

Let us now consider the reasons behind alterations to landscape detail form and identify their potential sources and causes both during the detail design process and afterward.

Why Details Change: A List of Causes

The causes of changes in details fall into three categories: those arising from *human actions* of numerous types, from *force majeure,* or unpredictable events, often described by the term "acts of God," and as a result of the forces of *climate and weathering.* They are broken down according to when they occur in the process of project development, in either the *detail design, implementation,* or *postoccupancy* phase.

Detail Design Phase

The following causes in this phase of work are considered to have arisen as a result of *human actions.*

- *Errors and omissions* occurring in detail design. These result from the inexperience of the designer or lack of resources in the preparation of detail design proposals.

- Poor detail design *practices.* These include wrong assumptions by the designer regarding the behavior of materials and products and the lack of precedents with which to compare detail solutions.

- Lack of proper *coordination* in the production of documentation. This includes mistakes and omissions resulting from the lack of communication between participants and a lack of time given to their preparation.

Implementation Phase

The following causes in this phase of work are considered to have arisen as a result of *human actions.*

- Lack of sufficient *site observation and quality control.* This includes failure to inspect and identify detail work not carried out in accordance with contract documents, as well as areas with potential detail design concerns not previously identified.

- Poor building *practices and workmanship.* These include carelessness or risk-taking while knowing the possible outcome—for example, the use of inadequate materials and implementation techniques.

- Outright *negligence.* This results from criminal or illegal acts in regard to building practices or the deliberate avoidance of the correct standards and codes of performance.

Postoccupancy Phase

The following causes in this phase of work are considered to have arisen from all three categories.

Human actions

- Physical *deterioration* from use or overuse. This includes changes as a result of continuous and reasonable wear by daily public use.

- *Vandalism* and wanton destruction. This includes all forms of intentional misuse by the public, including graffiti and physical assault such as vehicle impact.

- *Maintenance,* including lack of ongoing maintenance and—just as important—inappropriate or damaging forms of maintenance. This includes the avoidance of any ongoing site treatments, including general cleaning, supervision of weathering procedures, and regular replacement of damaged parts or the application of wrong cleaning and maintenance procedures, which cause even more severe or prolonged damage. Major culprits among these are the surface treatments to ground surfaces.

- Detail changes arising from design *revisions* to codes or design and programmatic alterations. These include the range of additions of new or revised detail forms to satisfy changes in legislation affecting the built environment, as well as the continuous transformations to built landscapes brought about by variations to program, seasonal use, or design intent.

Force majeure

- *Extreme* events. These include, for example, hurricane, flood, landslide, avalanche, tidal wave, fire, insect attack, and destructive wildlife. Such events not only affect detail design but may also induce major changes to entire built environments.

Climate and weathering

- Physical *deterioration.* This includes the normal aging of materials and assemblies that would happen if no human actions were carried out to prevent them.

- Moisture *penetration* and thermal *movement.* These include all changes arising from the actions of wind, rain, sun, humidity, snow, and ice.

Why Details Change: Summary

Among the three areas identified in the list of causes (see Table 5.2), those concerned with climate and weathering are of special interest to the designer in detail design. These produce most changes to built details and yet remain unpredictable. Although changes arising from human actions, especially in the documentation phase, are crucial, the development of good working practices can eliminate changes brought about as a result of poor communication, lack of observation, and quality control.

Table 5.2
Why Details Change

	DETAIL DESIGN	IMPLEMENTATION	POSTOCCUPANCY
Human Actions	●	●	●
Climate & Weathering	○	◐	●
Force Majeure	○	○	●

Time →

● Strongest
○ Weakest

It is also assumed that concerns about vandalism and destruction are addressed, as far as possible, as part of the detail design process through the choice of robust and durable materials and fixings. Extreme natural events create widespread damage and disruption in an unpredictable manner. The designer during the detail design phase, is rarely able to control this form of change beyond taking all reasonable precautions when designing a built landscape in an area where natural events are likely to occur, such as flooding or extremes of temperature or humidity. General weathering by climatic forces is one of the causes of detail change that can be more easily studied by the designer and then addressed successfully during the detail design process. In turn, this consideration informs the pattern and forms of detail development.

3. TYPES AND FORMS OF WEATHERING

Agents of Change

Wind, rain, sunlight, snow, and ice are the most easily understood and recognized sources of weathering that act on built landscape details. They behave in the following ways:

- Through *erosion* and *deposition*—altering detail surfaces, coatings, and applied treatments through fading, crumbling, cracking, or blistering, or inducing movement in soils by slippage, sedimentation, and buildup of granular surfaces

- As *sources* of live loads—wind action, snow, ice buildup, and standing water on detail surfaces and structures

- As *shear forces*—wind action that results in localized and general structural and mechanical changes to landscape details

- Through *thermal movement*—the result of the continuous actions of sun, rain, and humidity and the changes in temperature on a daily and seasonal basis

168

These forms of weathering are addressed by the designer through detail design concerns that include the following:

1. **Correct material selection**
   What landscape details are made from

2. **Structural and mechanical integrity**
   Where landscape details are located, their placement in relation to site conditions, context, and other site details, materials, and systems

3. **Specific detail design practices**
   How landscape details are formed, including:
   - An understanding of the detail parts that make up each landscape detail form, including their scale, size, and relationship to each other
   - Considerations of gravity and angles of repose for soils and granular materials
   - Knowledge of the endurance of surface finishes, textures, and joints to wind, sun, salts, and pervasive moisture
   - Attention to the juxtaposition, combining, and cutting of natural and synthetic materials
   - Diversion of water from detail forms and protection of sensitive junctions and joints from excessive exposure to sun and moisture

Figure 5.8
Time and weathering.

Time and the Types of Weathering

Time is implicit in all detail considerations about weathering in landscape detail design. Living natural materials used in landscape design (one thinks of plants immediately) grow, mature, and die within a known and predictable life cycle and, in doing so, alter both their own physical forms and the visible form and structure of the landscapes they inhabit. There are also daily and seasonal cycles of weathering, maturity, and decay in other landscape detail forms to consider, such as shown in Figure 5.8.

Inert landscape materials are less visibly altered and appear more resilient to physical change during their life cycles. However, they too go through periods of aging and decline. *This form of weathering is reversible and can be arrested and altered.*

There are forms of linear weathering that occur to landscape detail forms. They differ from the normal cycle of weathering by occurring as a continuous process, each stage dependent on the one before, in a successive and gradual *series* of changes *that are not reversible.* They may also be additive, each one a stage in an incremental process toward total decline.

Projects are altered intermittently over time by owners, clients, or authorities. Such episodes in the life of a project may be related to damage from climatic events, in response to social factors, including stylistic shifts or personal wishes, or cultural, legal, or economic concerns. *This form of weathering can be vigorously arrested and altered and is, in certain cases, with adequate resources, reversible.*

Finally, there is the destruction of a detail or detail condition that alters it irreversibly as unusable or unsafe. This form of weathering is likely to be the result of a total collapse of structural, mechanical, or material integrity caused, for example, by hurricane, earthquake, winter storm, spring flooding, or damage by vandalism. This type of alteration is *absolute and irreversible* and initiates a period of redesign and replacement.

In summary, in landscape detail forms there are four distinguishable types of weathering, each determined by the following:

• Time

• Period of recurrence of predictable change(s)

• The ability to respond to change(s)

These types of weathering are described as *cyclical, serial, episodic,* and *absolute.* It is rare, however, that a single type of weathering occurs in isolation; rather, it is common that more than one type are taking place concurrently, and acting with, rather than against each other. A short description of each follows.

Cyclical Weathering

The most common type of weathering relates to a variety of contrasting or degenerative processes that occur over periods of time, sometimes in parallel with each other. These produce conditions that slow down, reverse, or alter the progress and direction of weathering.

Daily, seasonal, and annual cycles involve the processes of heating and cooling, wetting and drying, freezing and thawing. In turn, these produce on landscape details the cumulative effects of expansion and contraction, seeding, growth and decline (of plants), erosion and deposition, chemical attack and decay, leaching and discoloration, corrosion and oxidation, and the surface growths of algae, mold, mildew, and lichens. As applied to landscape detail forms using natural materials, such as timber, stone, brick, and concrete, these result in the following functional, visual, and aesthetic detail changes:

• The progressive and incremental "coverings" by natural processes acting on and changing details in predictable patterns over time; the result may or may not be visually or aesthetically acceptable to the designer. These include not only deposits of soil, dirt, and airborne dust and soot particles, but internal changes to the composition of worked materials, resulting in patinas, surface residues, and films that camouflage and obscure.

- The deliberate selection, placement, and replacement of materials to take account of predicted alterations to their composition, surface textures, and colors. These changes are made with full recognition of the likely effects that weathering will have and, in fact, become a central part of the aesthetic motivation and character of the project and the design work. Here weathering and change constitute the source of the central detail design idea. As applied to landscape detail forms using synthetic or manufactured materials and assemblies—for example, plastics, metals, glass, and canvas—they also result in functional and visual detail changes.

- Alterations to the functioning of details by reactions within, or deterioration of, the material's main structure and composition. These cause fracturing, rotting, breakdown owing to corrosive attack in metals, discoloration, and the effects of ultraviolet light on polyvinyl chloride (PVC).

Serial Weathering

Serial weathering is similar to the cyclical type but differs in one important respect: *it is not reversible.* Incremental changes to an initial design proposal add up over time to affect the integrity and nature of detail forms. Each stage in serial weathering, although appearing insignificant, is part of a more comprehensive breakdown of the detail form.

As applied to landscape detail, this results in the following functional, visual, and aesthetic detail changes:

- Small-scale consecutive alterations to the functioning of details by reduction in their material thickness

- Realignment or displacement of detail parts

- Severe or partial collapse

- Finally, movement of materials

Episodic Weathering

The form of weathering most closely associated with cumulative incremental changes to initial design proposals is episodic weathering. Incremental changes occur over longer periods of time and are more likely to be associated with changes of ownership, stylistic changes, or alterations to codes and regulations in the built environment.

These changes produce a form of weathering that is irreversible. They create a potential layering of multiple forms of landscape detail within the project in a way that can be described as "organic," that is, happening as a result of a natural pattern of evolution and development. Many of the built public landscapes are the result of changes of this type. There are times, however, when such change is detrimental to an entire design project and exemplary landscape detail forms are entirely broken up and erased from the structure and fabric of a built landscape. This weathering type cuts across all forms of materials, installations, and detail configurations, including surfaces, transitions, and boundaries.

As applied to landscape detail forms, this results in the following functional, visual, and aesthetic detail changes:

- Complete and absolute destruction of detail forms, resulting from the elimination of the existing detail parts and the addition of either new or more historically or stylistically accurate landscape detail forms for the project context. This process may include the recycling of materials that were removed, the reuse of the detail forms in a different project, or the creation of workshop templates or molds to recreate them in multiple copies. Examples include the considerable work in the field of historic landscape and architecture preservation and conservation to correct landmark projects and landscapes where later additions of forms do not reflect current attitudes to detail authenticity and issues of historical integrity. This field is, however, made more complex by changing tastes and scholarship associated with older landscapes, the inevitable lack of clear documentation of each moment of alteration and change, and the repair required for cruder and more damaging types of restoration and conservation work.

- Manipulation and significant alterations that result in the adaptation of existing detail forms that form the underlying structure for subsequent aesthetic and functional expression. These take the form of coverings to existing surfaces and transitions, the addition of further quantities of similar materials and detail elements, or the careful insertion of complementary materials and detail forms. Examples include the changes brought about by the Americans with Disabilities (ADA) laws and the need for universal accessibility. All manner of ramps and sloped transitions have been added to every conceivable type of public building or outdoor space, irrespective of historical period, scale, or context. Timber handrails and decks are laid on stone stairs and walls; additional slabs of concrete are added to sidewalks and roads.

Absolute Weathering

Absolute weathering is the form of weathering most closely associated with large-scale changes, including the total and absolute destruction of design projects and their surrounding environments. The breakup of landscape detail forms in this case appears to be of minor significance in these events in comparison to the loss of human life or the disruption of entire towns and communities. However, two issues are significant in reference to this type of weathering: first, the forms of landscape detail that are part of the structures of flood controls, dams, levees, bridges, and barriers and that are required to withstand considerable forces and the structural, mechanical, and material criteria which are applied. Second is the ability of detail forms to be reconstructed after an event. This implies that due care can be taken at the outset to anticipate absolute weathering, with parts developed to deliberately fail and be replaced afterward—a process of "sacrificial detail."

As applied to landscape detail forms, these result in the following functional, visual, and aesthetic detail changes:

- Breakage, collapse, or, for example, inundation by water causing complete failure of detail parts

- Loss of functional integrity, with fundamental visual and aesthetic changes in appearance, form, and character

Summary of Types of Weathering

In describing the various individual types of weathering (with the exception of the absolute or catastrophic), it can be noted that these forms occur together in varying degrees of severity with differing results over the course of a project's life. In fact, it may be difficult at certain times to distinguish between the types of weathering taking place (see Table 5.3).

The cyclical type suggests detail design possibilities which, to the designer, make this an area of study and focus during the design process and the development of detail forms. It also brings certain detail design forms, considered static and inert, closer to the daily and annual rhythms of landscapes and their inhabitants.

Weathering is, however, more closely related to the issues of detail performance, the ongoing concerns for durability, and the successful development of landscape detail forms.

It is important now to address the issues of *detail design failure.* The discussion of weathering has illustrated that there are many types of failure that are considered the reverse of "successful" detail forms. However, in certain cases these are found to be unavoidable and, indeed, may form part of the evolution of a project over time.

WEATHERING TYPES	TIME	PERIOD OF RECURRENCE OF PREDICTABLE CHANGE(S)	ABILITY TO RESPOND TO CHANGES	RESULT
Cyclical	●	●	●	Reversible
Serial	●	●	○	Irreversible
Episodic	○	○	●	Reversible
Absolute	○	○	○	Irreversible

● Strongest
○ Weakest

Table 5.3
Summary of Weathering

173

4. ISSUES OF DETAIL FAILURE

failure (n): omission of occurrence or performance: a failing to perform a duty or expected action

Webster's Ninth New Collegiate Dictionary, 1988.

Learning from Landscape Detail Failure

What is failure in detail design, and how does the designer address it in the detail design process? The dictionary definition suggests that failure occurs both at a specific point in time (in the design or implementation period) and as a degenerative process (in the life of a project). Therefore, failure in detail design is the inability of a landscape detail to fulfill an intended purpose in its performance.

The process of studying the nature and role of failure in landscape detail design requires the following:

• Gathering of information about such failure

• Identification and analysis of the types and causes of failure

• Dissemination of results

Failure Studies in Other Disciplines

In other applied disciplines such as civil engineering, structural engineering, and architecture, investigations into the nature of detail design and construction failure have been performed using information obtained from insurance companies and federal and state appellate court summaries. In a 1985 workshop[2] on reducing failure sponsored by the National Science Foundation, among the findings was the following:

> That many of the lessons to be learned from failures in one discipline are equally applicable to other disciplines.

In the design and engineering of road structures, bridges, and buildings, the study of failure is central to the evolution of these disciplines, a subject of critical but open debate, and a frequent topic in professional journals and other publications. Examples include Thomas McKaig's 1962 book *Building Failures: Case Studies in Construction and Design* and *Performance Failures in Buildings and Civil Works*, produced by the University of Maryland Architecture and Engineering Performance Information Center (1991). In the latter, information and analysis are provided on approximately 8,000 building, civil engineering, and site projects implemented between 1970 and 1988. The goal of the study was

> The improved performance of our nation's existing and future building stock and infrastructure and, therefore, the increased

quality, longevity, and safety of the built environment through the identification of the failures presently being experienced.

Contained within this document is a range of information that includes the following:

• The type of project

• The size and cost

• The length of years of design, construction, and occupancy of the project

Information on failure types includes the following:

• Identification of the problem area

• In-depth information on the failed detail component, element, or material

• Type of service relating to the failure (whether structural, electrical, mechanical, etc.)

• The party holding responsibility

• Activity causing the failure

• Reasons for the failure

An example of a typical breakdown of information follows:

Structural/Civil Engineering Works [such as Causeways, Drainage Works, Embankments, Excavations, Highways, Park/Playing Fields, Parking Areas, Reservoirs, Retaining Walls]

Number of records = 2320

Property Damage Catalyst (Primary) — Edited

Water	31%
Loads	26%
Soils	10%
Impact	8%
Others	25%

Responsible Party — Edited

Civil Engineer	39%
Owner	17%
Contractor	9%

Architect	6%
Engineer/Architect	6%
Structural Engineer	3%
Landscape Architect	1%
Others	19%

Reason for Failure — Edited

Design Error	31%
Poor Quality Construction	11%
Poor Observation/Inspection	8%
Survey Error	7%
Poor Assumptions	6%
Practice Error	5%
Improper Specifications	5%
Poor Maintenance	3%
Communications Error	4%
Misuse of Area	3%
Natural Causes	2%
Others	15%

Detail materials in paving, fencing, roadways, and drainage, as well as plants, are noted but do not count in the final analysis of failures because of the limited number of recorded cases.

Case studies were drawn from failures in buildings, bridges, highways, and other infrastructure elements. The types of failure were simply organized according to size and scale of failure (from cosmetic/aesthetic to destruction), and causes were grouped according to the point in time in the process of designing, implementation, or occupancy each was believed to have taken place. Recognition of failure occurring in more than one phase or resulting from previous phases was not recorded. For further examples of sources of failure in engineering, see the references at the end of this chapter.

Summary: Failure Analysis in Landscape Detail Design
Attention to the implications of failure studies is important to ensure the future quality of the built environment of towns and cities and to protect the designer from costly legal action. Some of the forms of failure in landscape detail design are severe, causing the closure of public spaces and liability claims against designers. These include the structural collapse of paved sur-

faces and the erosion of slopes, resulting in landslides. Other failures are minor, appearing as cosmetic changes to surfaces and materials and requiring only the application of correct regular maintenance. Writing on the relationship between time and workmanship, designer and educator David Pye has remarked, "It all fails, to be sure: but it fails either sooner or later," [3] challenging the possibility of ever achieving true permanence in any built work.

This may certainly be the case in landscape detail design where the issues of climate, weathering, and design and implementation combine to render this form of detail work particularly vulnerable. However, to integrate a sensibility toward failure into the detail design process is a worthy goal for the designer and, as Pye suggests, is an essential aspect in considering exemplary and useful detail design.

5. ANTICIPATING CHANGE THROUGH DETAIL DESIGN

Let us return to the three questions regarding detail design, weathering, and durability that were posed at the beginning of the chapter;

1. What are the ways in which details are modified, and what are the probable causes?

Details are modified in four ways: materially, structurally, mechanically and aesthetically, and environmentally. Of greater significance are the three probable causes of detail change: human actions of numerous types, including detail design; force majeure or acts of God; and the forces of climate and weathering. Here, the part designers play in causing detail change is acknowledged and considered a positive rather than a negative attribute.

2. Why do certain details deteriorate and fail, and what can be learned from these failures in order to produce successful details in the future?

Deterioration and failure in detail design result from the inability of a landscape detail to fulfill an intended purpose especially in its performance. Details may fail as a result of the following actions: errors and omissions occurring in detail design, poor detail design practices, lack of proper coordination in the production of documentation, lack of sufficient site observation and quality control, poor building practices and workmanship, outright negligence, physical deterioration from use or overuse, vandalism, wanton destruction, lack of maintenance, including inappropriate or damaging forms of maintenance, design revisions to codes or design and programmatic alterations, extreme events, deterioration from the normal aging of materials and assemblies, moisture penetration, and thermal movement. Much can be learned and used in the future through the gathering of information about failures, the identification and analysis of the types and causes of failure, and dissemination of results.

3. Is longevity in detail design a worthwhile goal for the designer?

An understanding of longevity through a study of landscape detail failure can do more than avoid possible lengthy and costly legal actions for a designer. Of importance is the potential of anticipating detail change during the design development phase and contributing to the artful use of detail. To do this effectively and efficiently, the following steps should be taken by each designer to gain a general comprehension of the subject:

- *Disseminate information.* To learn from previous failures, designers should be aware of ongoing failures in their own built work and the work of others. To minimize the repetition of failures in the future requires active and open dissemination of individual findings and evaluations.

- *Encourage the development of innovative detail forms, as well as the continuation of appropriate traditional forms.* Many designers rely on standardized forms of detail and specifications. The introduction of new or untested materials or the deliberate choice to investigate alternative methods of forming or making landscape detail *does not in itself* indicate that failure is inevitable. To broaden the range of landscape detail forms eliminates those detail forms, whether traditional, standard, or innovative, that do not perform correctly any longer.

6. DEFINITIONS OF TERMS

The following key terms and phrases that were identified and discussed in this chapter are defined below.

Durability: soundness, constancy, and permanence of landscape details over periods of time.

Weathering: actions to landscape detail brought about by climatic forces and/or human use.

Detail performance: predictable way in which landscape details are expected to function over time.

Failure: inability of a landscape detail to fulfill an intended purpose, especially in performance or achievement.

"Sacrificial" details: in anticipation of weathering, those detail parts that are developed deliberately to fail over time and to be replaced cheaply and efficiently as part of future maintenance.

7. CLASSROOM EXERCISES

These exercises form part of a series of assignments to be carried out within the structure of a course on landscape construction, landscape technology and detail, or as part of a design studio.

Assignment 5: Weathering, Durability, and Failure in Detail

1. Develop a time line to describe the potential weathering of a set of landscape details in your locale. Establish graphically on the timeline the details that are most vulnerable to change and alteration. Determine whether they are of one type or geographically close to each other. Stretch out the duration of the time line over 1, 3, 5, 10, and 25 years.

   Record these weathering changes through photographs and notes. Find examples of details similar in age and compare the initial quality of construction where possible.

2. Select two landscape detail forms observed in the surrounding built environment. The details may consist of several materials and must be located at significant points of connection or transition within an outdoor space. One of the detail forms selected should display characteristics that demonstrate detail success, and one detail failure. The meaning of success and failure is for each individual to determine and is a central part of the assignment.

   Record the detail forms through field notes (dimensions, materials, finishes) and freehand sketches. Try a range of drawing mediums to describe the nature of material, junctions, and so on, and how they are used. What were the possible design sources available, or used by the designer? What was the cause of the failed detail—was it related to the initial design sources?

3. Investigate the consequences of extreme climatic forces on the details and construction of built landscapes in your region. Recent floods, hurricanes, droughts, ice, and windstorms, for example, should be examined for their short- and long-term effects.

   Develop a response in terms of traditional and innovative detailing procedures for future work. Which details can be considered "sacrificial," and which are fundamental to ensure public health, safety, and welfare?

4. Carry out short scientific experiments in the studio or workshop to test the ability of landscape materials to withstand extremes of moisture, heat, and cooling. Examples include soaking and drying repeatedly small samples of brick, stone, wood, and concrete, freezing samples over longer periods of time, and baking at high temperatures. Groups can be responsible for testing against field or standard samples in normal climatic conditions.

How can the results be used effectively in the field? Determine whether tests are carried out by designers or contractors in local projects to establish local performance criteria for a range of building supplies.

5. Research manufacturers and suppliers, current trade and technical literature to discover the range of tests carried out in laboratories and field sites.

Over what length of time are they carried out? To what standards do they conform, and how is that information translated into specifications and detail design?

8. REFERENCES AND SOURCES

Section 1. Introduction

1. In conversation with the author, spring 1997.

Section 4. Issues of Detail Failure

2. Noted in introduction of *Performance Failures in Buildings and Civil Works,* produced by the University of Maryland Architecture and Engineering Performance Information Center, 1991.

3. David Pye. *The Nature and Art of Workmanship* (New York: Van Nostrand Reinhold, 1972): 41.

9. FURTHER READING

Arnold, Henry. "Preserve the Present: It's Not Too Early to Protect Modern Landscapes." *Landscape Architecture* 84, no. 4 (March 1994): 50–51. Recent article on the weathering and alterations to contemporary urban landscapes by human actions; for example, Lincon Center Plaza in New York by Dan Kiley. Episodic weathering involving alterations to canopy trees' palette and their spatial organization, all caused by a mixture of mismanagement and incompetence by the owners.

Brand, Stewart. *How Buildings Learn: What Happens After They're Built.* New York: Penguin Books, 1994. A model taken from architectural design of how built work changes over time. Filled with photographs tracing the alterations and additions to built forms, with text that supports the idea of loose fit, flexible spaces that adapt to the requirements, desires, and whims of owners. A companion landscape architecture book for outdoor space is sorely needed.

Cohen, Eliot A., and John Gooch. *Military Misfortunes.* New York: Free Press; London: Collier Macmillan, 1990. Classic study in the field of military failure in war, indicating how and what one can learn from its examples. Identifies three principles to be applied to current military thinking: the ability to anticipate, the ability to predict, and the ability to learn. These appear to be reasonable principles to apply in any of the design fields.

Le Messurier, William. "City Perils: The Fifty-Nine-Story Crisis." *New Yorker Magazine* (29 May 1995). A fascinating, clearly written article for a non-professional audience on the work of engineer William Le Messurier to avert structural failure of steps at the Citicorp Center building in Manhattan. Related to detail, design, and structural performance as well as professional responsibility.

Mostafavi, Moshen, and David Leatherbarrow. *On Weathering: The Life of Buildings in Time.* Cambridge: MIT Press, 1993. The authors define architectural weathering as the "gradual destruction of buildings by nature in time." Photographic study and brief essay on the poetic implications of architectural form and materials in climate.

Olgyay, Victor. *Design with Climate.* Princeton: Princeton Architectural Press, 1963. Classic introduction to the subject of microclimate and the landscape.

Patton, Phil. "To Build a Bridge, You Must Cross Troubled Waters." *Smithsonian Magazine* (September 1996). A nontechnical article on bridge failures leading to human disasters: Tacoma Narrows Bridge, Washington, 1940; Silver Bridge, Point Pleasant, West Virginia, 1967; Mianus River Bridge, Connecticut, 1983; and overpasses during the 1994 earthquake in Los Angeles.

Petroski, Henry. *Design Paradigms: Case Studies of Error and Judgment in Engineering.* Cambridge, England; New York, NY: Cambridge University Press, 1994. Further study of the relationships between failure and design in engineering, focusing on human error.

Pye, David. *The Nature and Art of Workmanship.* New York: Van Nostrand Reinhold, 1972. An overview of the subject of design making and the issues of craft, craftsmanship, and workmanship. Written by an eminent educator and furniture designer, it goes beyond that single design field to address all design activities with daily concerns of materiality, design, and detail form. A wonderful introduction to the aesthetic and philosophical considerations of the designer's traditions and practices of working by hand and by machine.

Templer, John. *The Staircase: Studies of Hazards, Falls, and Safer Design.* Cambridge: MIT Press, 1992. Chapter 5, "Behavior on Steps," addresses movement on stairways and the concept of erosion and wearing marking the passage of humans ascending and descending.

Failure

The following examples illustrate the range of literature that has been written on the subject of failure in this and other fields. Attempts have been made to document and then to classify the types and causes of failure. Many of these resources include aspects of landscape architectural work as a general category within siteworks or infrastructure.

Blockley, David I. *The Nature of Structural Design and Safety.* Chichester, England: E. Horwood; New York: John Wiley & Sons, 1980. A work on structural failure identifying three general categories in the cause of failure: physical forces, environmental conditions, and a third that is concerned with forms of human activities.

Kirkwood, Niall. "Holding Our Ground," *Landscape Architecture* 86, no. 2 (February 1996). Short article laying out general issues of detail failure in the contemporary built landscape and discussing the preparation of students to study the subject.

Loss, John, and Earle W. Kennett. *Performance Failures in Buildings and Civil Works.* (AEPIC) Bethesda, Maryland: University of Maryland, 1991. Compilation of statistical information on recent failures within the construction industry. A survey prepared to define the nature of the future stock of built structures and infrastructure. Landscape architecture plays a minor part in the data that was collected and analyzed. Of interest are the categories of failures and their expected causes and effects.

Petroski, Henry. *To Engineer Is Human: The Role of Failure in Successful Design.* New York: St Martin's Press, 1985. Petroski's book on failure in structural design and civil engineering introduces the identification of physical forces and conditions versus individual human activity as the two main causes of failure.

Richardson, Barry A. *Defects and Deterioration in Buildings.* London: E. & F. N. Spon, 1991. A good technical introduction to the subject of maintenance and postoccupancy design and detail work in building structures.

CHAPTER 6

RESEARCH

THIS CHAPTER INTRODUCES the subject of detail research as an integral part of instruction and day-to-day detail work in the field of landscape architecture. It outlines the types of research that are used by design students and landscape designers who carry out detail studies. These research methods and their applications are presented to allow students to organize and complete their own detail research. Future research still to be carried out, which is of importance in the development of landscape detail design, is identified and outlined. A concluding section introduces the structure and organization of the detail case studies in Part Three. Students will be able to integrate research methods into landscape detail with their other courses of study. The tools of field and library detail research will be used to build a base knowledge of detail form, materials, and assemblies from which to draw.

1. INTRODUCTION

Previous chapters have outlined the importance of landscape detail and how the detail process is carried out, but have constantly emphasized the need for designers to carry out their own detail research as part of daily design practice. This is necessary to develop a comprehensive range of landscape detail for future reference and as an individual source of detail forms and elements. Why do you research landscape detail, what are the likely results, and how is the information documented, stored, and retrieved for future use?

Designers repeat details and reuse certain materials to ensure a continuity of landscape form within a single design project and between different projects. In this way, "learning by mistakes," rules of thumb, and various short-hand methods and detail practices are established over a number of years, to be repeated, elaborated on, or, as is sometimes the case, misappropriated and lost over time. The "research" of detail has previously been considered of little significance in practice. If research was carried out at all, it was done as part of a project. If it was engaged in outside a project by an enthusiastic designer working alone, or by an institution or company with narrow self-serving goals, the results of the studies were rarely made available to others.

The accompanying drawings and photographs shown in Figures 6.1 and 6.2 were developed by the author as part of an academic research project entitled "Landscape Patterns: The Woodland Gardens, Courtyards and Lanes of the French Village."[1] A series of streets, walks, entry drives and courtyards, terraces and gardens were laid out with single-family dwellings on sloped terrain within the Wissahickon Valley of the Schuylkill River in Philadelphia, Pennsylvania.

▲ Figure 6.1
Detail section. 7316 Elbow Lane, the French Village, Philadelphia, Pennsylvania.

▶ Figure 6.2
View of study area. Elbow Lane, the French Village, Philadelphia, Pennsylvania.

184

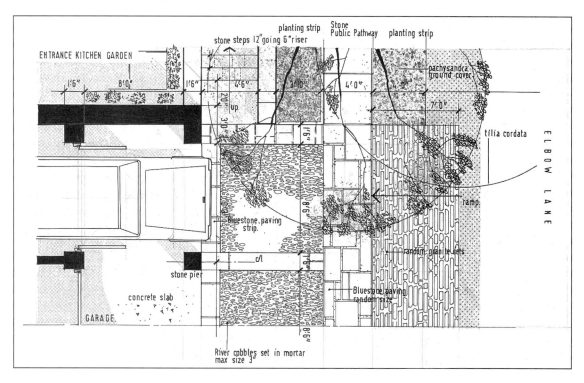

The detail study of the French Village area, a residential development planned and carried out between 1924 and 1929, had two initial objectives. The first was to investigate, through field study, measurement, and drawn analysis, the relationship between the natural and built landscape elements of which the site was composed. The second was to document those built elements present at key locations that constituted the woodland detail design idiom known as the "Wissahickon Style," as illustrated in Figure 6.3. Completed with dashed mortar schist walls, riven bluestone surfaces and gravel surfaces, and bounded by arched pedestrian gateways and enclosed forecourts, all the public streets and lanes were carried out in simple detail forms. This resulted from the original client's interest in the Wissahickon Style, which derived its architectural expression from the precedents of French Normandy vernacular building. The intention of the study was to describe and catalog selective landscape detail forms that contributed to the detail language of this particular built environment, both as a public streetscape and as a private residential neighborhood. The landscape detail forms focused on stone walking surfaces, step transitions from public pathways to private courtyards, and the layout of canopy trees and boundary walls.

Figure 6.3
Entrance paving detail.
7316 Elbow Lane, the French Village, Philadelphia, Pennsylvania.

Background to Research

The ASLA Code of Professional Conduct states, "The member shall encourage research and development and dissemination of useful technical information relating to planning, design, and construction of the physical environment." The meaning of *research* is "scholarly or scientific investigation or inquiry...a thorough seeking out or searching of a topic."[2] Research as applied to landscape detail has a distinct focus as a sustained investigation into an aspect of the built landscape, in which the detail is paramount, rather than a supporting feature. Research in landscape detail is rarely carried out and in recent years has not been considered an appropriate subject for academic study by students in design schools. Later, there is little time, energy, or inclination to engage in research in practice.

How can a designer develop an individual body of knowledge on the subject of detail? For those people entering the profession there has been little opportunity in their previous training to develop and establish their own approach to detail design; in addition, there has been little chance to formally study and research it as a subject.

The research of landscape details and detail forms is rarely considered of value until specific detail information is required, usually within a professional situation and related to a particular site or project. However, detail research has the potential to be carried out as part of ongoing professional development in landscape architecture. This may occur in much the same way as courses in project management, new planning techniques, wetlands regulations, and specific landscape types; for example, therapeutic gardens, landfill design, and golf courses are offered as part of the continuing education process within the profession.

An introduction for educators and students is laid out and explained here, with examples, including the following subjects:

• Types of research

• Participants and objectives

• Research in the field, library, and office

• Site tasks and methods

• Tools and equipment required

• Creation of case studies and their application

• Storage of documents and study information

The purpose is to allow individual programs, instructors, and departments to develop detail research and study programs that are appropriate to their location, context, student body, and available resources. To prepare for work in this area, it is necessary to consider the range and types of research that can be carried out.

2. TYPES OF RESEARCH

Research study of landscape detail falls into one of the following five categories: *descriptive, comparative, analytical, critical,* or *pictorial.* A short description of each is accompanied by examples of those most commonly carried out in landscape architecture.

Descriptive Study

A descriptive study is an in-depth study that focuses on the dimensional, perceptual, and formal properties of details and their juxtaposition with adjoining details and assemblies. This is particularly useful in considering discrete landscape elements such as fences, screens, and street furniture. It may go further and *prescribe* how an element may be applied or used in certain conditions or circumstances.

Figure 6.4 shows a study of the source of landscape details in a public urban landscape. It consists of a survey and documentation of landscape details of the civic realm in and around a grouping of public transportation subway stops. Sketches, scaled sections, and plans were made of stairways, walls, and paving treatments, and the careful depiction of wall tile, step, and railing elements accurately depict the selection of materials, the way they meet on-site, and the details of jointing. Particularly of note is the rendering of the runnel detail at the step edge, which allows the stairway to drain and acts as a transition between step and wall. Photographs, notes, and written descriptions were added to further describe these detail conditions. This descriptive study gives little information as to how and why these details were developed or about the choices or range of detail decisions that were made. It sets out to give a clear depiction of the found condition, the results of which may be used to form part of a further comparative or analytical study. The use of written notes mimics, in a way, the graphic conventions of the documentation process of construction drawings.

Figure 6.4
Descriptive study of public stairway and subway entrance. Central Square, Cambridge, Massachusetts. Courtesy of Patrick Maguire.

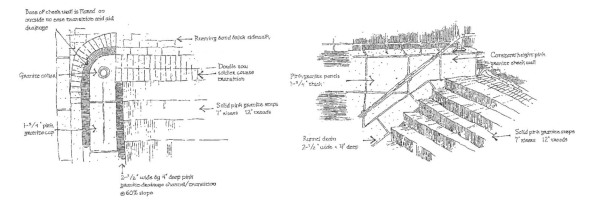

187

Comparative Study

In the comparative form of detail research, details from selected work, projects, or locations are identified and brought together for the purpose of direct comparison of the materials, detail expression, or motifs. This comparison can be made from the point of view of successful or unsuccessful, complete or incomplete, ancient or modern, private or public detail works and can range across all forms of landscape detail. The example in Figure 6.5 illustrates the development of road construction techniques from ancient to modern, all drawn at the same scale. In particular, there is a focus on the reduction in thickness of the subbase layers that support the final surface wearing course. Direct comparison can be made, for example, between the overall depth of Roman roads and that of the contemporary asphalt roadway.

Figure 6.5
Comparative road base sections, Roman to early twentieth century. Drawn by Sara Peschel for the author after *The Art of Roadmaking* by Harwood Frost, 1910.

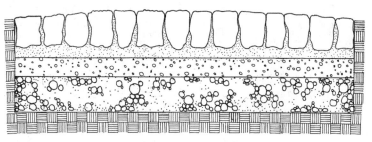

Ancient Roman Road

Early Eighteenth Century Road

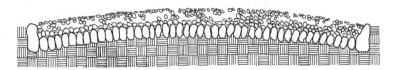

Late Eighteenth Century Road

Modern Macadam Road

188

Analytical Study

In analytical research, specific landscape details are studied from the point of view of their inner workings and organization, the assembly of their parts, and their relationship to other detail forms in the design project. The most common use of this category is in the exploration of the junctions and joining of an intricate detail assembly in which each individual detail part is held in a spatial and constructional relationship to the others. An "exploded" axonometric form of drawing clearly demonstrates the analysis of built detail forms where there is a hierarchy of inner and outer parts and demonstrates the relationships between substructure and final coverings. For example, in the analytical detail study in Figure 6.6 the combination of low parapet wall and bollard detail forms are disassembled to reveal the inner concrete core mass and thickness of stone cladding. Thus, the detail form is more clearly understood through this analysis of the spatial and tectonic connections and junctions.

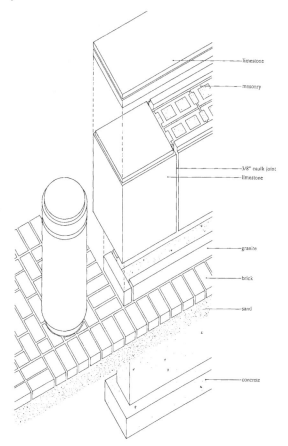

Figure 6.6
Inquiry into the sources of detail. Analytical detail study of the connection of paving and wall. Courtesy of Michael Fountaine and Shuichi Murakami.

Critical Study

Critical study is a type of research that evaluates the success or failure of a detail on its own terms or according to the set of conditions it occurs within. This is a valuable tool where the designer is taking a particular stance or position about a piece of detail work—for example, the evolution of an individual detail style or the development of detail applications across the work of different time periods. The architecture profession has always considered critical study in detail design to be of vital importance in understanding the evolution and development of internal space and building form since early times. Today there is a proliferation of books, magazines, and other writings on the details of architecture from every period, style, country, and design movement, either as case studies (The Architecture in Detail series from Phaidon Press Ltd., London), general books on the subject (*Details, the Architects Art,* Chronicle Books, San Francisco, 1991), or professional textbooks (*Architectural Detailing: Function, Constructibility, Aesthetics,* John Wiley & Sons, New York, 1993).

Of interest in this category is Edward Ford's classic 1990 study, *The Details of Modern Architecture* (a second volume came out in 1996), which closely examines, through photographs, detail plans, and axonometric studies redrawn in the same graphic style, how certain key late-nineteenth- and twentieth-century buildings were built. In particular, the relationships between individual architects, detail design, materials, and the changing methods of assembly and construction are critically examined through these drawn studies and the completed forms. A case is made for an evolutionary process of making in architecture seen through the critical focus of detail.

Pictorial Study

The final type of research, pictorial study, is concerned with recording and composing a range of detail forms or detail types. This is done in an attempt to "fix" or capture the spirit or essence of a particular place or type of work through the common associations of materials and forms. It is most often associated with photographic surveys, posters, monographs, or photo-essays of specific regions, cities, or cultural centers—for example, "New York Streets," "New England Fences," "The National Parks," or "The Southwest." Unfortunately, many detail studies included in this particular category are found in practice monographs or studies of the work of particular designers. Although visually rich, these are of limited value to designers in detail design work, other than as an assembly of "snapshots" of a subject.

Summary

No single method of research is used exclusively, and there are many forms that are combinations of these categories. Joint descriptive and comparative surveys of detail elements (bollards/lighting/curbs/benches) are most commonly illustrated in landscape construction books or articles. For example, Linda Jewell's *descriptive* and *comparative* detail research study "Stone and Concrete Bollards"[3] features 31 pedestrian bollards drawn in plan and elevation to the same scale and in a similar line weight and graphic style, with added dimensions of heights, widths, and diameters. The study also includes the materials the bollards are made of and their locations (Italy and the United States). The reader, by examining the whole group together, can discern, first, the range of bollard forms and expressions by size, location, or type. A second distinction can be made in the range of bollard forms and expressions by material; these also include "families of bollards" or groupings in the same location, for example, at the piazza at Saint Peter's, Rome. Comparisons can also be made between similar bollard types in different locations or between different forms made with similar materials. Finally, with some rough estimates of their creation and placement in situ (no dates are available), comparisons can be drawn between historical details, using the examples from the piazza at Saint Peter's and their modern reinterpretation at the entrance to the Boston Public Library. Therefore, from one set of details of this individual civic element, a large amount of information can be obtained.

However, such studies are rarely that exhaustive or critical, and no attempt is made to discern whether they are "successful" or "less than successful" examples, nor the economic, professional, and design conditions under which they were carried out, nor their postimplementation patterns of weathering and change.

In general, categories of research study focus on the following types of landscape design work:

• Work or projects of an individual landscape designer or office.

• A particular historical or stylistic period.

• A certain region or area of the country.

• A particular class of work that is carried out in landscape architecture or related design practices. These types of work can include built elements of the landscape and are as diverse as amphitheatres, highway sound barriers, marinas, small structures, and pavilions. They can also include types of landscape work such as office parks, resorts and entertainment centers, cemeteries, university campuses and parks, or, as seen in the Jewell study, a particular civic detail element. In all of these an in-depth study is conducted across different works in different locations and time periods.

The next section identifies the persons who carry out detail research and the objectives of such study. These are concerned with the initial design intent and the general circumstances of the project. Examples of detail studies carried out to support either academic or professional work are illustrated.

3. PARTICIPANTS AND OBJECTIVES

Participants

Although the number of people engaged in detail research today is quite small, they come from a wide variety of backgrounds: design and art students, design consulting offices and their staffs, design professionals, civic and historical organizations, and state and city design and preservation departments, as well as building trade and construction organizations. There are circumstances in which the federal government and its agencies, the military, or private companies or institutions require detail research to be carried out as part of larger design studies addressing particular sites or locations. Examples of the diverse forms of detail research include:

• The Disney Corporation's study of period garden and street furniture, planting structures, and signage as part of "imagineering" for resorts with particular themes. This approach includes the *descriptive, analytical,* and *pictorial* categories of research. Such investigation involves considerable field study and limited library research, using photographs and the reinterpretation of existing prototypes with new or revised material choices.

• The research of the accurate landscape details of historic landscapes by the National Park Service. This includes the *descriptive, analytical, comparative,* and *critical* categories of research. This type of study includes library and archival research, using drawings, photographs, paintings, and written records where available. The information gathered is compared with existing details on-site or fragments that may be left or uncovered. In cases where no documentation is available, other landscape sites of similar periods or types, or that were carried out by the same designer, are used as comparative models.

• Security and maintenance sitework details by parks departments or historic land authorities that require protection of ancient and/or valuable cultural amenities and built artifacts. This study includes the development of detail signage and barriers to provide increased protection against damage to sites from pedestrian foot traffic—for example, security devices to protect Native American burial sites from destruction and looting. Here, the research of landscape details takes the form of a *comparative* analysis of existing landscape details (guardrails, hidden barriers, reinforced grass surfaces) and their performance in similar conditions over time. In addition, proposed landscape detail forms involving the integration of innovative site technologies (trip beams, laser and vibration detectors) are the focus of *critical* analysis regarding their applicability and performance over time in the field.

Individual Designers

An example of the pursuit of a personal and professional interest in landscape detail forms and their variety and styles is Peter Joel Harrison's task over the last 18 years to document in the field, draw up, and publish site landscape details from the Georgian and Victorian periods in the United States.[4] *Descriptive* and *comparative* pattern books entitled *Fences, Brick Pavement,* and *Gazebos,* which he published himself, record an eclectic range of domestic detail in the author's own hand-drawn ink sketches with added dimensions and notes. Intended for home owners, they were first produced in response to Harrison's own needs for information on an accurate fence detail for his house in Raleigh, North Carolina (see Figure 6.7). More recently, some of his work has been published by John Wiley & Sons, including *Fences of Cape Cod* and *Trellises.*

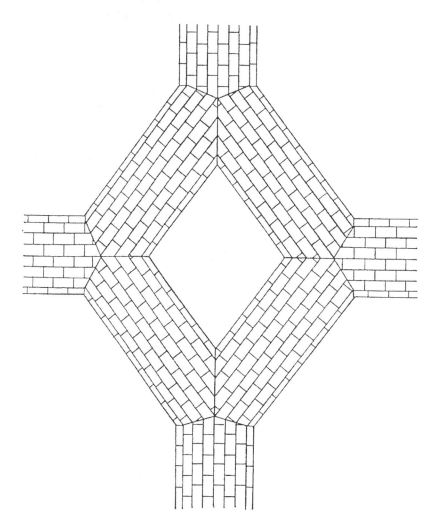

Figure 6.7
Brick detail illustration by Peter Joel Harrison. The Burgwin-Wright House, Wilmington, North Carolina. Courtesy of Peter Joel Harrison.

After visiting local and university libraries and the research library at Colonial Williamsburg, Harrison began to record in photographs and drawings eighteenth-century and nineteenth-century detail elements in different locations in the United States. His work has now blossomed into a thriving business in detail design pattern books. This is not a particularly new activity; pattern books were commonly used in the nineteenth century by suppliers to the building industry to document for commercial sale an extensive range of mass-produced items: terra-cotta forms, tiles, bricks, garden furniture, wrought iron gates and railings. Of particular interest here is the potential to extend Harrison's model to other landscape elements of the built environment and to other historical periods, including our own, with contemporary examples.

City Parks and Recreation Departments

The New York City Department of Parks and Recreation with the Central Park Conservancy published a management and restoration plan in 1987 for the rebuilding of Central Park, New York.[5] Included within this document is reference to the detailed aspects of the work, including an inventory of the built detail elements—the "detail language" of the park. The descriptive analysis of the park elements includes the park fences, drinking fountains, benches, luminaires, and trash receptacles drawn to a unnamed scale (possibly 1 inch to 2 feet). Redrawn within the text are other existing and proposed detail sections and plans covering drainage and vegetation. See Chapter 2 of the document for the development and use of the standard detail type by the New York City Department of Parks and Recreation.

Suppliers and Construction Trade Organizations

As the groups most closely responsible for the initial handling of raw landscape materials, as well as their completed and manufactured detail forms, suppliers and construction trade organizations carry out detail research with the purpose of demonstrating the correct use of their products. This type of detail research is either *descriptive* or *analytical* and is a good source of both technical and detail information for young practitioners to collect. Examples of such organizations include the Concrete Paver Institute, the National Concrete Masonry Association, and the Indiana Limestone Institute of America, Inc. (ILI).[6] The ILI serves as a coordinating agency, as stated in its handbook, for the "dissemination of accurate, unbiased detail information on limestone standards, recommended practices, grades, colors, and finishes." This publication, titled *The Indiana Limestone Handbook,* contains general information on limestone, recommended standards and practices with typical landscape detail forms of steps, platforms, wall copings, balustrades and balasters, and ashlar stone veneer. Documentation of case studies on the use of limestone in projects is included with specifications and cleaning and maintenance information.

Federal Government

A number of government agencies and affiliations are responsible for carrying out detail research. These include the Historic America Buildings Survey and the Historic American Engineering Record, which are of interest to designers.

Historic America Buildings Survey (HABS). Founded in 1933 as a division of the National Park Service, HABS is responsible for recording the built environment in the United States. It currently employs landscape architects, architects, and engineers, as well as photographers and historians, who together produce scaled drawings, text, and photographic documentation. The collection of approximately 30,000 documented sites is maintained by the Library of Congress. The drawings include detailed axonometric studies, detailed cross sections, and construction details. The following projects demonstrate to designers their wealth of information on detail matters.

• *Vietnam Veterans Memorial, Washington, D.C.* "Despite its relative newness, the national significance of the Vietnam Veterans Memorial easily justifies its inclusion in the HABS collection. Although only twelve years have passed since its dedication on Veterans Day, 1982, the memorial is already showing signs of damage and deterioration, due both to its exposed position and its large number of visitors." [7]

• *George Washington Memorial Parkway, Mount Vernon, Fairfax County, Virginia.* "The parkway is a lengthy scenic and commuter route that winds approximately 40 miles along the Potomac River shorelines of Virginia and Maryland, and around the national capitol. An interdisciplinary team made up of landscape architects, architects, an engineer, and a historian studied how the road and its features interact with the changing landscape, which includes the detail elements bridges, scenic overlooks, marinas, memorials and statuary." [8]

Historic American Engineering Record (HAER). HAER was founded in 1969 to document the country's industrial and engineering heritage. The following projects demonstrate the scope and range of HAER's works, which are germane to landscape detail forms and their expression.

• *Grand Canyon National Park Roads and Bridges, Arizona.* The documentation of approach roads, rim roads, and scenic drives, including detail layout, cross sections, and surfaces.

• *Acadia National Park Roads and Bridges, Handcock County, Maine.* "The first phase of recording, documentation consisted of an overview history of the roads systems and drawings of the Park's bridges. The second phase of recording will concentrate on road and bridge structure reports, drawings of road engineering, landscape features, and large-format photography." [9]

Objectives

After reviewing the participants in detail research, let us continue to examine the background to landscape detail research. It is necessary now to establish the objectives of a detail research study. These will depend on a number of factors related to the *purpose* of the research, the *scope* of the study, the *resources* at hand, and the *time frame* in which it is to be carried out.

Purpose

The categories of detail research introduced earlier in "Types of Detail Research" illustrate the intention of many of the research activities. There are two generic reasons for carrying out detail research. These are based on either a specific need related to a current design project, or the collection of information on landscape detail that has no specific requirement at the time but is gathered and stored for future use. The second approach, which is a reflective exercise, mirrors the actions of a mature designer who views and selectively records the built world around him or her, all with a certain attention and focus on detail interests. The first reflects the more common situation and is a reactive exercise, based entirely on the necessity of the moment.

Scope

The programmatic demands of what is to studied are determined by the nature of the detail forms, their location and type, how the information is to be used (for example, as it is produced, or as needed over a longer period of time), and who ultimately pays for it. Of interest to the designer is the precise placement of the detail forms to be studied, whether they are to be placed together as part of one single project or as individual forms scattered over a larger number of projects geographically. For example, consider the single detail forms (barriers and surfaces) that appear over a number of national parks and the local stone detail wall forms found only along the bridle paths of Acadia National Park in Maine (see the study on Acadia National Park Roads and Bridges in the section on the Historic American Engineering Record, noted earlier in this chapter). A series of rough survey notes may be all that is needed, depending on the final use of the information, or, at the other end of the scale, a set of dimensioned and formalized ink drawing records, notes, and photographs may be required. For most small and medium-sized projects, neatly sketched survey notes will suffice unless there are compelling historic or cultural landscape elements present on the site.

Resources

The three major elements to be considered in the execution of field research work are the expertise of the participants, the equipment available, and the funding or financial backing for the work (if any). As indicated earlier, the range of participants involved in detail research varies from individuals to large institutions and corporations. The *number* of participants, however, is of interest here—in particular, how many people will be working in the field. An individual can carry out useful initial research in the field, such as an early reconnoiter of the study site area, photographic documentation or dimensional surveys of specific details, using a retractable 6 foot metal tape or folding stick, or the collection of sample materials, soils, water, or plant material. For a more comprehensive detail survey, two or three persons, when coordinated, can carry out the work more efficiently. Two people are needed to handle cloth or steel measuring tapes; while one is recording the measurements, the other is locating the information to be taken. Three people allow the luxury of a coordinating leader with two assistants. Yet too many people working on a site together can be harmful and disruptive.

Time Frame

Although the study and documentation of hundreds of individual details and their relationships may be the initial intention of a study, the budget and time allowed to carry out the sitework will determine the final scope and form of the project. Attention must be paid to the seasonal nature of detail research outdoors, particularly bearing in mind the need to observe and record at different times of the year and under different conditions of temperature and exposure to sun, moisture, and wind.

4. RESEARCH IN THE FIELD, LIBRARY, AND OFFICE

Detail research is carried out in three potential locations: in the field, at the library, or in the professional office. It is necessary in certain cases to conduct research in all three locations, depending on the content of the study and the comprehensive nature and scale of the investigation.

Research in the Field

To carry out a comprehensive study, a field visit to the study area and site is necessary. If the site is local, it is possible to make repeated trips. For longer distances, a single trip may have to suffice. To obtain the most efficient use of time and resources it is necessary to plan your survey work. There are three areas of planning that must be addressed in off-site preparation: *equipment, site recording methods and techniques,* and *documentation.*

Equipment

To be adequately prepared for any research field trip, a researcher must have the tools and equipment required for the various tasks. A designer's collection or purchase over time of a personal field kit will be important so as to avoid relying on constant borrowing of office or institution equipment. A personal field kit should consist of the following basic tools:

- *Sketchbook(s)*. Hard-bound artists sketch pads with durable stiff covers, containing either plain or lightly gridded paper to suit individual preference. Sizes range from 8½ by 11 to 11 by 17 inches horizontal or vertical format for recording detail forms, written notes, and sketches. The sizes are determined by their ability to be photocopied for office and drawing board use and project files.

- *Base maps and Surveys* (where available). Folded paper copies or printed on waterproof paper at various scales, these help to organize, align, and identify the detail survey in the field.

- *Camera(s)*. To record the general context of the site, key detail parts and finishes, and their relationship to adjacent forms. Although the use of cameras by design students as an everyday tool is ubiquitous, it has now become a substitute for site observation and sketching. The use of a camera or video here is to provide a backup record.

- *Tape measures*. Metal and canvas tapes of varying lengths are required (6, 50, or 100 feet); particularly necessary are the small hand-held 6 and 12 foot variety.

- *Film canisters* (empty). The small black or gray plastic storage canisters for commercial 35 mm print and slide film make ideal on-site scoops and hand-sized sealable containers for collecting gravel and fine stone finishes from parks, roads, and sidewalks, as well as other smaller samples. In addition to their compactness, they are plentiful, cost nothing, and arouse little suspicion when used in public spaces or carried through airports. For a more airtight lock and seal, there are one-piece water test sample containers of a similar size made by the Eagle-Picher company of Miami, Oklahoma.

- *Sample bag*. For collecting larger samples of, for example, loose gravel and soils, plastic rezippable freezer bags approximately 9 by 9 inches are available in supermarkets (see Figure 6.8).

- *Profile gauge or lead bar*. The gauges, which come in a variety of sizes and materials, are all constructed in a similar manner. A row of finely arranged short metal rods are held by grooves in a central bar but can move freely up and down these grooves. Placed against any short profile in stone or brick, it replicates the profile on the opposite side of the bar. This accurate profile can be quickly transferred to graph paper. A small piece of flexible lead bar can perform the same function, but with less accuracy.

- *Plumb bob*. This inexpensive weight and line mechanism is necessary to confirm vertical alignments and placement of walls and structures.

- *Dividers*. Hand-held dividers allow minor elements to be gauged and repetitive small dimensions below 5 inches to be determined.

Figure 6.8
Field survey. Sample bags of loose gravel from Vaux le Vicomte, France, Christopher Columbus Park, Boston, and Parque Ecologico, Xochimilco, Mexico.

- *Clipboard, waterproof paper, and markers.* These are an added precaution in case of inclement weather when there is a need to protect valuable recorded information.

Site Recording Methods and Techniques

Tasks to be carried out on-site during a detail survey include the following:

- General documentation of site and surrounding environment. This can also be developed ahead of time through preparation of context plans and sections.

- After walking entire site area, the initial identification of key detail forms to be surveyed.

- The execution of these detail forms and their location and context within the site.

Two methods present themselves, depending on the nature of the project type in question and the size and quantity of the detail forms:

- A survey sequence moving across the site area, comprehensive but nondiscriminating of detail type, scale, or importance.

- The identification of specific isolated categories, based on the structure and organization of the detail forms on-site and their size and type. For example, all the horizontal walking surfaces, followed by the transitions in the ground plane, finishing with detail forms made off-site and brought to the site and installed.

Variations of the second method include using the actual sequence of detail implementation as a structure for the survey, the hierarchy of detail parts in terms of exposure to weathering, or the types of materials themselves. A complete listing of site techniques is given in Ron Brunskill's *Illustrated Handbook of Vernacular Architecture*[10] and in the *HABS/HAER Guidelines: Recording Structures and Sites with Measured Drawings*[11] and will not be repeated here. However, it is worth noting that in viewing the built landscape under scrutiny as a "structure," an external organization of detail forms arranged on the site in sequence (the second method), the detail survey requires an earlier analysis of the hierarchy of detail parts and their interrelationships.

Documentation

The completion of the field survey is not the end of the survey process. Notes, dimensions, and sketches are of little use unless they are properly organized both graphically and in terms of storage and retrieval at a later date by others.

Graphic organization. Field notes and sketches can be used just as they are, but for those who did not generate the original material, they can appear confusing and difficult to decipher. The development of clearly drawn field survey documents, either as groups of single 8½ by 11 inch sheets or on larger standard drafting sheets, is advisable if time and budget permit.

Storage and retrieval. Photographs and slides must be filed away to avoid damage and deterioration. The various filing systems are beyond the scope of this section. Readers can find further information on this aspect of professional practice in Bruce Sharky's *Ready Steady Practice* (1994).[12] A systematic way of storing and recalling slides is required, based on the categories in which they will be needed in the future. For instance, they can be stored by project name or geographical location — by state, city, or country — or by type of detail form — surfaces, walls, finishes.

Research in the Library and the Office

Literature on Landscape Detail

Landscape detail and detail design have not been served well by previous publications. Existing literature on landscape detail falls into one of four categories: publications dealing with implementation techniques, a range of catalogs/surveys of detail types, comparative detail studies, and illustrated monographs on the work of individual designers. It should be noted, however, that there is also a larger market of self-help or do-it-yourself books whose audience is the home owner. These are, in most cases, oversimplified and although well illustrated with colored diagrams, plans, and photographs, rarely address built work beyond the scale of the residential garden. Of these, the most influential in dictating a stylistic material and detail language was the Sunset Series, published initially in 1898. Of interest to designers were articles in the 1950s that featured outdoor rooms, pools, and elements of the contemporary residential landscape. A series of book titles was also assembled under headings related to garden detail elements. A selection of titles and other popular books of this type are listed at the end of this chapter.[13]

Work of this type has been carried out by individuals and organizations historically over long periods of time. What identifies these studies is an intense passion for the subject and the available time and resources. Examples include the work of John C. Shepherd and Geoffrey A. Jellicoe in recording and documenting in the 1920s an architectural appraisal of selected Italian gardens of the Renaissance.[14] Included in the book *Italian Gardens of the Renaissance,* which was first published in 1925, are photographs, plan and sectional drawings, and a concluding photographic study of selected details from the study sites.

Norman Newton, landscape historian and educator, between 1923 and 1926 at the American Academy in Rome, kept his "detail books," recording a comprehensive range of landscape detail forms observed during his travels. He also documented the site planning at the Villa Chigi and the Villa Medici through field measurement and watercolor wash drawings.[15] More recently, Linda Jewell, in addition to her published work in the areas of landscape technology, has tackled specific topics in detail form and implementation in the built landscapes of the early twentieth century. These include outdoor theaters constructed in the 1920s, combining the shaping of topography and the production of detail form with the development of social space.[16]

Technical Reports

From time to time, technical reports are issued by public agencies on the nature of landscape detail in public spaces. Examples include *The Park Management Series Bulletins,* published by the American Institute of Park Executives (AIPE) in its Park Education Program. Among these are bulletins like *Park Automobile Barriers,*[17] which examine in sketches and photographs such features as service barriers and boundary barriers in wood, stone, and concrete.

An earlier example is the report of George W. Tillson, consulting engineer to the president in the Borough of Brooklyn, New York.[18] This documents his visit circa 1912 to the cities of London, Liverpool, Glasgow, Edinburgh, Amsterdam, Brussels, Berlin, Munich, Vienna, and Paris to observe and document the installation, materials, and conditions of street and pavement surfaces. It forms an indepth survey of the state of landscape implementation, detail design, and materials in use at that time and as such now forms a valuable set of field observations and technical criteria from that period. Examples of work in progress and site execution were photographed in black and white and identified with typical detail conditions and material finishes. The costs of materials (in dollars) and maintenance and repairs are identified. Paving examples include wooden block, asphalt pavement, welsh granite, and asphalt. Examples of stone paving, dimensions of materials, and specifications are provided, as well as a series of suggestions, as follows:

1. Standard first-class paving material only should be used and the proper material selected for each street.

2. Work should be done carefully, with special care for small details.

3. The funds for new pavements should be provided in advance.

4. The number of openings in the pavement should be reduced to a minimum.

5. The surface of the pavement should be broken by any foreign construction as little as possible.

6. Repair should be made promptly and in a first class manner.

7. The city officials and those of street car companies should work harmoniously, so that railroad work will be done properly and permanent repairs or necessary reconstruction made at the time the streets are paved.

It is interesting now to note the appropriateness of many of these comments that were made back in 1912.

5. DETAIL RESEARCH EXAMPLES

A selection of illustrations, sketches, and photographs are presented here, taken from two examples of detail research. One is from an academic research project carried out as part of an independent course of study. The second consists of a preliminary detail study carried out as part of a professional multidisciplinary urban landscape design project by a large design office. Of the types of studies outlined earlier in this chapter in Section 2, the first example represents a combined descriptive and comparative study, the second, an analytical and critical study. Aspects of both studies are illustrated, with a focus on the types of drawings and sketches arising from each of them.

Academic Study

Title: *Grade Separations in the Landscape: Site Tectonics and Detail*
 Field Survey and Drawn Documentation[19]

This study addresses the issues of detail design in the built landscape in design school. It demonstrates the potential richness of this area of research, encompassing as it does the review of historical documents, a current examination of the built landscapes and their detail form, and, finally, speculative drawings about the nature of landscape tectonics and form. The study consisted of a number of individual field survey visits, archival research, and the development of exploratory drawings. A series of separate work efforts took place over a total period of 14 weeks. The subject of the study was roadway grade separations and their structures in the landscape. They were studied during their development from 1860 to 1930, a time frame that encompassed the anticipation, development, and mass use of the automobile. The study involved a drawn analysis comparing the issues of built context, site dimensions, and landscape detail forms. One study area was selected from each of the following locations:

1860s   Bridge E, 79th Street Transverse Road, Central Park, New York (1863)

1890s   Circuit Drive over Cemetery Entrance, Franklin Park, Boston, Massachusetts

1920s   Pondfield Road over Bronx River Parkway, Yonkers, New York (1922)

1930s   Riverdale Road over Henry Hudson Parkway, Riverdale, New York

On-site photographs were taken, along with field sketches and notes, as shown in Figure 6.9. Measuring devices included the human pace and steps, tape measures and rope. Each structure was broken down into a series of schematic plans, sections, and elevations. The intent here was to examine and compare site design, details, and construction methods from four site conditions. This was done to test a hypothesis that the progression, historically, from tunnel to overpass related to the passage from horse-drawn carriages to automobiles and changes in the site detail and implementation methods that developed accordingly.

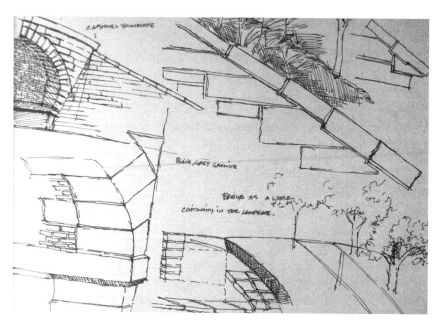

Figure 6.9
Grade separation. Underpass sketches and field notes. Courtesy of Timothy Mackey.

203

The methods selected during the preliminary organizational period were as follows:

• Visit each of the site areas in turn.

• Take photographs and measurements.

• Sketch possible ways in which the details were assembled and structured.

The historical archives of the Central Park Conservancy, the Westchester Historical Society Library, and the Triborough Bridge and Tunnel Authority Archives, New York, were found to contain a range of original blueprint and linen drawings of the bridge, wall, and road structures, with progress photographs taken of field tests of materials, implementation techniques, and the finished built landscape in use. The study was then narrowed to compare the construction of two of the detail conditions, Bridge E, Central Park, New York (1863), with a brick arch, granite abutments, and timber crib foundations, and the Bronx River Parkway, Yonkers, New York (1922), with a concrete rigid frame, concrete retaining walls, and granite wall facings (see Figures 6.10 and 6.11).

Anoxometric drawings with layers of material peeled back show the buildup from substructure in brick and concrete to the finished veneers and coverings of soil and stone. The drawings illustrate the relationships of the detail parts and how they were assembled as a complete built landscape element. The drawing was done, in a sense, to attempt to reconstruct the process of the making of the built element, and certain features came to light tangentially as a result of this research process. First, it was discovered that the foundations of the brick structure of Bridge E in Central Park rested on massive timber crib footings. These presumably were to provide support in localized wet areas liable to settlement. Second, in the Bronx River Parkway Bridge the development of new construction techniques combining steel and concrete as a bridge substructure still relied on a cladding of stone veneer. Both discoveries resulted from the ability to pursue research into these built landscape elements down to the detail form, materials, and structure.

Professional Study

Title: *White River Park, Indianapolis,* by Sasaki Associates, Watertown, Massachusetts. Sketchbook Detail Research[20]

In contrast to the academic study (A), the White River Park detail research, which produced a group of sketch drawings, was carried out over a much shorter period of time as part of a daily working method.

Although still speculative in nature, the sketches in Figures 6.12 and 6.13 are precise regarding the *selection* of key details, the few detail forms whether existing or invented, on which the project would thematically focus. It is the

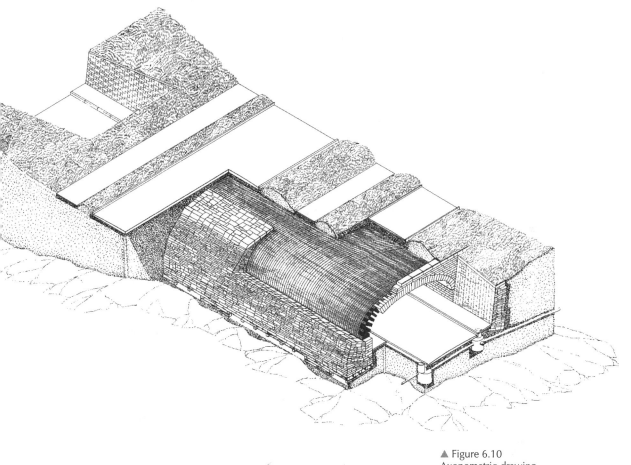

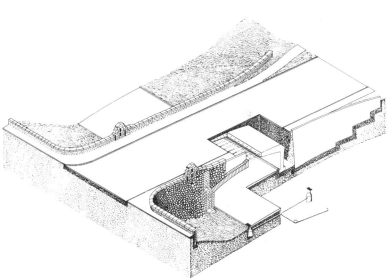

▲ Figure 6.10
Axonometric drawing.
Grade separation, 1863,
Bridge E. Central Park, New
York. Courtesy of Timothy
Mackey.

◀ Figure 6.11
Axonometric Drawing.
Grade Separation, 1922.
West Pondfield Road over
Bronx River Parkway,
Yonkers, New York.
Courtesy of Timothy
Mackey.

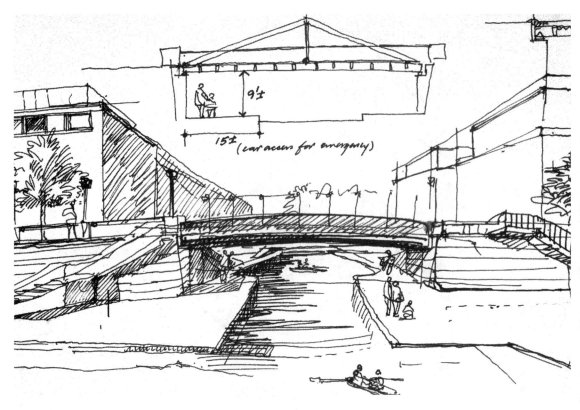

▲ Figure 6.12
Detail sketch study. Central Indianapolis waterfront, Indianapolis, Indiana. Courtesy of Alistair McIntosh.

▶ Figure 6.13
Detail sketch studies. Central Indianapolis waterfront, Indianapolis, Indiana. Courtesy of Alistair McIntosh.

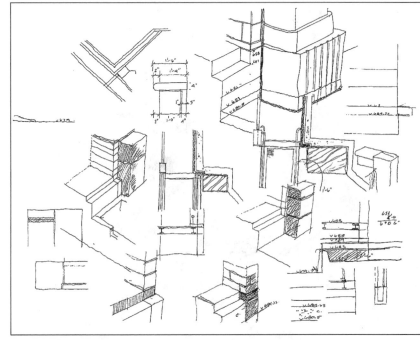

ability to directly focus on these few detail forms that distinguishes the work of an experienced designer. The detail sketch technique also indicates that it was developed over time with a concern for maximum clarity in the spatial information and relationships of the detail parts while maintaining personal graphic conventions.

These detail sketches were done at irregular intervals within the daily workings of a design office, including periods of travel away from the office environment. They document a critical method of detail research. This method is based on the nature of a civic landscape within a city, an urban edge, and the ability to develop over time a response to this condition and the concerns and constraints of a transition between the river and the city. It represents the work of a designer, working in a multidisciplinary office design environment, who is critically examining and reinterpreting through the detail sketches the actual physical transitions and boundaries found on the site.

From the pages of the daily working sketchbooks of Alistair McIntosh, the sketches shown in Figures 6.12 and 6.13 record the progress achieved in moving backward and forward between specific historic detail boundaries and

Figure 6.14
Detail of promenade. Central Indianapolis waterfront, Indianapolis, Indiana. Courtesy of Sasaki Associates.

transitions—for example, the floodwall and bridge structures and the general layout and framework for the site. Detail forms are based on the introduction of a new program and the reengineering of the flood control system. A promenade alongside a canal is created, as shown in Figure 6.14, that acknowledges, through landscape detail forms, both the local conditions of this site and place and the landscape condition of a transition between urban land and water. This is a working method grounded in both the poetics and pragmatics of landscape detail.

Further Work to Be Done

This book has addressed one particular aspect of the field of landscape architecture, and in the areas of landscape technology and implementation. In the process, other subjects have been touched, for which there are gaps in information or further study is required.

Designers are increasingly separated from the developments in landscape technology and participate less and less in initiating and carrying out research in this area. Developments in new materials, for example, in modifying conventional details, or in reinterpreting their applications in the area of landscape technology are likely to be the result of work by manufacturers, trade organizations, project management, and construction companies. The following are a number of areas of work in landscape detail and detail design to be addressed in the future:

- *A history of landscape technologies and site detail.* The history of landscape implementation, the development of landscape technology, with the changes in labor techniques and site machinery—from manpower to horse-drawn power to steam and then to diesel—and the changes in materials and industry practices (including nursery practices).

- *Regional case studies in landscape detail.* The development and documentation of local exemplary built landscapes, illustrating the use of native materials, building techniques, and regional detail expression. Case studies representing the climatic, cultural, and geographical range of built landscape detail forms will be significant not only for local practitioners, but for comparative studies nationally of individual detail forms and their variations across the country.

- *Detail durability.* Postoccupancy evaluations of landscape materials, detail forms, and the influences and effects of weathering over time. An obviously worthwhile study would be an examination of the American Society of Landscape Architects (ASLA) Design Award winners published in *Landscape Architecture* magazine over the last 25 years, with a before-and-after photographic survey and a review of critical detail forms and their subsequent weathering and changes.

6. INTRODUCTION TO CASE STUDIES: ASPECTS OF THE DETAIL DESIGN PROCESS

> case study (n): an exemplary or cautionary model; an instructive example.
>
> *American Heritage Dictionary,* 1994

The detail design case studies in the following chapter will provide an insight into the design motivations and working styles in detail design of a number of landscape design practitioners. The intention is to allow the designers themselves to explain their detail ideas and their concerns about the issues of detail quality. In addition, the case studies examine how the individual projects contribute to our understanding of the art of landscape detail through their detail approaches and themes. For the student and young practitioner, the studies also illustrate the detail knowledge and experience that have been gained over many years of professional work and how they are applied in a variety of project types and at a range of scales. The discussions with the practitioners confirm that exposure to the subject of landscape detail started early in their careers and that their knowledge continues to evolve and develop today. In addition, the structure of the case studies will serve as a basis for students to carry out their own studies.

The *case study* method of teaching is central to instruction and practice in other professions—for example, medicine, law, civil and structural engineering, economics, business, and the military. It allows habitual or established practice (praxis), the cumulative effect of knowledge resulting from practice, to enter into and support study in educational institutions. In turn, this knowledge is returned to the field through the training of informed graduates. The profession becomes more aware and critical of its level of performance, the general body of evolving practical applications, and the exercise of its own branch of learning.

Within landscape architecture, case studies are commonly found in regional planning or site planning books. Detail design and landscape detail are seldom discussed and infrequently form part of these case studies within the evolution of planning or site design processes. One rare example is Kevin Lynch's *Site Planning*[21] in which, in Chapter 1, the development of siteworks at the ARCO Research and Engineering Center, Newtown Square, Pennsylvania, is documented and illustrated in plan and sectional detail construction drawings and final site photographs (see Figure 6.15).

These drawings, however, appear at the end of the documentation process, and Lynch notes that "plans and sections were made for the site works that needed to be detailed in a form beyond what could be indicated on large site

Figure 6.15
Landscape detail form.
ARCO Research and
Engineering Center,
Newtown Square,
Pennsylvania. Courtesy of
Hanna/Olin Ltd.

plans." The next page of the book illustrates, in photographs, the final executed project. The details appear at the conclusion, rather than as part of the design thinking of the whole project from the beginning. The ARCO case study has a clear purpose—to demonstrate the elements and relationship of parts of the entire site planning process. In the detail design case studies that follow, it is proposed to focus only on that aspect of the entire site process that is related directly to the conception and development of the forms of landscape detail.

The Use of the Case Study in Landscape Architecture

As background to the next chapter, it is worth noting that the case study has not been an integral part of instruction and practice within landscape design and construction. The reasons are as follows:

• The temporal nature of landscape work and the length of time needed to achieve completion or intended maturity in a work of landscape design.

• Lack of postoccupancy evaluations of completed projects as part of the normal full service between a landscape architect and a client.

• Absence of available comparative and comprehensive data on the design, documentation, and execution of landscape architecture projects by professional bodies such as the ASLA and other institutions.

• The privileged nature of information on design and construction failure derived from past and ongoing litigation and the insurance companies that assign professional liability for the landscape profession. This information is currently unavailable to the landscape practitioner.

Selection of Case Study Projects

There are thousands of landscape projects that can form suitable subjects for case studies. They are located throughout the country and represent a range of landscape design work, from the scale of a large public park to the smallest community space—whether street, square, or public garden. In addition, they are sited in varying climatic and cultural regions. To narrow the choice of projects to illustrate and compare, the following criteria were applied:

- Each project had to present the highest level of design craft and attention to quality in landscape detail form.

  The projects were selected from previously published examples of exemplary landscape design work. Many received recognition from the American Society of Landscape Architects Awards Program at either the Design Honor or Merit level, or comparable awards from outside the field.

- Access to the original designer(s) of the project, so as to understand and review the sources, background, and development of the landscape detail forms.

  Such access was vital in order to identify the evolution of the landscape detail forms and to discuss the decisions that were made in establishing a detail language. In addition, the detail aspects of the project that were never realized or were altered in middevelopment could be examined. The study of these detail ideas and forms was as important as the study of those that were finally carried out. It illustrates the search for a suitable landscape detail language and expression under the constraints of budget, codes, regulations, and, in some cases, a client's preferences or prejudices—all valid concerns in the professional environment in which a designer works.

- Projects to have been implemented in the last 25 years.

  The projects were implemented within the same general time period, employing similar forms of professional practice and construction procedures.

- Drawn and photographic project information to be available.

  The background studies, sketches, and completed documentation of the projects, including photographs of on-site progress, were necessary to illustrate the detail working methods and interim phases of the project that were unable to be traced by looking at the final project.

- Public access to all case study projects, to allow interested students and practitioners to carry out their own site visits and subsequent evaluations.

  No written or drawn study can substitute for the experience of visiting these projects and observing firsthand the extent and scope of the built landscape and studying close-up the landscape detail forms. The intention is to encourage frequent visits to these and other exemplary built landscapes to record and comment on their durability and evolution as they are altered over time.

In creating an initial list of projects, no attempt was made to deliberately search for obscure or unpublished landscape projects. For that matter, projects that were well known through constant exposure in magazines and design monographs were not dismissed simply on these grounds. Built landscape projects whose planning ideas and design motives had already been documented in modest depth were ideal subjects. Although they were recognizable through photographic images (usually taken just after they were completed), little had been written or studied about the design development and execution of the detail parts that were featured in the magazine color images. In addition, their site programs concerned the resolution of particular detail problems and issues that were of interest, and the resulting details were either highly visible or had become identifiable through repeated documentation and publication.

Method of Presentation

The method of presenting the case studies exposes the processes of conceptual design, design development, and elaboration that were undertaken in each of the projects by the designers and the design practices. Although they are deliberately varied in scope and scale, the case studies are limited in terms of their type of work: parks, plazas, and waterfront promenades located in predominantly urban contexts. In addition, they have been carried out by landscape architects from the private sector.

Any selection of projects will almost certainly fail to include familiar works by a known designer or will include projects that, in the opinion of some, do not warrant inclusion. Many of our more familiar designers or design practices are not represented here, or if they are, the project selected is not considered to be their most significant work. Of the firms selected, three are no longer part of the configuration that existed when the work was carried out (the offices associated with Dan Kiley, Laurie Olin, and Martha Schwartz). The distribution of projects geographically does not cover large areas of the profession or the country. Offices in the public sector are not represented, nor are the large areas of landscape work that come under the heading of preservation and conservation. It was not the author's intention to exclude or include examples purely to cover every part of the country or every form of work currently carried out by the landscape profession. Instead, there was a careful selection and matching of a range of detail practices and landscape detail themes. These represent, for a student or young professional, models or exemplars they can start to study and from which they can develop their own individual methods of working.

In time, students or young professionals will be able to develop their own lists of favorite projects based on regional, cultural, or personal interests. It should be noted that it is not intended that these examples represent, by their selection, the best or the only detail practices that are present in landscape architecture. Indeed, there are cases where there are inconsistencies or areas where the final details do not match up with the original detail expectations of the designer. In fact, the most instructive cases are those in which there is a tension in site design and landscape detail between what is desired and what is possible.

Understanding the regional aspects of detail work is vital, as is concern for how the detail design under study relates to the larger public landscape. Professional practice is now able to extend to wider geographical areas and across national and international boundaries. It is the hope of the author that a significant increase in detail case studies from all regions of the country and sectors of the profession will arise, building into a more comprehensive collection of work from which all professionals can draw inspiration, irrespective of their own scale of operations.

Structure of Case Studies

There are nine parts discussed for each case study, although the attention to each part will vary according to the project type and the available drawn and written material on each:

- Project Title

- Project Background

- Conceptual Detail Sketches

- Introduction

- Discussions with the Designer(s)

- Detail Development

- Implementation Documentation

- Site Implementation Photographs

- Postimplementation Detail Photographs

Project Title

The project title identifies the main detail characteristic of the project, related to the range of detail approaches and themes described in Chapter 3.

Project Background

The project background includes the name of the project, the site and its location, the client organization or authority, the composition of the design team and consultants, and the construction and completion dates. The total execution costs are included where available, although this is regarded as privileged information and most designers and their clients are reluctant to disclose it.

Conceptual Detail Sketches

The full range of representational techniques, including sketches from the designer's personal notebooks and sketchpads, constitute the conceptual detail sketches, along with yellow trace drawings from the corners of the studio. Also shown are rough initial idea models, scaled and unscaled.

Introduction

The designer or designers are briefly introduced, as well as the professional circumstances under which they carried out the project. The general areas of the detail focus of the designer and the discussion are outlined, along with an overview of the site and project conditions.

Discussions with the Designer(s)

The author carried out interviews with each designer over a period of two years. Follow-up phone calls were also made to clarify certain issues brought up during the interview discussions. It is important to note that the interviews have been edited by the designers to most clearly represent their point of view regarding details and detail development. The interviews focus on three questions: How is landscape detail and the processes of detailing carried out in the designers' respective practices? Why is landscape detail important? What is their understanding of detail in relation to design? The questions include discussion on detail influences and comments on implementation processes, contemporary design practice, education in detail design, and a range of professional issues arising from the implementation of built landscape work. It should be noted that there are a number of contradictions regarding what was said in the discussions and what was done. In defense of the interviewees, the ability to clearly remember aspects of one project carried out some years ago requires a mental recall beyond most people, particularly as these projects represented only a fraction of the ongoing work at that time.

Detail Development

A selection of images are drawn from, in most cases, the exhaustive collection of sketches, drawing, and redrawing that has been accumulated during this period in the design process. Of special interest are the exchanges between designers and manufacturers or contractors on the nature and specification of details, particularly those that require particularly close attention because of their complexity, use of new materials, or need for specialized connections and finishes.

Implementation Documentation

The precise communication of the information that enables detail design work to be executed in the field is illustrated in a selection of pertinent detail drawings at a variety of scales. These include hand-drafted work, computer images, and combinations of both.

Site Implementation Photographs

Central to an understanding of the implementation process is documentation of the field procedures through photographic records. These portray either the extent of progress in terms of a general sequential group of dated images taken at regular intervals over the whole site area, a specific record of a particular detail under implementation on-site, from inception to completion, or an account of detail decisions made on-site.

Postimplementation Detail Photographs

Of most use in fully understanding the implications of detail design are the photographic records of subsequent site visits after occupancy to view the use of the space, any detail issues that may arise, and the general opportunities for reviewing critical details in place. A number of these photographs are included, taken since the project has been occupied.

Notes:

1. Although the detail process is shown as a sequential progression, it is not the intention to portray it as a linear process; rather, the case studies should be viewed in total, with certain actions and events happening at the same time, or in reverse order. As often happens, a series of detail explorations occur that do not result in any applicable results, however fruitful as a study. In certain cases these have been included to demonstrate their potential use for future work.

2. An appendix is included to provide further information on the case studies, containing additional background, references, and articles on the projects and the designers.

7. DEFINITIONS OF TERMS

The following key terms and phrases that were identified and designed in this chapter are defined below.

Detail research: a sustained investigation in which the detail is a primary focus rather than a supporting factor.

Descriptive study: a study focusing on the dimensional, perceptual, and formal properties of landscape details.

Comparative study: selected work, projects, or locations brought together for the purpose of direct comparison of their materials, detail expressions and styles.

Analytical study: specific details are studied in regard to their inner workings and organization and the assembly of their parts.

Critical study: evaluation of the success or failure of a detail in its own terms or the set of conditions it occurs within.

Pictorial study: recording and composing a range of detail forms in an attempt to "fix" or capture the essence of a particular place or type of work through the common associations of materials and forms.

Case studies: established process of the study of exemplary detail design from practice.

8. CLASSROOM EXERCISES

These exercises form part of a series of assignments to be carried out within the structure of a course on landscape technology and detail or design detail.

Assignment 6: Researching Landscape Detail

1. Create a detail design case study for a built landscape within your locality or region. Select a project carried out by a local landscape designer or design office. Follow the structure established for the case studies in this chapter. Interview the original designer(s) or the people involved with the detail design process. These can, in addition, include the contractor, client, owner, local site inspector, and the occupants and users of the project, if possible. Follow the development of the detail design process through the stages as documented and as completed.

   The intention is to establish clearly how the decisions regarding detail design were made, what the detail concerns of the client, designer, contractor and user were, and whether the project as executed reflected the design as documented by construction drawings and specifications. A range of similar projects by a selection of offices, public or private, can be compared across the class.

2. Carry out one of the following forms of detail research for each of two built landscape projects in the locality: descriptive, comparative, analytical, critical, or pictorial.

   Compare and contrast, among the class selections, the types of information and drawings required to carry out each type of study.

216

3. Select and document a single built detail in the landscape—for example, a surface type, transition, or site boundary—across a range of types of landscape work: public garden, commercial plaza, community park, or waterfront.

Examine how the scale and form of the detail alters according to the project type. Do detail forms from one type appear in another? Is this a deliberate design intent?

9. REFERENCES AND SOURCES

Section 1. Introduction

1. The study was carried out under the guidance of Carol Franklin, Graduate School of Fine Arts, University of Pennsylvania. The French Village landscape and buildings are featured in the following publications:

    Willard S. Detweiler, *Chestnut Hill: An Architectural History* (Philadelphia: Chestnut Hill Historical Society, 1969).

    Robert A. M. Stern, ed., "Chestnut Hill." *Architectural Design* 51 10/11 (1981): 22.

2. *American Heritage Dictionary of the English Language* (Boston: Houghton Mifflin, 1971).

Section 2. Types of Research

3. Linda Jewell, "Stone and Concrete Bollards," *Landscape Architecture* 76, no. 4 (July/August 1986): 93–96, 112.

Section 3. Participants and Objectives

4. See Peter J. Harrison, *Fences: Authentic Details for Design and Restoration.* (New York: John Wiley & Sons, 1994). Also by same author, *Brick Pavement* (1994) and *Gazebos* (1995).

5. See Elizabeth B. Rogers, *Rebuilding Central Park: A Management and Restoration Plan* (Cambridge: MIT Press, 1987). Part I, "Parkwide Analysis and Recommendations," includes research and survey methodology and the topics of circulation, topography, soils, and drainage, including diagrammed detail sections and plans with notations of surface drains, seepage basins, paths, lake edge shorelines, water edges, and prototypical sections of the park's perimeter showing the detail relationship of paths, catch basins, swales, retaining walls, slopes, and plantings.

6. The ILI can be contacted at:
    Indiana Limestone Institute of America, Inc.

Stone City Bank Building
Suite 400
Bedford, IN 47421
Telephone: 812-275-4426

7. *1994 HABS/HAER Review* (Washington, D.C.: 1995): 38.

8. *1994 HABS/HAER Review* (Washington, D.C.: 1995): 32.

9. *1994 HABS/HAER Review* (Washington, D.C.: 1995): 41.

10. See R. W. Brunskill, *Illustrated Handbook of Vernacular Architecture* (London: Faber and Faber, 1972). Working methods of studying and recording vernacular buildings and their detail. Can be adapted to assist study of built landscape elements.

11. See Joseph D. Balachowski, *HABS/HAER Guidelines: Recording Structures and Sites with Measured Drawings* (Washington, D.C.: U.S. Department of the Interior, National Park Service, Cultural Resources, Historic American Building Survey (HABS), Historic American Engineering Record (HAER), 1994).

12. See Bruce G. Sharky, *Ready Steady Practice* (New York: John Wiley & Sons, 1994).

13. Sunset Books, published by Lane Publishing Co. of Menlo Park, California, include titles such as *How to Build Walls, Walks, Patio Floors* and *How to Build Fences and Gates.* For more information on the history of Sunset Publications, see Michael A. Keller, *Sunset Magazine: A Century of Western Living, 1898–1998* (Palo Alto: Stanford University Library, 1998).

   Ortho Books, published by Chevron Chemical Company of San Francisco, include titles such as *Basic Masonry Techniques, How to Design and Build Decks and Patios,* and *Garden Construction.*

   HP Books, published by Horticultural Publishing Co. of Tucson, Arizona, include titles such as *Fences, Gates and Walls* and *Patios and Decks.*

14. J. C. Shepherd and G. A. Jellicoe, *Italian Gardens of the Renaissance* (Princeton: Princeton Architectural Press, 1986).

15. See Norman T. Newton, *Design on the Land: The Development of Landscape Architecture* (Cambridge: Belknap Press of Harvard University Press, 1971); see also William J. Thompson, "A Persistence of Talents," *Landscape Architecture* 79, no. 3 (April 1989): 92–97. This article on Norman Newton also includes illustrations of his measured detail studies.

16. Linda Jewell, "Great Siteworks: Two California Outdoor Theaters," *Places* 10, no. 3 (Summer 1996): 64–71. Drawn detailed plans, sections, and photographs of examples of two built landscapes: the Sidney B. Cushing Amphitheater, Mt. Tamalpais, Marin County, and the Nature Theater, Mt. Helix, San Diego County.

17. See, for example, *Park Management Series,* Bulletin 1, produced by the Park Education Program and Michigan State University, 1955.

18. See George W. Tillson, *As a Result of an Examination of City Streets and Pavements in Certain Europian Cities in 1913* (New York: Borough of Brooklyn, 1914).

Section 5. Detail Research Examples

Additional information on the two detail research examples and their authors are as follows:

19. *Study A,* by Tim Mackey, landscape architect. "The Separated Landscape" was part of an independent study carried out under the author's direction in 1995. The scaled illustrations drawn by Mackey in ink on mylar formed part of a larger comparative analysis of the selected study areas. After graduation, his first employment was documenting bridge structures in Washington D.C. as part of the HABS (Historic American Buildings Survey) Summer Program.

20. *Study B,* by Alistair McIntosh, landscape architect. The pages of a daily working sketchbook record the progress of detail development of the proposed White River Park in Indianapolis carried out by Sasaki Associates, Watertown, Massachusetts. Of interest to us here is the type, variety, and consistency of detail investigation in these sketch drawings, a potential model for students to study.

Section 6. Introduction to Case Studies

21. See Kevin Lynch, *Site Planning* (Cambridge: MIT Press, 1986).

10. FURTHER READING

Burns, John A., ed. *Recording Historic Structures.* Washington, D.C.: The AIA Press, 1989.

Leach, Sara Amy. "The Rock Creek and Potomac Parkway Model: Tailoring HABS/HAER Documentation to Historic Landscapes." In *A Reality Check for Our Nation's Parks,* a one-day symposium on Preservation Planning for Historic Landscapes, St. Louis, Missouri, September 1993. The National Association for Olmsted Parks, The National Trust for Historic Preservation, and The National Park Service.

Radde, Bruce. *The Merritt Parkway.* New Haven: Yale University Press, 1993.

Russell, Caroline H. *Secretary of the Interior's Standards and Guidelines for Architectural and Engineering Documentation.* Washington D.C.: HABS/HAER, National Park Service, 1990. Available from HABS/HAER, National Park Service, P. O. Box 37127, Washington DC 20013-7127.

PART 3

CASE STUDIES

The search for principles that guide any art soon becomes lost in the embarrassing realization that art itself is a mystery. It may be described and circumscribed by precepts like unity and variety or rhythm and balance, but these are all qualifications that evade the main issue of the substance or the tissue we would like to understand as a human gesture. Art is merely a way of performing any act, a manner or style of carrying on; and fortunately it may be sensed by reading about it or practicing it.

STANLEY WHITE,
A Primer on Landscape Architecture, *1957*

In Part Three, a series of eight case studies highlight a range of detail approaches taken by designers during current landscape design projects. They illustrate a number of interpretations to the approaches that were presented earlier in Chapter 3, used either singly or in combination. The application of these approaches in practice is demonstrated within the limitations of the time constraints of a professional office. In addition, individual designers' views on the subject of landscape detail are illustrated through comments on the role of landscape detail in daily design practice and the sources of, and influences on, their detail ideas. They show how these constraints can be overcome to produce exemplary landscape detail work. Chapter 8, "Postscript," returns to the relationship of landscape architecture detail design and making and comments on the implications of the designers' discussions.

CHAPTER 7

ASPECTS OF LANDSCAPE DETAIL DESIGN

IN THIS CHAPTER designers discuss their attitudes toward landscape detail design in professional practice, their influences, and their working methods. The projects they describe demonstrate a range of themes and approaches to landscape detail and detail design. Here the application of the *fundamentals* of landscape detail and the concerns and idealized *practices* of landscape detail in the field are tested against the client's needs, program, site, and restrictions of time and budget. This involves the study of the evolution of detail form and the designer's detail aesthetic with concern for materials, craftsmanship, and durability in implementation.

INTRODUCTION

Projects

The following projects were selected as case studies for this book, based on the criteria outlined at the end of Chapter 6. Landscape architect, project name, location, design office, and awards are identified.

A. Recessive Details in a Historic Public Setting
    Landscape Architect: Laurie D. Olin
    Bryant Park Restoration and Improvement, New York, New York
    Hanna/Olin, Ltd., Philadelphia, Pennsylvania
    ASLA Design Merit Award, 1994
    AIA Design Honor Award, 1994

B. Scaling of the Civic Landscape Detail
    Landscape Architect: Stuart O. Dawson
    Christopher Columbus Waterfront Park, Boston, Massachusetts
    Sasaki Associates, Watertown, Massachusetts
    Honor Award, The Waterfront Center Awards, 1987

C. Landscape Detail Improvisation in the Parking Lot
    Landscape Architects: Martha Schwartz, Ken Smith, and David Meyer
    The Citadel, Grand Allée, Commerce, California
    Schwartz/Smith/Meyer, San Francisco, California
    ASLA Design Merit Award, 1991

D. Organic Evolution: Concept to Detail
    Landscape Architects: Dan Kiley and Peter Ker Walker
    Allied Plaza, Fountain Place, Dallas, Texas
    Kiley-Walker, Charlotte, Vermont
    ASLA Professional Award of Excellence, 1987

E. Contrasting Surfaces and Edges: Expression and Materiality in Detail
    Design
    Landscape Architect: Michael Van Valkenburgh
    Phase I, Allegheny Riverfront Park, Pittsburgh, Pennsylvania
    Michael Van Valkenburgh Associates, Inc., Cambridge, Massachusetts
    Progressive Architecture Award, 1997
    ASLA Design Merit Award, 1998

F. Abstracting Nature's Details: A Planted Path Along a Cove
    Landscape Architect: Susan Child
    South Cove, Battery Park City, New York, New York
    Child Associates, Inc., Boston, Massachusetts
    ASLA Design Merit Award, 1992

G. Beyond the Wall: Surface Details for Public Access
    Landscape Architect: Henry F. Arnold
    Vietnam Veterans Memorial, Washington, D.C.
    Arnold Associates, Princeton, New Jersey

H. Landscape Details of Culture, Tradition, and Abstraction
    Landscape Architect: Mario Schjetnan
    Parque Ecológico, Xochimilco, Mexico City
    Grupo Diseño Urbano, Mexico City
    Design Award, The Waterfront Center, 1992
    ASLA Design Merit Award, 1994
    Prince of Wales/Green Prize in Urban Design, 1996

RECESSIVE DETAILS IN A HISTORIC PUBLIC SETTING

What we didn't want was to introduce new elements that would jump forward and come away from the background. We wanted the new elements to just remain part of the fabric, so that meant suppressing a lot of the details.

LAURIE OLIN,
Interview with author, 1996

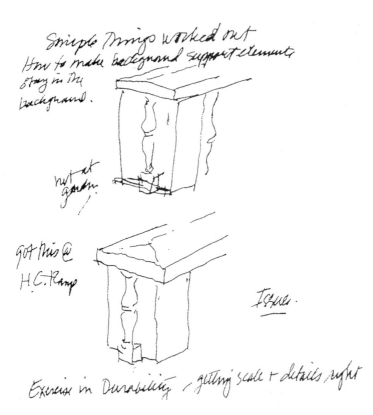

Figure 7.1
Sketch of balustrade detail form. Bryant Park restoration and improvement. Courtesy of Hanna/Olin Ltd.

PROJECT BACKGROUND

PROJECT
Bryant Park Restoration and Improvement

LOCATION
Sixth Avenue between 40th and 42nd Street, New York, New York

PROJECT SIZE
5 acres

LANDSCAPE ARCHITECT
Hanna/Olin, Ltd., Philadelphia, Pennsylvania
Partner in charge: Laurie D. Olin

CLIENT
Bryant Park Restoration Corporation

ARCHITECTS
Davis Brody & Associates, New York, New York
Kupiec & Koutsomitis, New York, New York
Hardy Holzman Pfeiffer Associates, New York, New York

ENGINEERS
Joseph R. Loring
Robert R. Rosenwasser

OTHER CONSULTANTS
H. M. Branston & Partners (Lighting)
Lynden B. Miller (Planting Design)
William H. Whyte (Sociological Study)

DESIGN PHASE
1981–1989

COMPLETION
1992

COST
$8.9 million (includes library expansion)

INTRODUCTION

Laurie Olin, landscape architect, currently a partner in the Olin Partnership in Philadelphia, Pennsylvania, was a partner in the landscape architectural office of Hanna/Olin, Ltd. when this project was carried out. The restoration of Bryant Park in New York formed part of a larger preservation and restoration effort around the public library and included earlier design detail work at the Fifth Avenue Public Terrace.

The main concerns of the designer regarding the landscape detail development of this project were "whether there was a precedent or not, and how to make supporting elements stay in the background." What does this offer for the student reader as an "exemplary or cautionary model" in detail design? Did this integrated detail approach allow the designer the flexibility to creatively develop detail forms within a historic public setting? How does the use of the recessive detail theme—the "background surrounding elements" and motifs, particularly those ideas of detail order, craft, and craftsmanship, and the shaping of profiles—lend itself to support artful detail design? This particular case study illustrates that creative landscape detail work *can* take place as part of a detail continuum and an evolving tradition of detail design, while still addressing contemporary design issues.

Detail invention is as much a part of landscape restoration and conservation projects as it is in built sitework that explores new landscape design ideas and themes. The case study demonstrates aspects of the art of landscape detail through a concern for spatial and visual continuity and a consistent use of detail precedents. These precedents were taken either from the existing Bryant Park site or from the body of built work within the history of landscape architecture. For example, early curb studies for the grass panel and the balustrades drew on examples from the Carrère & Hastings Library building, the stonework of Union Park, New York, and the Luxembourg Gardens in Paris. Although this seems appropriate for landscape design work that is located clearly within a historic setting, it is not necessarily the only alternative available to a designer. There are opportunities, for example, to introduce innovative detail materials and forms. Therefore, when designers choose to work in this idiom, it is done with the understanding that they are working within a potentially rich but constrained detail language. It is the evolution and development of these precedents for students that present the greatest challenge and the spatial and visual continuity in detail design achieved by a limited palette.

The focus of this landscape detail study is the assembly and support of simple transitions and the issues and problems of carrying out new landscape detail within a historic setting that already contains distinctive detail materials and forms. The discussion addresses the landscape detail process and the role that detail precedents play in generating new and imaginative detail forms.

SITE DESCRIPTION

Located in midtown Manhattan on the east side of Sixth Avenue, Bryant Park, adjacent to the New York Public Library, is an oasis in the heart of one of the world's densest commercial centers. In plan, the park is a straightforward and symmetrical design. Raised above street level, it is enclosed by a granite retaining wall crowned by balustrades at the raised terrace area and by cast and wrought iron railings. The focal point of the park is the depressed central lawn area that is surrounded by a promenade and enclosed by balustrade railings. Rows of London plane trees form allées lining both the 40th Street and the 42nd Street edges of the park. Narrow flights of steps admit people from the sidewalks to each of the allées. The trees shelter flagstone walks, which are separated by beds of ivy and bordered by benches. The land the park currently occupies has historically been used as a graveyard, a Victorian park, and a city dump; it was redesigned in 1934 in the Robert Moses Period as a public park in a formal French style.

Figure 7.2
Site section toward New York Public Library, 1986. Bryant Park restoration and improvement. Courtesy of Hanna/Olin Ltd.

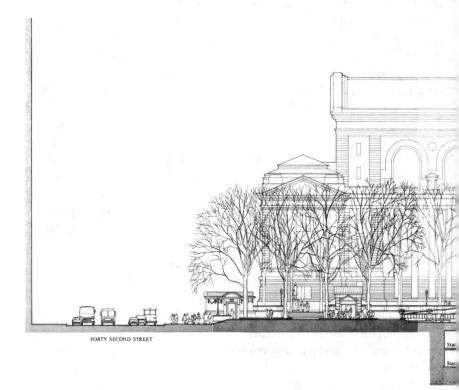

FORTY SECOND STREET

Cross Section A-A

Park Reconstruction·
Hanna / Olin Ltd., Philadelphia, Landscape Architects

Library Stacks Expansion·
Davis Brody & Associates, New York, Architects

Park Pav
Hardy

226

The Bryant Park Restoration and Improvement project consisted of two basic components: (1) the restoration and reconstruction of the park itself and (2) the construction of six small park pavilions and kiosks, intended to improve park life by providing enhanced security and new foci for legitimate park uses. The goals of the park restoration were to increase visibility into the park, increase circulation within the park, enhance the existing formal French landscape design, increase public seating throughout the park, and increase security. Circulation within the park was increased by creating openings in the balustrade surrounding the lawn, thus improving north-south access. The Sixth Avenue entrances at 42nd and 41st Streets were redesigned to improve sight lines into the park. The Bryant statue was restored in place on the library terrace overlooking a combination stairway/ramp, providing barrier-free access to the entire park. Stone buildings at either end of the terrace were restored to serve as a public rest room and service building.

(Adapted from project report by Hanna/Olin Ltd., 1986.)

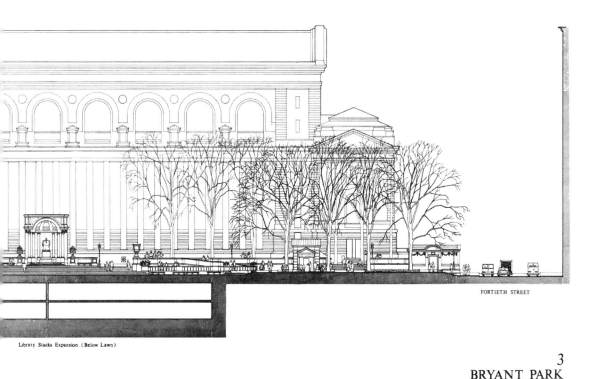

FORTIETH STREET

Library Stacks Expansion (Below Lawn)

New York, Architects   Date: 27 August 1986

3
BRYANT PARK
THE NEW YORK PUBLIC LIBRARY

DISCUSSIONS WITH THE DESIGNER

LAURIE D. OLIN, *Landscape Architect*

The interview was carried out in the library of the Olin Partnership in Center City, Philadelphia, on June 6, 1996. Participants are identified as Laurie Olin (LO) and the author (Q).

An Overview of Detail and Detailing

Q: First, how is detail design carried out in the office?

LO: Detail design happens as the logical development and outcome of a notion, it comes from how something is supposed to feel.

The first thing which happens in our office during the first sketch, is to start sections as well as plans. The section cut is absolutely critical to us. From the first doodle: a plan, grading, sections, and alternate details on how to make edges. Then thinking of it in the larger context, getting to the larger spatial structure. I immediately go from the doodle to a plan, to dimensions, to materials, to a perspective, to a section, to a detail, sometimes all in the matter of an hour. They are all inextricable. To see them all, you step back, change, transform, eliminate, and throw away.

Q: Directly from those sketches?

LO: Yes. I bring them into the office and pass them around, and then it gets drawn and I sit with it, and it gets drawn again, and we work back and forth. So that the sketches are inevitably about how things are made and put together. I have been interested in the relationship between the larger thing and the subelements, and then what the physical expression of each piece might be to make that continue.

When someone draws something in my office, I quite often draw it larger; I make it wider, or thicker, or longer, because I think they're being too timid, or they're not making it substantial enough for the full extent of what's required, and I know where that comes from. I grew up around construction projects, really large-scale construction projects that have to do with infrastructure: roads, highways, drainage, rivers, dams, bridges, airports. It really does come out of this sense of largness that I had as a child, in this enormous landscape of large-scale infrastructure and physical construction.

Q: Could we identify the work as being the work of Laurie Olin through a specific detail, or a way the detail design is done?

LO: There is a habit about how I approach material. I'm very fond of stones—it's the earth, you know, "rock is the bones of the earth" just as "water is the blood of the earth." It's hard to imagine a good landscape project being made without a strong sense of surface and ground. How the parts are formed, their shape, and how one thing sits on another is something that is very important to me. The underlying strata for any detail development is the conception of materiality. I think that comes first.

That's one of the reasons why landscape architects either have strong feelings for and the ability to manipulate the ground surface, or they don't. There are a couple of details that I worry about. One example is support, how things support each other. It's led to all sorts of trials and tribulations, to try to come with the right kind of soil mixes so that we can plant trees in pavement and not have the pavement collapse, and have the trees get air. I've been fussing about how to put together gravel mixes for years.

Q: What is the relationship between detail and craftsmanship?

LO: Craftsmanship has to do with just the love of making things. I mean, making things for the joy of making. Detail design is the sense of "how do things reach their final form," and "what is final expression of an idea?"

The detail is the physical expression of some situation. The relationship is something like this — don't ask for things people can't typically do, or ask for things that are out of proportion to the gesture in some way, whether it's economic or physical or psychological. Try to get the degree of effort and precision involved in something commensurate with the role that it has to play, and that's both in the local physical situation and in the larger psychological situation.

Detail Workmanship

Drawings I do to execute work in Italy are different from the drawings I do in Germany, and different from the drawings I do in America. The ones that have the most instructions in them, the most legal documents, are the ones for America. Here there are wonderful products and terrible workmanship generally. Whereas in Europe, in Italy, they have terrible products and fabulous workmanship.

I've had a marvelous marble fountain built in Rome, for the American Academy, where I did a sketch and then just drew a half-full-size profile and sent it off. They sent me back a metal template full-size to see if they had it right. I sketched on it, made changes, and sent it back to them, and the next thing I saw was a completed fountain. It was made by hand. It's beautiful; it was totally understood what I was trying to do. I had looked at a series of measured drawings in a book on fountains in Rome, and looked at some real profiles of fountains I knew, thought about it, and drew a new one that was slightly different but related to them. Back came an understanding by the craftsmen [in Rome].

Q: Because you were working within a tradition?

LO: What I sent them came from a tradition. In Germany, you hand over your design development drawings and they produce fairly crude but precise shop drawings. They have almost no feeling in them, but a lot of content. The Germans have good materials and very patient, thorough contractors, and the workers are very skilled. Our drawings have a lot of feeling, but sometimes they're a little shaky on precision. In America, it's not that you don't have well-skilled workers; if you can get the interest of the particular work crew, of the particular subcontractors, you get good work.

Bryant Park, New York

Q: What were the detail issues you were addressing at Bryant Park, and the scope of detail?

LO: Bryant Park—it's about simple things being worked out in a particularly consistent way. There was the curb, the central grass panel—all the issues had to do with structural support. They had to do with water and frost action and the movement of materials, they had to do with connections, joints, thickness. That is, the various cuts and assembly of stone, and how things were set. Most of the thought went into that, it went into gravel; there were some plants, there was some grading, some subtle grading, but that was really it. It had to do with whether there was a precedent or not and how to make support elements stay in the background. It was an exercise in durability, how to get the scale and detail of something right enough for that project.

At Bryant Park we began trying to figure out how to make something seem like it was done whole, and yet we were having to cut it up and interrupt it and change it and reorganize it. How to work with materials and forms and details that seemed to come or to flow naturally out of the Carrère & Hastings work with the New York Public Library and the earlier work done by the New York City Parks Department under Robert Moses. It's a sort of thing that modernist architecture does quite often. Some of the best modern architecture suppresses certain connections, joints, details, and makes them go away so that your eye will look at other things.

Q: Which is actually the opposite of articulation, where you're pulling out details.

LO: There's a suppression of things in order to express something else that quite often gets lost. At Bryant Park, having concluded that the building and the park were really derived from the spirit and products of the École des Beaux Arts, the question of how to do additional details, or revise and change details, that would be in keeping, and not jump forward as "wrong period" or "too shiny or bright," became an issue, especially since there was no precedent for some of the details.

The Search for Detail Precedents

For instance, there are no handicapped ramps in the École des Beaux Arts or in Carrère & Hastings libraries. So how do you do a handicap ramp? You had to figure out those transitions, when you're dealing with cut granite balusters that are square in section at the base to start with, and they're on a slope. So there are two ways to do it: either step them up, or slice them all on a bias, and there's precedent for both in French architecture. The question is which to use. What would Carrère & Hastings do? You can't ask them, and even if they had done one, would it have been the right one? If it was meant to be background, a support element and not a "star turn," now that's very important distinction: When is a built piece meant to come forward and when is it meant to recede?

There were big walls that did come forward physically, and you have to try to figure out how to suppress them visually and psychologically. So we picked one. We picked one and not the other, and did it. We purposely took some of the old balusters and mixed them in with the new ones so there was a range of color. When we cut through the walls and we salvaged stone, then we got new stone to match, and we carved profiles. We would blend the new ones with the old ones along their lengths so that there wasn't a bright, shiny one in the middle. So there's a real careful sleight of hand.

Detail Influences

While working on Bryant Park I realized part of the inspiration for it was certain aspects of the Luxembourg Gardens in Paris. I looked at slides I had from there because it's a place I knew. I went to look at it one more time to look at a couple of details, which, although we didn't physically copy in any way, just helped me get the scale right.

I was troubled by some of the existing pieces at Bryant Park that I thought were unsuccessful. For instance, there's a railing done by Robert Moses's agency that runs along the two side panels of the garden, which I had always thought was too thin and wobbly. I believe the railing is limestone, although it looks like precast concrete. If the balasters had been respaced slightly, it would have looked better.

Q: The notion of sketching, researching work from the past to inform the present—did that derive from your architectural training?

LO: I don't know how much is school and how much is my childhood background. I grew up in a place that was detail-rich. The whole world is, but we don't know it. Growing up where I did, I had an acuity of the telltale detail.

I think it may go with life on the frontier that "Ah, this is the new scheme of here since an hour ago" sort of thing, the notion of "see that broken twig?" or "See this footprint here?"—the notion of "See that little puff of wind over there? That means the weather is changing." Although the world is stuffed full of information, certain pieces of information are more revealing about trends, events, or something else that is not present or visible.

I remember the first night I was in New York. I had been out all night, we arrived and went out with friends, and I was very excited. I grew up on the West Coast, I had never been to New York City before. We went out to a couple of jazz clubs and stayed up all night. At about 5:00 A.M., we decided to go somewhere and find breakfast, so they took me to some place, and I don't remember how I even got there, but it appeared to be below the sidewalk level, and a nice dining room, and we were ordering meals—you know, "Here we are in some place." And then I was sort of sitting, looking around, and I turned, and about 10 feet away from me there was a wall with a door, and I saw on the door that there was a door handle, and I looked at it and I said, "Oh, we're in the Seagram Building!" and people looked at me and they said, "How do you know?" and I said, "Because Mies Van der Rohe designed that door handle, that lever action handle, as a special custom design for the Seagram Building," and I remember looking at it and thinking about when it was published. There's that sense of the giveaway detail that shows the hand behind the bigger thing.

Detail and Design

These projects are really very carefully and tightly designed and constructed as built works. They're really not "soft" projects, they are tectonic projects. They're put together more like buildings. They have a lot of living material, and there is drainage, grading, and irrigation, but all is in very set situations. How does detail design really happen? Well, I realize that all the pieces are very simple, they seem simple, they're meant to seem simple. In fact, they're meant to be background for the substructure of some spatial or other phenomenon.

Quite often the built pieces are not really meant to call attention to themselves, but are meant to support some other thing, some other visual, spatial, or physical phenomenon. The decision of whether to make something thick or thin, or whether direction [of movement] should be changed, or how we should support something, quite often has to do with what role we want it to play in that larger picture.

Detail and Designers

The truth is that all the designers I know and that I'm interested in have been interested in the big picture and the fine-grain detail. They never thought, "Oh, I'll do this one, and then later I'll get to that." They're always thinking of them all together simultaneously. So, whether you're looking at the work of people from the eighteenth century or you're looking at Frank Lloyd Wright, it doesn't matter who, they're always thinking about a specific material while thinking about form and the other ideas. The relationship between material properties and other conceptual considerations is that they're inextricably linked, you cannot separate them.

The actual physical substance of formal expression changes the formal expression. The way things are physically made does physically affect you, you feel the difference.

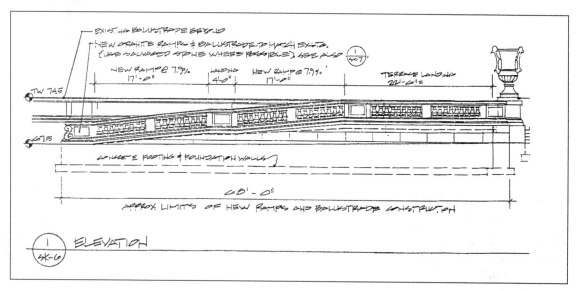

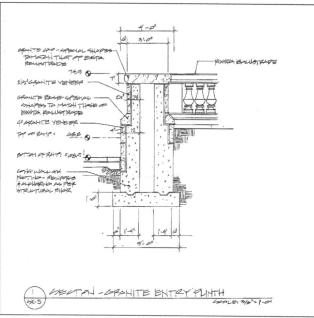

▲ Figure 7.3
Ramp elevation. Bryant Park restoration and improvement. Courtesy of Hanna/Olin Ltd.

◀ Figure 7.4
Section—granite entry plinth. Bryant Park restoration and improvement. Courtesy of Hanna/Olin Ltd.

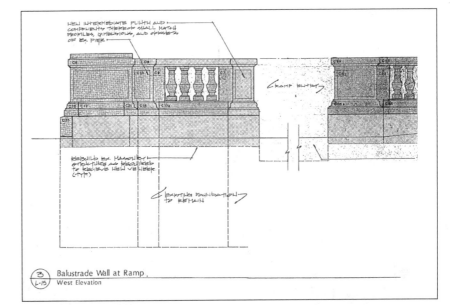

▶ Figure 7.5
Balustrade wall at ramp.
Bryant Park restoration and
improvement. Courtesy of
Hanna/Olin Ltd.

▼ Figure 7.6
View of balustrade
restoration. Bryant Park
restoration and
improvement. Courtesy of
Hanna/Olin Ltd.

▲ Figure 7.7
View of ramp. Bryant Park restoration and improvement. Courtesy of Joseph Disponzio.

▶ Figure 7.8
View of ramp. Bryant Park restoration and improvement. Courtesy of Joseph Disponzio.

SCALING OF THE CIVIC LANDSCAPE DETAIL

Dexterity is key, which of course leads you to having millions of different design details. So our standards have always altered and changed because we do so many different kinds of things.

STUART DAWSON,
Interview with author, 1996

PROJECT BACKGROUND

PROJECT
Christopher Columbus Waterfront Park

LOCATION
Waterfront, Boston Harbor, Massachusetts

PROJECT SIZE
4.5 acres

LANDSCAPE ARCHITECT
Sasaki, Dawson, DeMay Associates Inc. (now Sasaki Associates), Watertown, Massachusetts

Partner in charge: Stuart O. Dawson

DEVELOPER
Boston Redevelopment Authority

CLIENT
The City of Boston

DESIGN PHASE
1974 Park
1988 Rose Kennedy Garden

COMPLETION
1976

COST
$2.5M.

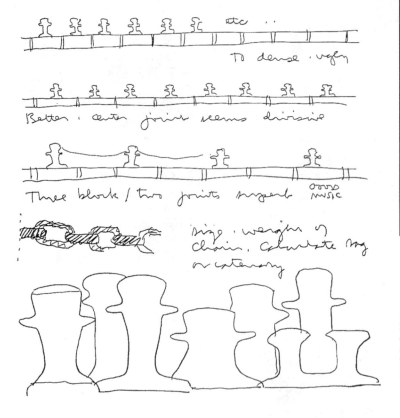

Figure 7.9
Sketch of alternative water edge detail transition. Christopher Columbus Waterfront Park. Courtesy of Sasaki Associates.

INTRODUCTION

Stuart Dawson, landscape architect, is a partner in the multidisciplinary office of Sasaki Associates. The office combines the discipline of landscape architecture with planning, architecture, and engineering in carrying out urban design projects. The detail design work at Christopher Columbus Park was concerned with the establishment of an appropriate scale for the civic landscape elements in relationship to the context adjacent to the harbor front and the public activities that take place. Aspects of detail design that are illustrated for the student reader are the concerns of the designer for a simple and clear landscape detail language and the development of detail motifs that address the nature of the surfaces at the water's edge. These include detail motifs about durability, craft and craftsmanship, and the expression of the detail joints. The search for a simple detail illustrates the use of customized detail forms that, by virtue of their repetitive use, can be thought of as the standard detail elements of the harbor front. What is role of these built forms in establishing detail scale relationships in the public realm?

This case study, although now more than 20 years old, stands as representative of a model set of detail practices that address the nature of contemporary public civic space. The practices mentioned by the designer include the use or misuse of standard details, the short time periods for the detail and development process, and the issues of both the quality of execution and maintenance. For the student, the aspects of the detail process that are most revealing are, first, the relationship between the need for individual detail expression and the establishment and use of standard detail forms in a large landscape practice and, second, the use of detail scale to establish a spatial order at the pedestrian level, particularly at the water's edge. In addition, when this scale is deliberately expanded and built forms are enlarged, it constitutes a means of ordering on the site, for example, at the civic scale of the pergola. In the words of the designer: "The scale of the two wings of the pergola element doesn't appear in any other project along the waterfront, which all tend to be very domestic in scale.... This large-scale element organizes the park." This indicates the ability to use the landscape detail elements simultaneously both to organize the design layout and to arrive at a considered built expression.

The focus of this landscape detail study centers on the two detail conditions. Two forms are of particular interest: first, the water's edge transition between the public promenade and the harbor, a barrier of marine bollards and chains, and second, the oversized timber pergola at the high point of the site, which acts as a boundary between the waterfront and the city. Here the issues and concerns of generating landscape detail forms for a public waterfront promenade are contrasted with general discussion on the professional office's use of standard and nonstandard detail forms. In particular, the research of materials, the nature of public work, and the quality of detail execution are reviewed.

SITE DESCRIPTION

The Christopher Columbus public park is located in downtown Boston adjacent to Quincy Market, the North End residential area, and Boston's historic harbor. It therefore acts as both a continuation of the waterfront edge of the city and an extension of the urban open space down from the City Hall Plaza. Built within an extremely short time schedule for the Bicentennial celebrations in 1976, the park is composed of two main parts. These consist of an

Figure 7.10
Evolution of water edge transition detail forms. Christopher Columbus Waterfront Park. Courtesy of Sasaski Associates.

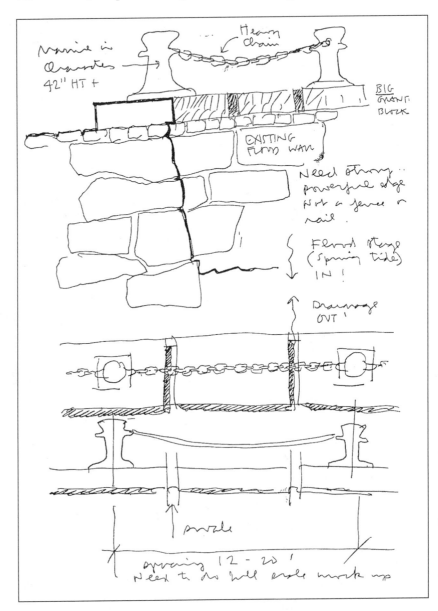

open 400-foot frontage to the water's edge and a community park and garden—a "park within a park"—at the rear. The frontage consists of an upper walkway under an enlarged public trellis, grass lawn panels sloping down to a granite paved promenade, and a water's edge transition composed of an overscaled stone ledge and pedestrian marine bollards and chains. The community park to the rear replaced a mixed-use development that was originally planned there, and addressed the concerns of the local residential neighborhood with the provision of playgrounds, a fountain, sitting areas, and groupings of locust trees. Although the reworking of adjacent vehicular circulation, the rerouting of utilities, and the strengthening of pedestrian access from the city to the water were the driving urban design forces, the park as realized contains certain detail elements of interest. First, there was a concern for the development of an overall detail language for the park that would echo the detail precedents found in the surrounding maritime environment. Second, the designers focused on the evolution of landscape detail forms that would support public activities at a scale appropriate to the individual and the larger waterfront landscape. Finally, they worked toward the establishment and elaboration of detail motifs that could be continued along the length of the harbor front.

DISCUSSIONS WITH THE DESIGNER

STUART DAWSON, *Landscape Architect*

The interview was carried out at the offices of Sasaki Associates, Watertown, Massachusetts, on Wednesday, July 31, 1996. Participants are identified as Stuart Dawson (SD) and the author (Q).

Detailing and the Design Process

Q: How is a project developed in the office, from the initial conception of the idea through the design development?

SD: We're going through a tremendous debate here at Sasaki with the advent of CAD [computer-aided drafting]. It's almost like you go from schematics to working drawings. The design development is sort of a joke. It's a slice you take through the CAD work if you need to reevaluate costs and specs. But it's not what it used to be in the old days; then you first had a sheet of freehand schematics, then you had several sheets of what you call semidrafted design development drawings, and finally you had drafted working drawings. The way people talk to each other in our profession now—making a contract for schematics, then design development—we're really saying, "That's schematics, and after that we do CDs." This is what really happens.

Q: In an office of 10 people, for example, the principal may be very closely involved in all aspects of the project. In an office such as this [200 persons], at what point do you engage in a project and at what point do you pull back?

SD: I'm very much involved through the whole project. I don't go out and bring in projects and then disappear. I like to be out in the field. Design is in the detail, particularly in public work. You've got to be almost a brutalist through the duration of the project to be certain that what you draw is built.

This is especially true with public work. It was a little easier in the old days when we were doing corporate headquarters, where you had one boss, and if you visited the project every two or three months and saw something you didn't like, you could change it. In public work, you've got to be one step ahead of the contractor all the time. I cannot overemphasize the importance of good detailing and good specifications. It's almost double on my priority ladder, once you go public...because you almost always get the low bidder, and the low bidder almost always wants to cheapen things. And if you don't hit him hard up-front with your standards, the whole project is vulnerable. The whole project is vulnerable once the contractor feels he can get away with it. He'll continue to get away with it, and if you haven't caught it, you'll never catch it. It's too late.

I think what this has caused us to do is to have full-size mock-ups built for everything. Mock-ups are protected by fences, 8-foot chain link fences with barbed wire if we need to. I think we even have decided now that we need to do the same thing with asphalt. Once a mock-up is approved, it's very simple: if anything on the job doesn't conform to the mock-up, you rip it out. I don't care if it's an acre of asphalt or an acre of granite. If it doesn't conform to the mock-up, it's out.

Q: In terms of you as a principal within a much larger design office, where there are a number of principals, first of all, is there anything that one could identify as a Sasaki method of detailing or an identifiable Stuart Dawson way of detailing?

SD: We have developed a series of standard details in the office, and standard specifications. So you might say that's a typical Sasaki approach to detail design. The downside of that is that a lot of the stuff we do, particularly with our engineers, tends to be public-works-level curb and concrete detailing. The designer of every project has got to be responsible for reading through our standard specs and details to be certain that what is standard is acceptable and fits the detailing and quality that the designer wants in the individual project. That's very hard to monitor. We've had a lot of designers who don't really care about specs; the last thing they want to do is to sit down and read specs and try to understand what we mean by standard details.

If there's a hard thing to do in the office, it's getting someone to get away from soft pencil and model making to the real nitty-gritty of what is really going to be a legal contract. Dawson detail design is probably driven by the many years I spent in Illinois, influenced heavily by Mies van der Rohe, where design was really in the detail and had to be very rational, and ideally repetitive. It had to be bulletproof, bombproof, while at the same time not overdoing the structural requirements. I guess one thing that's for certain is that almost every project has a whole set of different details, so you can say that it's a many-faced style. It's more related to the individual I'm working with within the office, or in some cases the client, who may be an architect, who likes to approach things differently.

Also the geographic situation requires that you look at details differently. Indianapolis is a lot different from Boston. There you're dealing with limestone instead of granite.

Detail Design Influences

Q: You mentioned Mies; I was wondering who, with the exception of Mies, has influenced you in terms of detailing design?

SD: Frank Lloyd Wright was a very important person for me. The Robie House is what really got me interested in landscape architecture, rather than architecture, because of the way the walls and everything about the structure really fits the Prairie scale.

Ed Barnes, I think, was another strong influence on me. I found that not only within the building but outside the building there is this incredible fluidity of color and simplicity of detail, even when he deals with the exterior — most architects don't worry a lot about how the building meets the ground. Barnes, in today's terms, is the one who really knows how to let the exterior wall meet the landscape. Pete Walker, of course, influenced me considerably.

Q: He was a peer of yours?

SD: We worked together for two years, and we've been friends ever since. I remember joking with Sasaki when Pete had done a sketch, and you'd measure the length of the bench that he had drawn, and it was 120 feet long! Hid [Hideo Sasaki] and I had always said, "benches are 8 feet long." But it was at that point that I think both of us began saying, "That looks pretty good though!" There's nothing wrong with a 100-foot or 200-foot bench, if the scale says so. And that's what Wright was about too. A retaining wall doesn't have to be 6 feet long. It can be 300 feet long.

Q: So what you took from Pete was scaling?

SD: Yes, think scale; don't worry if the bench is vast, there's nothing wrong with that. I've been influenced by a lot of things that I've seen: from Eliott Noyes to the Roman Empire. I think that probably says a lot if you were looking for a Stu Dawson- or a Sasaki style. In the way we approach a project, you could say there really isn't a common denominator. Every project looks quite a lot different from the project before, even by the same designer.

I think you can almost tell a Pete Walker project, you know, but you can't tell a Stuart Dawson project. I think ours tends to be a lot more flexible. We tend to do more what the client wants, more what the community wants, without giving in on certain issues! Sasaki has always believed that if someone wanted a French garden, you should give the best French garden that a twentieth-century landscape architect could do.

And we'll start the same way: If we want something more Miesian, or more "tour de force," then we should be able to do that, better than anyone else. So, something like the Christian Science Center [in Downtown Boston] is extremely powerful, compared with the John Deere [headquarters]. They're both about the same dimension. One is about French formal design and the other is about soft English landscape.

Detail Precedent

Q: Here is a question actually regarding detail precedent, which is a discussion that comes up time and again. If you travel around the world, if you go to the famous landscape spaces—Piazzo San Marco, the Tuileries—and if you look, in the corner of your eye you'll see earnest students or professionals sketching details, photographing things that no one else is photographing. If one takes Piazza San Marco, one takes any number of spaces, how does one actually use precedent, how does one translate detailing quality into contemporary landscape?

SD: I don't think it's so much the detail itself, as it is the scale. Because if we don't have the hand labor, we don't have the artisans, even if we could afford it, so things are a lot different these days. There is one good example I've always loved, and it's more of an architectural example but it translates to sitework as well. We were doing some work for the University of Colorado years ago. We walked on campus and saw that a lot of the buildings built in the 1950s were detailed with a horizontal native sandstone, stratified, very stratified. Yet that was the same stone that made Charles Klauder's earlier beautiful sandstone buildings famous. It was the way it had been laid that turned it into a 1950s ugly building, rather than the material itself.

Basically, we took a photograph of how nicely Klauder had done it, which was random ashler big blocks with fat joints, more Italian-hilltown-style. Then we took a photograph of the stratified perma-stone: same stone, same material. We recommend that from now on all the buildings on campus should be built with big stone, random ashler—we gave some dimensions minimum, some dimensions maximum, and, it's done. I've always looked at things that way.

I would always like to do basalt paving like you see in Piazza Navona, but forget it!

Christopher Columbus Park

Q: In this project on the Boston waterfront there is a sense of simplicity, scale, magnificence, and public spiritedness, particularly the water edge detail, which consists of solid, large, generous stone slabs, and the sloped lawn that has held up over what must be 20 years now?

SD: Yes, it was finished for the Bicentennial [1976]. I love that project even though the maintenance is lousy and I would do things a lot differently if I could do it today. But I still love certain things about it. You've already touched on one giant success, and that was keeping it simple. The whole triangular level, I don't know if you're aware of that, is topped over at spring tides, and whenever we have a good moon tide, the whole triangle fills in with tidal water. It was done intentionally, a sort of interpretive event. There's the scale of the pergola element, the two wings. This scale doesn't appear in the other projects along the waterfront, which all tend to be very domestic in scale. Our primary use of the pergola structure was to recall the old industrial wharf buildings that were there, which were basically built of granite, wood, and brick. It organizes the park.

It became a division separating Boston Harbor from all the small-scale stuff that the community wanted on the urban side of this space, closer to the neighborhoods. The abutting users, the older Italian community and the residents of the Harbor Towers complex by I. M. Pei, wanted a lot of elements in the park. Originally, there was pressure to put in tennis courts and squash and bocce. The gravel surface still allows the bocce lobby to play.

There were many things, many pressures, not the least of which was the short two years to go from the master plan to completion. So, we had the advantage of needing to move quickly.

The BRA [Boston Redevelopment Authority] couldn't slow up decision making. We reminded them that we had to have a decision in three hours, not three weeks. So that helped. But we had to put up with the usual community concerns. For instance, the bollard chain and the granite block at the water's edge were seen as a dangerous cross section to family groups.

There was a lobby that wanted to have a 5- or 6-foot fence along the water's edge because "little Johnny" might fall into Boston Harbor and either die of poisoning or drown.

But we were able to get this through, and, to the best of my knowledge, no one has fallen in. In fact, it's probably better than a fence, because kids climb fences.

243

Q: And if someone did fall in, you could actually get to them?

SD: Well, that's right also. We actually did this at Long Wharf [a later project on the Boston harbor front by Sasaki Associates adjacent to Christopher Columbus Park], and that's a much more difficult situation, tide-wise. The detail changes there, the chain simply turns into a sea wall, and in some cases the steps go right down into the water. Those were historic steps, we simply preserved them.

Q: In defense of your decision, I remember Sir Peter Shepheard always said that if you go to Amsterdam and look at the traditional old canals, there is not even a lip, or a chain, and people are not really falling like lemmings into the water. A car goes in maybe once a week and has to pay to be pulled out. It's about the notion of perceived danger that has now been lost in the public realm. That people perceive danger, that if you go close to the edge, there is a possibility that on a windy day, or if it's icy, you may fall in. They have a primal recall just to stay the 5 or 6 feet away. He was arguing, of course, for no barriers whatsoever.

SD: I agree with that. In fact, I helped WRT [Wallace Roberts & Todd, Planners and Landscape Architects] as an expert witness on a drowning case in the Cumberland River, and basically they had no barrier. They've had also had two drownings in Baltimore, a wheelchair that was pushed over the edge, and then another one, a kid walked in over by the Venetian piles, down by the steps into the water. I'm happy to report that at least in two states water has been identified as a hazard, like a semi truck on an interstate highway: if you're dumb enough to sit down in front of a truck, or dumb enough to walk into the water, you're on your own.

So there's some hope out there that water may be considered something more than a litigious trap.

Q: Returning to the Park project, I think, just in terms of the other pieces here, that the steps and the ramp seem very calm, very straightforward. They're where they want to be. There's really very little attention paid to them in terms of making them extraordinary. They're workmanlike, straightforward. One knows how it works, for example riser/run relationships. You have a very interesting way with corners, because you do a reentrant detail where every corner is turned so you don't have a piece of granite coming back. Was that intentional?

SD: I never thought of that. You know, the thing was done so quickly. I would have loved to have studied some of these things a lot more. But we really had to get the working drawings out, and get it bid. And so I think I'm glad when something comes off on this project, and sad when it doesn't. Like the curbs around the grove of trees. Those received a bias. We hadn't specified cut granite faces and they ended up with very irregular split granite faces. So every time you got a curved end butting a curved face, you have a tremendous gap between the two pieces of granite. Although you can't really see it and it looks pretty good, it's little things like that that really bother me.

Q: As a working method, did people who were on this design team work up in sketch form some of the parts for you, or did you, like some designers, have a little sketchbook where you personally worked out the details and then handed them out?

SD: I have sketches back in my book collection, but we built a 3-inch to 1-foot scale model of the pergola, for instance. We were back into building models in those days, full-scale mock-ups of these bollards. With these we actually worked on the spacing relationship to the sagging chain, and came up with some 17 feet. That had totally to do with a full-scale model. We also had a model of the whole park. In fact, we started with a glass gable structure, beautiful crystal, because we felt it was more like the old mill building vault. But the community didn't want that, they wanted the rain to come through the structure. So we went from the glazed structure to open construction and ended up with a truss, which is a more contemporary structure than a simple gable.

Q: And now it's covered in wisteria?

SD: Yes. Also the community were worried that Boston Parks wouldn't keep it clean, and the rain would help keep it a little more clean, and they were probably right about that.

Detail Research

Q: At the present moment, does the office do any specific research or study of details/detailing other than on a project-by-project basis? Do you, for example, do research on materials that may not have any obvious use right at that time, or are you simply driven by the project?

SD: I think we're always looking at things. We're just by nature a very curious office, so whenever one of us sees something interesting, it's circulated around the office. We have manufacturers come in a lot with new stuff. We're constantly looking for something better, especially with things like lighting. We're looking for a lot of help to get rid of sodium vapor (anything we can use to get rid of sodium) and bring in another halide. We're constantly pressing the envelope on, say, the 12-volt lighting system, to see if we can't do a lot more with it.

With regard to materials though, being from New England, now I use granite whenever I can. Having grown up in Illinois, I never saw any granite for 22 years until I moved out here and fell in love with it. I have some prejudices about some natural materials, when we can afford it. I love the native out-of-the-earth materials. I probably like asphalt least.

So I think in the office we tend to be wanting to do something that's more permanent, timeless, when we can afford it.

Q: Would there ever be a situation where you would start a project, it might even be a speculative project, where you have an idea about a detail, about how one piece of one material meets another, and then from that, the project would grow? What I'm doing is reversing the design; I'm saying can one start with the part instead of the whole, whether it is a material or a detail of an idea of how that material is used?

SD: We've done it many times, I think, maybe not knowingly, but many times. Earth is the most common. If you think of a material that you know right away, that you're going to manipulate, its the earth. It's a clear one.

I think it actually happens a lot, inspired by what we see. You know, the Frito-Lay project [Frito-Lay corporate headquarters] is a good example. Texas around Dallas is pretty flat and boring, but the site was a genuine beauty, laced with groves of trees, and a little stream ran through the middle of it, exposing lots of limestone. Even before we were interviewed, we made a pitch for the limestone in the stream to be amplified, not only in the base of the building but in other ways as well. We said that if you do a courtyard, waterfalls, and ponds, the limestone is really important. You've got a landmark site in an area which usually has no landmarks. So I find it very helpful in interviews to have a concept like that. It's very important, actually.

Figure 7.11
Study model of park.
Christopher Columbus
Waterfront Park. Courtesy of
Sasaki Associates.

246

▶ Figure 7.12
Study model of pergola.
Christopher Columbus
Waterfront Park. Courtesy of
Sasaski Associates.

▼ Figure 7.13
Plan layout of pergola
structure. Christopher
Columbus Waterfront Park.
Courtesy of Sasaski
Associates.

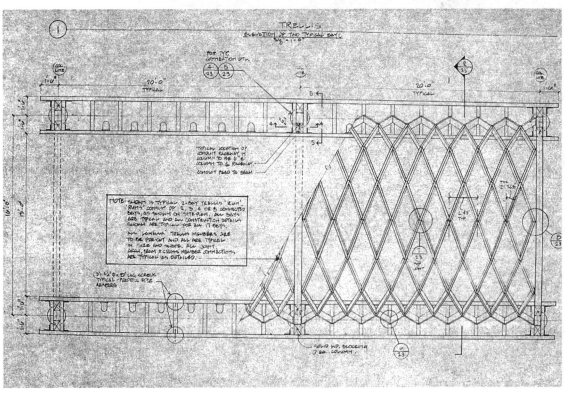

Figure 7.14
Water-edge transition
under construction.
Christopher Columbus
Waterfront Park. Courtesy
of Sasaski Associates.

◀ Figure 7.15
View of water-edge
transition. Christopher
Columbus Waterfront Park.
Courtesy of Sasaski
Associates.

▼ Figure 7.16
View of water-edge
transition. Christopher
Columbus Waterfront Park.
Courtesy of Sasaski
Associates.

LANDSCAPE DETAIL IMPROVISATION IN THE PARKING LOT

I come up with some detail image, and then we spend half the time in this office calling up people in the Yellow Pages all over the country, you know, "Do you have this?" "Can we do that?" "Is it off-the-shelf?" "If it is off-the-shelf, can we bend it, can we make it longer?" So we spend a lot of time researching detail in order to accomplish an image from out of the blue.

MARTHA SCHWARTZ,
Interview with author, 1997

PROJECT BACKGROUND

PROJECT
The Citadel Grand Allée

LOCATION
Commerce, California

PROJECT SIZE
lot 700' × 150' (masterplan 35 acres)

LANDSCAPE ARCHITECT
Schwartz, Smith, Meyer Inc., San Francisco, California.
Partners in charge: Martha Schwartz, Ken Smith, David Meyer

CLIENT
Trammel Crow Company

ARCHITECTS
The Nadel Partnership, Inc. (Prime)
Sussman/Prejza (Retail)

DESIGN PHASE
1990

COMPLETION
1991

COST
$1.3 million

Figure 7.17
View of "tire" tree surround.
The Citadel Grand Allée,
Commerce, California.
Courtesy of Martha
Schwartz, Inc.

250

INTRODUCTION

Martha Schwartz, Ken Smith, and David Meyer, all landscape architects, were together as partners in the landscape architecture office of Schwartz, Smith, Meyer of San Francisco when this project was carried out. Since the project was completed, the partnership has ended and two separate design offices have resulted from the original group: Martha Schwartz Inc., Cambridge, Massachusetts, and Ken Smith, Landscape Architect, in New York City. David Meyer continues in landscape practice at the offices of Peter Walker and Partners, Berkeley, California.

The main detail concern of the designers was to establish a detail language for a common landscape program—a parking lot—without the use of an established set of standard detail forms. Therefore, innovation and improvisation in the evolution of the landscape detail design was concerned with the exploration of new materials and techniques of implementation, coupled with research into the viability of both new and old detail forms and their subsequent expressions.

This involves issues of risk and detail. Martha Schwartz relates the exploratory nature of this process in her comments on the benches at Jacob Javits Plaza in New York: "If I had known how to make those benches, I probably would have been too scared, because it would have been way too extravagant."

The improvisation carried out here also illustrates approaches to a contemporary craft, the "off-the-shelf" items that use materials and products that are readily to hand but may fall outside the conventional range of the sources of landscape mediums. This particular case study illustrates that exemplary detail work can take place outside the traditions of detail design where there are few or no precedents. Such details, in turn, become models for development and future reiteration.

Of particular interest to the student reader is the interaction of the three partners in this process, indicating flexible overlaps of activity and focus. In addition, there is the use of the detail process as an opportunity to carry out meticulous research as part of the design development process. Finally, there is the continued emphasis on drawing and model making as a central part of this process.

The student reader will recognize the conventional approach of concept to detail—one form of the detail design process—that operates here. The richness of the themes that are brought to bear, however, suggests that this is more an integrative process, combining detail and conceptual ideas, whereby early investigations of detail forms support early conceptual design decisions.

251

Site Description

The Citadel site, formerly the Uniroyal Tire and Rubber Plant, has captured the imagination of generations of Southern Californians. Like an ornate movie set, the decorated Assyrian temple and bas-relief front walls have inspired a sense of mystery and awe since the factory's construction in the 1920s. The developer preserved the front wall of the factory's exterior but demolished the rest of the site in preparation for a multiuse development, which would include four office buildings, an outlet retail mall, and a hotel. The designers attempted to retain the Assyrian wall and create a compatible context, maintain the fantasy and mystery created by the wall, and produce a strong design that would attract users to the mall. The landscape design was to create a powerful visual axis that would unify the different uses within the site. At the center of the wall is a breach that reveals an oasis of date palm trees aligned in rows on a patterned plaza. The buildings are located along two sides and at the terminus of the central plaza. Specially designed tire-shaped rings that surround each of the palm trees separate pedestrian and vehicular spaces. The checkerboard paving is composed of a series of colored concrete paver rectangles that visually slide under the plantings and other plaza features.

(Adapted from project description by Schwartz, Smith, Meyer Inc.)

Figure 7.18
Landscape plan. The Citadel Grand Allée, Commerce, California. Courtesy of Martha Schwartz, Inc.

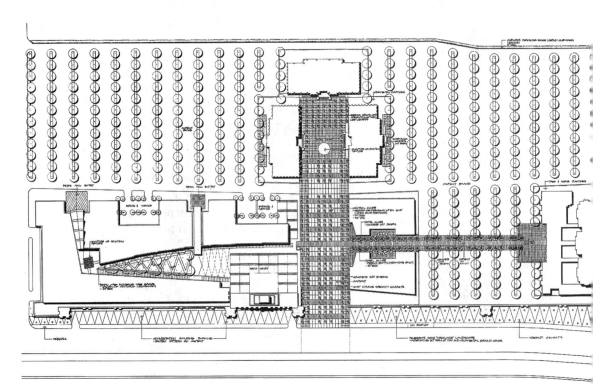

DISCUSSIONS WITH THE DESIGNERS I

MARTHA SCHWARTZ, *Landscape Architect*

The interview was carried out at the office of Martha Schwartz Inc. in Cambridge, Massachusetts, on May 29, 1997. Participants are identified as Martha Schwartz (MS) and the author (Q).

Drawing and Detail Design

Q: How does a project develop in your office, from a conceptual idea to physical detail?

MS: Drawing for me is a big part of it. It's the drawing that enables me to really focus, concentrate and give form. It's very important that I sit down quietly and draw, then I will come up with a number of different ideas. It's hard for me to focus and know what is the right way to go. I'll usually come up with a kind of sketchy outline of what I think ought to be done, and what the parts are, what the structure is, what flavor it ought to be, and philosophically what we're trying to accomplish. I'll come to the office and we'll sit around and have a meeting, and I'll describe what it is that I'm after, and describe several routes that we might take, then ask the various designers to explore different routes of inquiry. We then have big pinups and take a look at what we have. That either helps reinforce one direction and eliminate another, or it may just keep the process open.

Q: How is that physical form initially expressed?

MS: First of all I have to go see a site. That's very important. I'm always totally scattered after having seen the site, because it's such a big physical entity that I always feel kind of squashed. Once I've talked to people and seen the site, I use the plan as an organizing and focusing device, a way of starting in terms of organizing the elements. Earlier in my career I was basically responsible for developing all the ideas, so that lately, now when we have many projects, it's difficult coming up with brilliant ideas on all levels. I like to work with people who are strong, talented designers who can initiate and bring ideas to a project. There are some kinds of tricks that you learn that seem to work in terms of organizing space and manipulating space, and getting people to do things that you use. I still love the use of hard-edge geometry. It's hard for me not to do that. But now the forms are starting to break up, I see myself going off in a slightly new direction.

I usually do give initial form to a project because of my first contact with a client. I'm usually the one to go and to talk and to develop a relationship with the client. The design process really begins when you find out what the client needs are, what their wishes are, their dreams.

Q: Do you consider the design and its detail as the same thing?

MS: I do absolutely consider detail as part of a design continuum that is equal in importance. How one conceptualizes the detail of the project is really part of one effort. The detail may in fact influence my approach to a design, so I don't see it as separate from the design process at all.

Q: At what point would an idea about a detail emerge?

MS: Ideas come at different scales, and it is not really a linear process. I might stumble across a material I think is particularly wonderful, and which is something we can build an idea around. I think that designers build a repertoire of images: of things that they've seen, materials they've used, and of ideas used in projects they've tried and haven't succeeded in building, but they want to still do something with. I think that we actually carry the majority of what we do in our heads already, and compose out of that bank of knowledge. I think that the structure of any project could be expressed in different palettes.

I find that in our work, because we have often been in tough budget-constraint projects, the actual gist of the project, the structure or organization, has been conceived of in two or three palettes of materials.

I often come up with an image unrelated to a particular detail. I hunt madly to try to shoehorn a material into the image that I have in my head.

I typically go ass-backwards; Pete [Peter Walker] and I are always having arguments about this, how obviously the wrong way of designing is to come up with an image and then madly go about trying to make it. That's certainly what happened with the benches at Javits [Redesign of Jacob Javits Plaza, New York]. If I had known how to make those benches, I would have been too scared to suggest them, because it would have been too expensive.

Q: How is the image formed in your mind?

MS: By thinking and drawing. It may be the result of making a drawing or finding a photograph of something which represents what I'm getting at. Then we try to develop it into something.

Q: What, then, is the relationship, at a much more philosophical level, between design and detail?

MS: I think it's very important that the parts be expressive of the whole, and the whole be expressive of the parts. There needs to be a consistency, because big ideas are not more important than simple little ideas. The little ideas add up and become the big idea. I think landscapes do not work well where only the basic scheme is expressed. Where you sit, touch, and walk, there's another kind of attitude expressed which is more intimate and ultimately results in how you feel about the space.

How people experience a space has to be carefully considered. People see things up close, and they see things from a distance. You have to think about how you convey an attitude, a feeling, or an idea to people in a consistent manner.

Your design has to add up to something. The other side of it is, that if the concept or the big idea doesn't work, the detail will not work either. The projects that you feel best about are those which have a strong idea, convey a real sense of place, and are still detailed in a way that supports the feeling of that space.

Detail and Photography

Q: In the most recent book about your work [*Transfiguration of the Commonplace*, Spacemaker Press, 1997] your projects are represented through very tightly cropped photographs; you see the parts. Was this deliberate as a graphic convention, or were you wanting people to see these small, very tight detail pieces of the project without perhaps seeing the whole?

MS: I think that seeing a project through photography is really different than seeing a project when you're there. So I think the intent was to allow people to see the whole thing.

When you're photographing a project, you are in fact interpreting a project; you're not bringing the real project to the viewer, you're bringing an image. The challenge is to convey the mood of the space. A photograph is something more than just a graphic.

It's an interesting topic. There's always the discussion about photography when you're looking at works of landscape, in juries, or in symposia. People often complain a designer has a professional photographer to photograph their work and therefore their work should be discounted. But how does one actually portray a space in the most forthright and telling manner where there's no measure to interpret anything but the image itself? A clumsy or badly composed photograph of a space is no more truthful than an artful photograph. It would be much more effective if people really thought more about how to convey a design through cropping, composition, and through the medium of photography.

Q: Do you also ascribe this to the real project?

MS: I think that's true in the real world as well. I think that you have to think of other things than just mere composition when you're designing. You can use the art form of photography to convey what your space is about. "Cropping" a detail that somehow comes to be emblematic of what you're getting at—that's a valid way to develop and represent your design.

Influences in Detailing

Q: Who has influenced you in your detail work?

MS: I wouldn't say I have a great ability to answer that. You know, that's the other side of it. I have always felt that it's an area that I particularly have lacked in my training.

I depend very much on other people in working those things out; I work in collaboration with people who really know how to build things, who are craftsmen.

It's kind of a sore spot with me. I wish I knew how to do that better myself. I wish I had the training in the field and spent time as a young person building things.

Q: Your father is an architect?

MS: My father's an architect, but I think that's different from being out onsite. My training is in art. I spent a lot of time with photography, silk screening, etching, lithography. I know how to do those things and how to make things by hand. Now I spend a lot of time directing people to make things.

Immediately, when I started landscape architecture, I was working at a conceptual level without knowing how to detail. The only training in landscape I had was from school up. I would say I got beyond myself very quickly.

My training as a landscape architect was first influenced by working as a member of the SWA office. It was the school of detail design most closely associated with Pete [Peter Walker] and his subsequent offices; an austere kind of minimalism, very pristine, very intellectualized.

Q: What would you say that training consisted of?

MS: Pete's training was demanding in terms of making things work and look beautiful with a minimum number of moves. Whatever moves you did make had to be done absolutely perfectly. There's not a lot of room for fudging when you have one move. The design philosophy behind detailing was that the detail should support a concept and an individual sensibility. Minimalism, in terms of the bigger picture, is a statement about the use of constraint in both your expression and use of resources.

What's the least you could do and still transform the space? Whatever you may be reduced to doing had to be done correctly. Details were very taut, very cool. The office was able to work on projects that had big budgets and allowed one to explore ideas. I have had to devise a philosophy about materials, which comes out of necessity given the types of projects I do and their low budgets. What if I don't have any budget? Do we just quit, refuse to do it, or do I go over to Kmart and pick out what's best there, and try to make something out of that?

I do whatever I can, given the budget. I know I run into trouble when I try to do something that requires precision but I often just don't have the budget to pull it off. It's frustrating, because I haven't quite learned when to go really "shaggy and lumpy," because that's basically what the process is going to turn out to be.

The project in New York City [Redesign of Jacob Javits Plaza] was a public project. We knew we were going through a process where the low bidder was going to get the job. As it turned out, the low bidder had never done colored concrete work or dust-on colors. I produced a job that was very demanding so I hold myself responsible for not taking into consideration what the level of workmanship was going to be. We should have designed and detailed it so that a gorilla could have put it into the ground.

I was overly ambitious. It would have been better to have come to grips with that issue earlier. That's my assessment of it.

Durability

Q: What is the role of time and change in your work?

MS: The values that people have for a project are expressed in the amount of money that they wish to spend on it. Money describes the client's own long-term objectives for the space. My work is not able to transcend the government's or the developer's valuation of the space, or his idea about how long something is going to last. If one wants to institutionalize a design, one has to pay a lot more money for more permanent materials. People see the materials I use as transient and temporary. The materials I use are an expression of our culture itself.

There's a relationship between money, commitment, and materials. If one does not want to commit to spending a lot of money, then one has to choose from materials that are going to be more or less temporary. There's a whole palette of materials that are very durable, but you usually have to spend money up-front for them. In my projects, the client talks about what level of commitment they are making to the project. The client will say, "This is a very important project, it has to last forever, and I'm going to give you seven dollars a square foot to build it."

What that translates into for me is the client saying, "I'm only committing to doing a very inexpensive outdoor area. Do the best you can because in 10 years I won't be here. I'll be someplace else and it'll be somebody else's problem." The commitment to longevity is not there. I hear a lot of double-talk on that issue. What they want is the look of permanence, not the cost that permanence requires. My budget is a loud and clear description of what the collective value is for the project.

The collective value for a space that we hold as a culture is what I have to deal with in as straightforward a way as possible. I have a choice. I could say, "Well, seven dollars a square foot is not enough to do a proper outdoor civic space for the front of the old City Hall and the new Federal Courthouse Building in the middle of Minneapolis. One should have more value for this public space. Well, that's only what I think, it's not what the collective culture thinks. It's not what

257

the voters think, it's not what the people who they voted into office think, it's not how the planners think nor how the project has been structured. The bottom line to me is that nobody really cares. So I say, "Well, seven dollars a square foot. What can that buy me? It's paint, dirt, and concrete."

Q: Colored concrete?

MS: Well, it's colored concrete if you don't put anything else on the plaza. But it's plain concrete if you do. I could say, "I'm not going to be involved in the design of an important civic plaza if it has to be made out of concrete and not stone. I will only be involved in projects where our culture makes a proper commitment to a civic space." According to my values, what does that mean? It means I'll never do a public project. The public doesn't value civic space the same way I do. We as a culture don't care about our public spaces enough to imbue them with money. We are not institutional. If you don't want to entertain this lack of value, you just go to work for very wealthy people who want private gardens. I'm an optimist. I think, by force of either an idea, a concept, using whatever cheesy materials are out there, I can still make a design that will make the space important or memorable.

It's pretty clear what the choices are when a project is budgeted. But they're not necessarily my choices, or reflect my values. I have to decide whether I'm going to work on projects where the client and I don't share the same values for the space. I often try to do with it what I can because I like the challenge. In Atlanta, for the Rio Shopping Center, the developer had bought a great big piece of land he wanted to develop. In order to tame this area he decided to put an anchor on the corner in the form of a shopping center. The building was a complete throw-away. The whole corner would eventually be torn down and redeveloped in 15 years. It wasn't meant to last longer than that. How long is a parking lot supposed to last? How long is a parking garage supposed to last? We have to confront our own values. We're always saying, on the one hand, "Materials are so important, lasting a long time is so important," but on the other hand our culture doesn't act that way.

We have lost our value for public space, and we have little value for our landscape. I wish we could require that there be a percentage for landscape in all the projects. That would put our money where our mouths are. If we think the landscape is so important, then we have to pay for it—especially in the urban environment, where it costs so much more. In the RFP [request for proposal] process, where landscape architects are subconsultants and buried inside the team structure, the landscape component of the project suffers. If landscape is so important, why not make a separate project, with its own RFP and its own budget. There, you would have a chance to get at the client and make an argument for more money and be the proponent for the space.

There is no great virtue in using cheap materials if you have the option to use higher quality materials. The use of good materials is a good idea, if the goal of the client is to have the project last a long time.

The Citadel Grand Allée, Commerce, California

Q: Your involvement on the project was with the Schwartz, Smith, Meyer office?

MS: That office worked as a very efficient little machine. I usually came up with the concept and the idea, and Ken [Smith] worked out the various design permutations. We worked together on the development of the concept. Ken took it from schematics, working through issues such as proportion, spacing, and materials. David [Meyer] became involved in design development to develop details. However, we always worked together in all phases. There was never a point where there was any real handing off of the project.

Q: What about motifs?

MS: I think they do appear. It's not anything that necessarily was done in a purposeful way. I carry around a series of forms I've been working with, consciously and subconsciously. When I come to a situation, I don't come to it clean. I come with all sorts of things in my head, and I apply them.

There are a couple of ways that artists work. One is that you stick with one idea or motif and you basically keep on developing that. Joseph Albers painted that same picture, but he varied the color. Rothko was very much like that as well. They worked in-depth, in terms of exploring color, and kept the format the same. Then there are other artists who go from one completely different idea to another. Frank Stella is someone who's worked like that, and Bryan Hunt, Larry Poons, or Joel Shapiro. One day they're doing polka dots, and next they're doing cast water fountains. It takes a lot of guts to go from one thing to something completely different. I tend to be a combination. There are things I just keep on grinding away on, and you also see new things appear.

However, because you've done them once, from my point of view, doesn't mean you can't do them again.

Q: The surrounds of the trees, the concrete bumpers, they keep reappearing in different guises in other projects as a motif.

MS: It's the same person, it's the same you. You don't have to toss out an idea, especially if it's a pretty simple one, because you've done it before. "Well, I used the circle so I can't use circles any more." There's nothing like a circle. There's nothing that even approximates a circle except a circle!

Craft and Making

MS: The craftsmen get very excited doing something that derives from what they do over and over again. They really get into it. Here is somebody who's delighted just to take on the issue of fabricating a metal frame structure. Figuring out how to make it fit into our concept challenges them and creates some variety from what they've been doing in the past. It gives them an opportunity to show off their skill and they enjoy producing something more than just the standard stuff. In almost every project there's been a champion craftsman who's taken on for himself the making of these new things. He's just into it.

DISCUSSIONS WITH THE DESIGNERS II

KEN SMITH, *Landscape Architect*

The following interview was carried out at the Graduate School of Design, Harvard University, in Cambridge, Massachusetts, on December 3, 1997. Participants are identified as Ken Smith (KS) and the author (Q).

Q: In the office of Schwartz, Smith, Meyer Inc., how did you actually work on a day-to-day basis on the Citadel project?

KS: Overall the project consisted of three main spaces: the allée, the parking lot, and the retail court.

We ended up doing design development, construction drawings, and field observation for the allée. In addition to the final scheme, there was an earlier long scheme that was interesting that had a series of great big circular planter constructions. These were things that Martha had drawn....I was working through the allée scheme and figuring out how the big checkerboard worked with the trees and with the tree spacing, with the dimension of two lanes of cars.

Q: At this time, had you chosen the materials?

KS: Originally the intention was that it not all be the same material. In the early design development, there were unit pavers but there was also cast-in-place concrete. Basically, the idea was to vary the materials to get differences of texture and reflection. The project had a very tight budget, and the developer got a very good buy on concrete unit pavers. We were told that it all had to be unit pavers. Then it became an issue of how you could get the most out of unit pavers.

We were doing this very large section across the whole site. It was 70 feet wide, I don't remember exactly, but we were actually drawing at a very large scale, like a half inch to a foot, and actually drawing every paver, and studying how you could vary, how you could use 4 by 8s, and the 6 by 12s, and how you could mix a couple of colors…

Q: To get a large checkerboard?

KS: Yes, how you could also play with the pattern. It had to herringbone because of the interlocking properties. Then we studied how you could actually use that limited vocabulary to get the most "jump" between different parts of the herringbone. If you look at the project, the different bands are composed of 4 by 8s and 6 by 12s, and also there was a variation in the herringbone. We were doing these studies where you could jump the pattern. David was really involved by this point because we were already working materials, and David was always putting together the estimates of probable construction costs.

Q: So it was done predominantly through sketches, through drawings?

KS: Yes, there was a model made at the end of schematics, pretty early in design development once we had the scheme set. But that was just colored paper. One of the things that was interesting about the office was the idea that you were doing certain things, not necessarily for the first time, but you had no detail language necessarily to fall back on. It wasn't as though you could pull out your standard details.

On the laying out of pavers, there was a whole wall of pencil drawings on trace looking at different arrangements of how you put the pavers together.

Q: How long did that process take?

KS: It was about six weeks. We were working on the drainage. The drainage was really critical on the plaza because there were no curbs, and the rings around the trees were, in fact, the barriers that made the whole thing work.

Q: With area drains?

KS: Originally we thought there would be area drains, it was going to fit into the checkerboard. But, of course, the budget didn't allow for that. In really cheap suburban projects, like Kmart, they have these really long slot drains, basically a corrugated culvert, and they weld a channel on the top, and they put this in the ground, and they asphalt up to it. Basically, it's the slot drain and the drainpipe all in one unit. They're really cheap, and because we had a long project we were able to put in two of these so that the center part pitches, and then there's a slot drain, and then it pitched back up. So it was a big flattened out W, with pitches of between 2% and 2.5%.

Q: The bumpers, where did the idea for those come from, the things that are always referred to as "tires?"

KS: Why, the Bagel Garden of course! Initially, the idea was that they were going to be precast concrete. But precast concrete was too heavy and GFRC [glass fiber-reinforced concrete] was actually cheaper, so they were hollow. We did drawings, and then David was working with a fabricator on those. The footings were complicated because we had to get the palm trees in. Palm trees have a very small root ball. The rings were in two pieces, and then they were bolted together. They had kind of a neoprene caulk seal. Originally, they were supposed to be green. The developer was really afraid of color! So in the end white was what we got. They wouldn't go for safety yellow or anything. Actually, in the end white was beautiful.

Q: Was it you or David who followed it through on-site?

KS: David followed it through on-site. It wasn't exactly that clean-cut, because David would always be involved in schematics, and Martha was involved in construction documents. Everybody was involved in all phases.

DISCUSSIONS WITH THE DESIGNERS III

DAVID MEYER, *Landscape Architect*

The interview was carried out by e-mail between November and December 1997. Written questions sent by the author were answered by David Meyer from San Francisco. Participants are identified as David Meyer (DM) and the author (Q).

Roles in the Design Process

Q: What was your role in the Citadel project?

DM: Ken [Smith], Martha [Schwartz], and I worked together as a team, from schematic design to construction observation. Citadel was no different. The extent of our individual involvement would vary based on the phase of work. My role [in the Citadel project] intensified during design development, when I worked closely with Ken crafting the design. After that, I directed the production of construction documents and then performed the construction observation services.

Q: The Schwartz Smith Meyer approach to detail design—was it consistent?

DM: We approached every project the same in that it should speak to our intellect as well as having a strong aesthetic. Perhaps this project could be categorized as appearing more conservative than our other projects. Given that we were working for a conservative client, giving an edge to the design was a bigger challenge.

One distinctive thing that happened on this project is how a landscape concept led the way for architectural organization. The concept of a landscape gesture, a central piazza-like space, was the impetus for the entire site design. This was set up by preserving the existing perimeter walls, which were quite beautiful. Next, the walls were breached to create a central arrival space, an oasis of palms. This space then organized the architecture around it. After this basic but strong move, our challenge was to make it special and memorable. Although the patterned paving design and palm oasis transformed the space, the rings at the base of the palm trees (the ghosts of tires past) gave the project its edge.

Q: What specific detail issues did you address?

DM: Grading: A good concept was essential because of the patterned paving design. The site was composed of a series of slightly tilted planes that were pitched to slot drains. The slot drains were carefully placed at the seams of the paving patterns, eliminating pattern breaks.

Paving: Originally we wanted to use colored concrete to create the pattern. The cost of colored concrete was up to $8.00 per square foot, but we only had $10.00 per square foot to do the whole site! We were offered unit pavers at about half the cost of the colored concrete, due to the aggressive nature of a manufacturer. Although we fought to keep the brighter concrete, perhaps the unit pavers ended up being more successful; the texture and reduced scale of the unit pavers feels right.

We composed the plaza out of three different colors (orange, charcoal, and white) and two sizes, a blend of six different paver units that became a layout nightmare.

It was a complicated puzzle to get the 6-by-12-inch units to modulate with the 4-by-8-inch units in two directions, utilizing only full or half modules, while maintaining a relationship with building columns. A lot of time was spent with the contractor during layout. Cutting pavers was not allowed except at the base of the tires.

Tire curbs were made out of a thin shell of GFRC painted with an acrylic polyurethane enamel. We originally proposed that they be painted bluish green to brighten the space and punctuate the tires. However, the client balked at this color.

As a follow-up, we recommended that they be painted glossy white, once the color of inner tubes, to pay homage to the old Uniroyal tire factory. The glossy white was compatible with the orange and charcoal pavers and, most important, still made the tires "pop."

Plant Selection: We originally proposed that the plaza be planted with a grove of Italian cypress trees. The client rejected this proposal as he felt that the look would be "cheap" or "funereal." Although the palms look good, the cypress trees would have been more striking.

Q: Were there any installation difficulties on-site?

DM: Installation of the tires became a critical issue of construction sequencing. We had assumed that these would be put in place first and then have the palms put in afterward. We had to plant the palms within their planting season, they had to go in well ahead of everything else. That left us with a problem: How do you install the tires?

The owner suggested that we eliminate the "odd-looking tires" and replace them with the more traditional cast-in-place curbs. This would have solved the installation problem, minimized potential criticism, and created a substantial credit. Fortunately, we hung tough by suggesting that we tightly tie up the palm fronds. With the use of an extendible forklift, we were able to barely slip the tires over the palm trunks.

A fascinating marketing bonus resulted from the early planting of the palm trees. While the buildings were just beginning to rise out of the ground, a grand oasis of palm trees had instantly popped up. This stunning landscape energized the marketability of the development. Before the buildings were completed, the client had leased 100% of his development, something never accomplished previously. The palms sold the space.

Q: What were the weaknesses and strengths of the Citadel project in terms of detail design?

DM: Weaknesses include the trench drain grating, which was a galvanized expanded metal welded to the neck of the drainage slot; this has failed. This is a case of a product, typically designed for highways, not being appropriate for a pedestrian-sensitive area.

The product was not carefully built, which made installation difficult. This, along with a contractor who had never installed this product before, resulted in excessive wobble in its horizontal and vertical alignment. Fortunately, a tight tolerance was specified in order to fit the rigor of the paving pattern, so a lot of pipe was removed and reinstalled.

The strengths were the grading, drainage, and paving, which were well designed and built with a minimal 2-inch exposed slot laid out as a seam between the paving modules. The paving was well executed with close attention to field layout. The tires are noticeable! They are vulnerable to being hit by poor drivers, and I was concerned about their durability, especially when we switched from precast concrete to GFRC. So far, however, they are holding up quite well.

Still, in terms of the whole project, we got a lot of mileage out of a small budget.

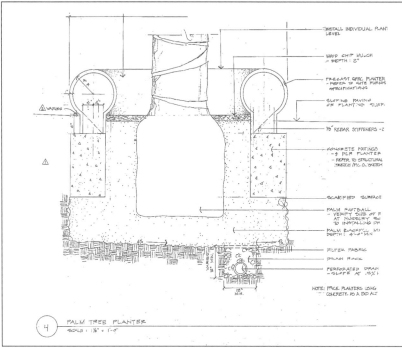

▲ Figure 7.19
Paving color samples. The Citadel Grand Allée, Commerce, California. Courtesy of Martha Schwartz, Inc.

◄ Figure 7.20
Palm tree planter. The Citadel Grand Allée, Commerce, California. Courtesy of Martha Schwartz, Inc.

▶ Figure 7.21
View of surface drainage, combined slot drain/drainpipe. The Citadel Grand Allée, Commerce, California. Courtesy of Martha Schwartz, Inc.

▼ Figure 7.22
View of checkerboard paving surface. The Citadel Grand Allée, Commerce, California. Courtesy of Martha Schwartz, Inc.

▲ Figure 7.23
View of tree planter. The Citadel Grand Allée, Commerce, California. Courtesy of Martha Schwartz, Inc.

▶ Figure 7.24
View of plaza. The Citadel Grand Allée, Commerce, California. Courtesy of Martha Schwartz, Inc.

266

ORGANIC EVOLUTION: CONCEPT TO DETAIL

Detail is not a separate item, it's an organic evolution from the design, just like your arms and your legs, and ending up with your fingernails, integral and part of the total design.

DAN KILEY,
Interview with author, 1997

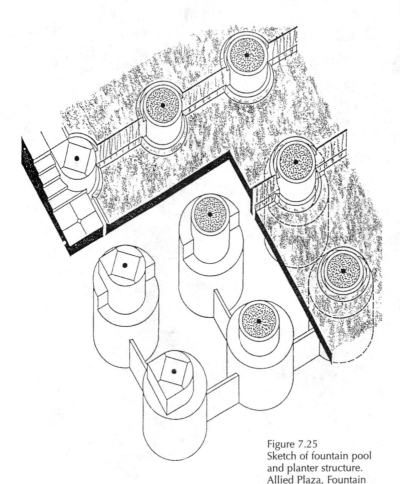

Figure 7.25
Sketch of fountain pool and planter structure. Allied Plaza, Fountain Place. Courtesy of Office of Dan Kiley and Office of Peter Ker Walker.

PROJECT BACKGROUND

PROJECT
Allied Plaza, Fountain Place

LOCATION
Dallas, Texas

PROJECT SIZE
6 acres

LANDSCAPE ARCHITECT
Kiley-Walker
Partners in charge: Daniel U. Kiley and Peter Ker Walker
Design Principal: Dan Kiley
Project Principal: Peter Ker Walker

DEVELOPER
Criswell Development Company

ARCHITECTS
I. M. Pei & Partners, Architects and Planners
Harry Weese & Associates, Architects
Architectural Consulting Services, Inc.

ENGINEERS
CBM Engineers, Structural
(First Interstate Bank Tower)

OTHER CONSULTANTS
WET Enterprises Inc. (Fountain Design and Technology)
POD (Planting Observation)

DESIGN PHASES
1982–1986 Fountain Place Development Plan

COMPLETION
October 1986 (Dedication)

COST
$ (withheld)

268

INTRODUCTION

Landscape architects Dan Kiley and Peter Ker Walker were partners in the landscape architecture office of Kiley Walker during the conceptual and schematic design stages of the project. After the partnership ended, the project was continued by Peter Ker Walker's office through the preparation of the design development drawings. The designers describe the project thus: "The Allied Plaza, Fountain Place, stands midway between a fledgling arts district and a revitalized warren of warehouses and commercial buildings known as the West End Historic District. Unrelated formally to either, it nevertheless acknowledges its urban responsibilities through the plaza, which may be a key to unifying this entire area as a kind of garden office district, unlike anything else in the city."

This case study illustrates the most commonly understood approach to detail design and one that student readers will find most familiar. It starts with the initial overall design concept and works through to the smallest part of detail form. The focus of this landscape detail study is on the transitions between the public walkways, water elements, and trees. The detail issues of the resolution of the water weir, the provision of adequate planting conditions for the trees, and the technical concerns of building over structure are reviewed. The general discussion focuses on maintaining the integrity of an architectural landscape detail language that is both minimal and rich throughout the evolution of the design process.

SITE DESCRIPTION I

In the center of downtown Dallas, Fountain Place combines an office tower with elements of a fountain and a European public garden to produce an urban plaza where the detail focus is on the landscape elements of water, pathways, and trees. Most urban plazas, especially in hot climates, end up as reflective, hard pavements with few trees, creating a hostile environment for people. Here, 70% of the plaza's surface is water, so that from above the office tower appears to be floating. Instead of the pedestrian looking at the fountains and trees, the pedestrian is an integral part of the design. Some areas are dark and tranquil, like the surface of a swamp, whereas others froth and roar with bubblers and cascading waterfalls, like miniature upland landscapes. A dramatic computerized fountain sits in the center of the plaza, surrounded by hundreds of swamp cypress trees in soldierly rows and interlaced with a grid of walkways. People can stroll through, sit and watch the fountain displays, or drink and eat at a cafe that is sunken opposite the building.

The details of the plaza result from a rigorous classical design. The alignment of the built surface of the pathways with the water results in a detail transition of clarity and simplicity. The resolution of the pathway edge with weirs allows the water to roll over before it meets the paving while maintaining it precisely coplanar with the paved walkways. Traversing the completed built surface is like walking on water.

(Adapted from a project description by the office of Dan Kiley.)

SITE DESCRIPTION II

This project is particularly interesting in its collaborative nature. It reflects a very important intention on the part of the client, who wanted this project to be, in all respects, unique and to make a contribution to the amenity of downtown Dallas that transcends, by far, the contribution made by typical commercial office buildings. The result is an urban park that clearly reflects a thoughtful integration of the work environment into the fabric of the city. Significantly, the focal point is a water garden, which maintains the overall geometry and design established for the project. At the plaza level, on a deck above the parking, is a grid of swamp bald cypress trees *(Taxodium distichum)*, 15 feet on center, that form a canopy over the formal water garden. Within this framework, acres of pools have been structured into three different areas, and a personality is established for each through the selection and blending of the water elements used. Water cascades robustly emphasize the natural contours of the site; water is serene, water is ceremonial. Water is spectacular at the center court plaza, truly giving life to the name Fountain Plaza. Here a highly complex computer-controlled fountain of 160 water jets ensures an infinite variety of forms. When these jets, set below the plaza parking level, are turned off the center court can become the setting for major outdoor events. Bubbler fountains are positioned at the center of each cluster of four trees, enhancing the ordered harmony of the stone-paved walks and plazas stepping and weav-

Figure 7.26
Site organization of fountain pools, pathways, and planters. Allied Plaza, Fountain Place. Courtesy of Office of Dan Kiley and Office of Peter Ker Walker.

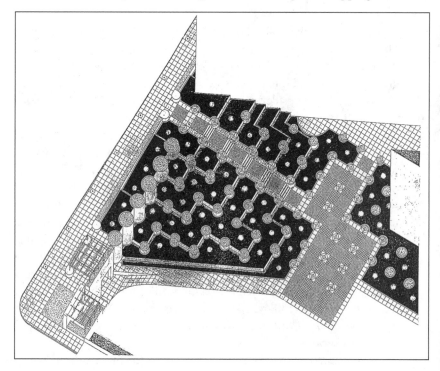

270

ing throughout. At dusk a transformation is created by fountain lighting and water effects, giving the area an entirely different look. Fountain Place is a plaza in which its detail elements are primal. Its parts have descriptive titles, specific forms, and textures, but, essentially, it is for people, providing a refreshing outdoor setting unrivaled in Downtown Dallas.

(Adapted from a project description by Peter Ker Walker.)

DISCUSSIONS WITH THE DESIGNERS I

DAN KILEY, *Landscape Architect*

The interview was carried out in the office of Dan Kiley, East Charlotte, Vermont, on January 6, 1997. Participants are identified as Dan Kiley (DK) and the author (Q).

An Overview of Detail and Detailing

Q: How do you develop a design in your work, at the scale of the detail?

DK: Well, it shouldn't be thought of as a separate item at all. I mean it shouldn't be all of a sudden you're talking about a detail. Detail is like your fingernails on your body. You know, if you don't have the right diagram, no amount of detail, however clever it is, is going to help your design. Detail just naturally is an organic flow of the rest of everything you do. It's a result.

Drawing and Design

Q: You didn't draw—you were able to let the people draw for you, through you?

DK: I was too impatient to want to draw too much. That's one of the few drawings I finished *(pointing high up on the office wall)*. I had a sensitivity of line, but I didn't like design ending up looking pretty. I worked for Warren Manning as an apprentice. Manning couldn't draw, aesthetically he was terrible. He grew up with his father's nursery, and he had no sensitivity but he could copy nature very well because he knew plants. In Manning's office, although he didn't know how to build, he had A. D. Taylor. A. D. Taylor was the construction man. We've been fortunate in our office in the past to have some beautiful draftsmen, who were fast, who were straight draftsmen. My office has been good all along because I've had wonderful people working for me, like Peter Ker Walker, Henry Arnold, Ian Tyndal, Peter Schaudt, and many others.

I remember the first job I had, I hadn't done any working drawings. I remember the fellow who worked with me, he had done some plans. I've forgotten how it was, whether he did it for me, but anyway I didn't have him, I had his plan, and to see how it worked, I copied everything! That's how I learned; it's probably a good way, because it sticks with you.

I now draw like this! I draw how I want to see it, *(sketching)* like this. I draw like Mies van der Rohe did, not quite but that's all you need. His details are what made his buildings. It's just the joining, the placement, and the columns. He was getting it down to the "bones"—the body again, how your body works, your knuckles, your tendons. The people then developed the design. You know, it's life, it's nothing to do with some stupid little drawing on paper.

The Detail Process

DK: You're searching always, searching, searching, searching. Le Corbusier said, "Creativity is a patient search," but I'd add to it, "It's a choice that's covert!" Because the search is to discover something.

Well, we have no idea of what the detail is going to be to start with, it's an evolution. Incidentally, I think a simple way of describing my design process is as an evolutionary process, starting with the knowns and working through with an open mind, and taking for granted that you know something about the history of what's happened in the world, not only in landscape design, but architecture and sculpture and the whole business.

I think my greatest value wasn't going to any school—you know I quit Harvard after two years, and I couldn't get a degree because I was a special student. Walt Chambers was our construction professor. I remember he was reading out of a book about how to build, and I said, "Hey, Walt, you know, I can read, just give me the book!" There we are just sitting, he reading the book to us!

When I first went to Europe, and then subsequently on different jobs, I would always take side trips, and what I've seen are the most inspiring and exciting spaces. In school that pompous little head of the department used to sit there and show these slides, the dreariest thing you can imagine, and nobody was interested in looking at anything abroad after those slides. And when I went there, I said, "My god, why didn't somebody tell me!"

Q: You went to Italy, then France?

DK: I was at the Academy of Rome a couple of times, and took the students around; they were looking, seeing but not what I was seeing, at all. I was interested, just like you say, in detail. I'm interested in how things work, oh, everything, like the drip-cap edge of a window. I'm interested in seeing how you could do it better maybe. So I was fascinated not only with the spatial design of what I was looking at how it was developed and formed. I was particularly interested in the detail of how it was carried out.

Structure and Building

DK: Design presupposes a good knowledge, a competent knowledge of structure and building. I didn't learn how to build roads until some basic training in the army: we had machines, and we'd ram, bulldoze, bump into each other. We actually saw a road being built. If you know how to build, details just roll off your fingers.

I keep saying that detail design should be open. In the process of construction you're going to find something that doesn't work with the reality of the site that you had worked on earlier. So you're constantly adapting, changing things on the ground. Detail is a result of what you're doing, and detail doesn't come from knowledge of detail, it comes from common sense and knowing how to build as much as you can.

I'm always amused by young designers coming out of school who have probably never touched a 2-by-4 or piece of steel, and they try to tell a carpenter on a job how to do it. The carpenter has been working for 40 years, doing everything, you know; he'd just laugh at the young guy coming in. When I worked in Franconia, New Hampshire, I did a lot of houses as an architect and I had wonderful carpenters. They were master builders. They knew all the terms for the different moldings. I wouldn't say, "Do it this way!" I would say, "How would you do it?" Because, you know, you're a kid and he's been through it. A great carpenter is also open. You might suggest other things because you're doing it the so-called modern way and so forth, and a good carpenter will listen to it if it's common sense, and if it isn't, if it's stupid, he'll tell you.

Q: Same for stone construction?

DK: Building stone walls, let us say it's very difficult, because the whole tradition has died out. For instance, every cellar here was built in the 1800s. The walls are beautiful because they have to work, they're designed to hold up and to work; they knew how to do that. None of us, no matter how long we live, have had enough experience. It's like drinking wine; you know, I've been drinking wine since I was, say, about 18, but I still don't know much about it, even though I'm a great devotee and I know a lot about it, but not enough about it, or what you could know.

I think what we're saying is it's imagination, an open-mind respect for the builder, and interchange, and not being afraid to take his way of doing it along with an ability to suggest how you might do another detail. I was working with one of those great carpenters, and I wanted glass coming to glass at an edge, and everything clear and simple. The easy thing would be to put a post in the corner, but that would be so dull. So I was talking with him: "How do we cantilever this thing out, how do we get the structure to work?" And he designed the truss, a beautiful truss going up to the attic, which completely freed the wall and the glass. It was his design; he made it possible.

Allied Plaza, Fountain Place, Dallas

Q: I thought we could talk now specifically about Fountain Place in Dallas. At first appearance it seems very straightforward, but it is actually complex: the interrelationships between the planting, how those trees grow, the water, the materials.

DK: All of the projects, really, are that way, I think. We've also had the advantage of working with architects like I. M. Pei, Harry Cobb, and Harry Weese. A lot of the construction details got worked out by the architects, and not directly by us. We did the design details, and they did the working drawing details for the contractor. Construction documentation for the plaza was done by Architectural Consulting Services, Inc., Dallas, Texas. POD was the local associate on Fountain Place for planting observation.

We wanted Fountain Place to be an architectural complex. The design was so simple, one fountain repeated 220 times—I wanted the edge flush, so that you appeared to walk on the water. That's why there are weirs all around the whole thing. In order to make sure that those weirs had an even flow, a bronze spline was embedded in the concrete. The level was adjusted with a screwdriver.

Q: Do you ever go back and revisit projects to look at specific details?

DK: We'd like to do more; the only thing we find is that most clients don't come back to you for changes. At Lincoln Center, when they were ripping out the trees, they never came to ask me, and the same thing at Ford Foundation. Irwin Miller is one of the few who consults our office about ongoing maintenance, and his work has precise, meticulous results. Fountain Place did come back—I went down there about six months ago to consult. When we put the trees in, we were worried about whether they were going to grow, or get big enough. I remember talking with I. M. Pei about the soffit which came out, 70 feet up in the air. He said, "What about the light, Dan, in there?" I said, "I think they get plenty of light." But they still wanted to put lights in the soffit, which they did, and now the problem is that the trees are growing too strongly...

Q: Too well?

DK: 70 feet high! They're pushing the soffit up there now. These bald cypress planters on the surface are 10-foot circles, but 10-foot squares underneath, and they go down 6 feet. The plant boxes were to be reinforced concrete, but during construction they were changed to concrete block allowing the roots to penetrate and thus their growth was not limited.

Q: Is this is a case of a detail being too successful in terms of the right environment for the plant?

DK: Many places in the city have a hell of a time getting anything to grow, and I didn't dream that they'd grow that much. We may need to get new, younger trees and put them in, or transplant some of the trees that are inside and put them outside, and then put new, smaller trees inside. That's the way it's going right now.

Q: Have you continued to evolve these details in other projects?

DK: On a house in Connecticut recently, we did a beautiful detail: concrete walls topped with a water channel retain a lawn terrace at 7 feet above grade. I didn't want the water to touch the concrete walls, so we installed a bronze pad, a channel in a sense. The water flows over the bronze lip set 2 inches from the concrete face, so you see a very nice edge of water rather than a crude edge of water. It's very beautiful.

I was a little leery of poured concrete, about 200 to 300 linear feet of 7-foot-high wall, not having the capabilities and the control that I. M. Pei's office has on concrete. I decided to make it precast to make sure that we were going to have beautiful, clean work; we had it all detailed. I think it was $180,000 more just to clad the walls. I said, "Look, this is ridiculous to pay that…let's just go ahead and pour it, and we'll cover it with vines," and actually the walls came out quite well, and we saved all that money. We still have Boston ivy growing up, and it's striking. This is a case where you admit that you're not sure how the walls are going to turn out, but you say, "The cheapest and simplest way to do this is plain concrete. Otherwise you can overdo something.

Q: How do you integrate all the things that projects have to deal with now, ADA for example?

DK: It must be done. The worst thing is the ugly ramps they put in, especially in those beautiful old churches. At a local church dating from 1780 they put the big ranch-house ramp up to the front door, and that's terrible. Well, I'm 84; and I say, "You shouldn't make it easier for old people [to access], you should make it harder. Make them work, make them use their bodies. The walk to my house is rough with boulders, and for a while I thought of putting wood stairs at certain places to make it easier. But then I said "I'll lose my tactility and I'll lose my alertness. By going up and down in the snow when it's slippery, I stay close to the earth and connected.

Q: In conclusion, is your work intended to be permanent?

DK: Nothing's permanent; many times it's wrong to build too permanently because of that. There's a certain point where you have to be careful of how far you can go. The whole thing is common sense, and it's building; there's something of sensitivity, and imagination. The imagination can solve problems that you find during construction by a discrete leap from here, and you jump right over the problem by what you propose. Instead of fighting nature like this, I say, "Go with nature," always go with nature.

DISCUSSIONS WITH THE DESIGNERS II

PETER KER WALKER, *Landscape Architect*

The interview was carried out in the office of Peter Ker Walker, Burlington, Vermont, on April 9, 1998. Participants are identified as Peter Ker Walker (PW) and the author (Q).

Fountain Place, Dallas: Initial Design Detail Ideas

Q: Where did the initial design and detail idea for the project come from?

PW: It has always been of little importance to me where the idea came from, other than that Dan [Kiley] and Harry [Weese] have always been interested in the pursuit of some ideas with water. The early sketches, I remember, were of Harry Weese's hotel having an impluvian roof; water came into the central courtyard, and then all of a sudden the water came out onto the plaza. There were basically two driving design elements here: the desire of the client to have something unique, which is always a good beginning, and the ability to pay for that uniqueness.

Detail Language

Q: The critical issues in terms of detail design were to clarify and ensure the horizontality of the water, and that the spaces people move through and occupy have a seamless flow. Where did the detail language develop from?

PW: The plaza, in many ways, is the facade of the building laid on the ground, in that it is all one place. The original model showed a building skin that had no articulation apart from its form. The mullions were minimal, for structural necessity only. From that aspect there was a consistency one to the other.

Q: How was the overall project organized?

PW: We took initial schematic drawings through design development. When the Kiley Walker partnership broke up, I was asked to continue to look over the preparation of the design development drawings; I was not asked to do any of the site observation. The project was in three parts: an office complex, a hotel complex, and a landscape carried out over two phases. The office building on the corner was rotated to become the other building—an identical plan. Because of its faceted appearance, you would never recognize the two buildings as twins.

There was universal agreement that it was the landscape element that would hold the whole project together, the ingredients that make this thing spectacular. This was particularly important in Dallas, where the client wanted some big feature that would make his development different from anything else around, and it encouraged the use of the external space, which was six blocks in size. There was a large cardboard model that spent most of the time in Dallas and was shipped up and down to the office, and we would actually work on that model to demonstrate directly to the client what was happening.

The client wanted something spectacular, and at some point in time he decided that the design we were pursuing was fine but dull; he wanted more. We had succeeded in making something like the Moorish tradition, a water element that reduces the atmospheric banality of the climate; then we have the trees, which are deciduous, but in full leaf in the middle of summer when you need maximum shade. The basic idea had to be taken further—what do people do in the space after you have provided these two very important elements that change the microclimate? We could not ad infinitum or ad nauseam treat this plaza as something that was just a canopy of trees coming out of water. I, at the request of the client, met two times with a group called WET [fountain consultants]. A meeting was held over one weekend in Los Angeles, where we had a brainstorming session, and I then flew to Dallas for a Tuesday morning meeting to present a series of ideas that would enrich the basic space and provide the variety that the client had requested.

Q: The client brought in WET after having seen a piece of their work?

PW: The client had made inquiries about WET because he had been to Disney and seen their "leapfrog fountain." I don't think Dan fully understood the implications of that. We had really a very difficult time with WET being later characterized in magazine articles as technicians, downplaying their participation in the design. I almost lost Dan as a friend because I could not support his attitude, because I was instrumental in participating with them on this particular design.

Schematic Design

PW: The schematic design indicated a table of water with trees coming out of it. For all practical purposes, it was a flat plane that was topographically sculpted to create a series of flat planes. There was a 14-foot drop from one corner of the deck to the other. It gave a spectacular opportunity to play with that water. The idea was to get down as quickly as possible, otherwise we would waste a great deal of area above which we did not need; also there was a tunnel that ran right through there, which connected to the rest of downtown.

Q: We are talking about a concrete deck, with parking and utilities below?

PW: A deck, with parking below, and a plenum where there has to be space to provide the root development for trees. Part and parcel of this idea was an emphasis on the horizontality of the water and the trees coming out of the water. Just like swamp cypress would, indeed, come out of the water. The trees were located in self-contained cylindrical concrete "bottles" [bottle-shaped concrete pits], located every 15 feet. The buildings were expected to have reflective surfaces, and there was interest on our part; if there were no trees at all, the buildings would be invisible [with nothing to reflect]. When the trees were put in, the forest would be exaggerated. Also we were able to convince the client to take the trees under the building, the overhang. At that time there was less concern about the use and economy of "grow lights."

Q: At that time, had you been working very closely with the structural engineer of the deck?

PW: No. We had previous experience with this entire thing at La Defense in Paris in the early 1970s. We were engaged by the French government to look at a concrete deck that was 1 kilometer long and 100 meters wide, and our mission there was to humanize it. It was the same issue here, to humanize the space. We knew from past experience what you could do, which was much more than the engineer would accept on the first pass. At La Defense we were able to take entire floors out for complete tree growth and still maintain the integrity of the structure. From that past experience we knew that by placing trees on a 15-foot grid related to the 30-foot grid of the structure, we could suspend or hold as a point load every second tree, and because we were using water, which is the lightest element you can use on a deck system, the technical problems were not great or insurmountable.

We stepped the site in 2-foot increments and made an interesting topography to do that. The handrail goes down the center of the steps, not on the edge. We were aware of the safety issues; other than the one drop that is 14 feet, which has a handrail in that particular situation, each of these other drops is within code requirements. Also, the water depth itself was only 6 inches. We used the tree as the point of change at 90 or 180 degrees. We were able to bring pathways, albiet almost suspended between the trees, so that you were actually walking on the path at the same grade as the water, and the tree was at that same grade as well.

The space was further subdivided, after the arrival of WET, into a rich pattern of three areas. There was the "robust" area, where there are areas of maximum drop at the top of the site, where pedestrians would come from downtown Dallas to arrive at this site. A clear platform was called the "ceremonial" area. This retained open joints in the surface to have a computerized fountain system coming out of that flat bed of pavement. In the project, there were a lot of little spaces confined by the 15-foot grid—a nice intimate scale, but the client wanted to have a bigger space for events. The problem with most of these open spaces is that if they get too large, they are hardly used 24 hours a day. What other built-in activities could we create? So we arrived at a space that is maybe too small but that has an intensity, an activity of people and interchange, and the accommodation of water as well.

Originally, there were three 20-minute computerized versions of what you could do with the fountain system. On the opening night, there were all these guys in tuxedos convinced that they could anticipate where the fountain patterns would be; of course, they got absolutely soaked.

The opening date was October 9, 1986. Only 50% of the project was realized at that time, the robust and ceremonial landscape elements and one tower were built; the second tower and the hotel, to date, have never been done. However, the ingredients that make this thing spectacular were already there. The third landscape part would have been similar in character to the robust area. A lot would therefore have depended on what the second tower building would have been.

Q: At what point did you start to look at the specifics of each of the detail junctions?

PW: There was a good dialogue between Pei's office and ourselves. There was tremendous interest by Harry Cobb [I. M. Pei] on how the building was going to meet the ground and what these paths would be. We generated sketches and I. M. Pei developed a lot of the sections. Paramount, always, were the edge condition, the weir or gutter, and the paved surface at the same level. The detail interest in water being at the same level as the paving and the trees was resolved by weirs. These are only 6-inch-wide channels that hold the water away from both the tree and the paving. I think there is an inch differential [between paving and tree edge] as more persuasive security to prevent the trees, rather than the walkway, from getting flooded.

Q: There was a scupper with some form of covering?

PW: No covering! There was always this concern about legal suits arising from someone putting an ankle in there. There are other examples in Dallas, water walls by architect Philip Johnson, and other separations of water from paving that are carried out by channelization, but I do not think anyone has ever taken it to the extreme as was done here.

Q: The general material on the walking surfaces?

PW: Basically, granite, slate inserts in a pattern, and little granite squares on a precast slab. There was concern on our part about pedestal supports and slabs of granite spanning between.

Q: The concern being?

PW: Open joints, and the drainage systems all being perfectly flat. That technology we had pursued in France, where we had developed all these precast concrete units. For the slate and the granite, we gave up eventually on the open joints, and everything just washed onto the water element itself. In the process of going from the design development to the actual implementation drawings, major changes took place in the finishes. In the end the granite paving became precast concrete, because of pure cost cutting and problems of the granite bedded in mortar absorbing water.

Q: What implication did that have for the detail design of the edge?

Figure 7.27
Site plan. Allied Plaza,
Fountain Place. Courtesy of
Office of Dan Kiley and
Office of Peter Ker Walker.

PW: To begin with, the water edge profile in granite was a knife edge, and later, because it became precast concrete, it was easier to do it as a half-round. The tolerance required of the knife edge at 45 degrees is impossible, even using the highest-grade concrete.

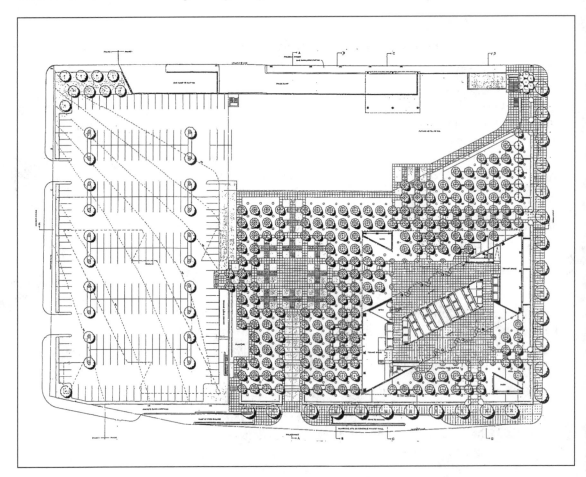

Design Development

PW: We prepared design development drawings for the client, and for costing purposes. The basic elements still remained—the grid and the movement through the trees. These were modified time and time again as they were developed, but each time the basic idea was reinforced. In time the bottle [planter pit] became square, not round. Drawings were done to illustrate the series of steps from the bottles, on the plenum, so that we could take all the service lines through between the trees. The trees were now in a concrete box, 10 feet square. Later these were changed to concrete block surrounds. I found the trees in Savannah—swamp cypress, which is just what we wanted.

Note: The plaza went through a hard time in the change of ownership. There were a lot of leaking problems, and materials didn't stand up as well as they should have, but it's reassuring to know that the plaza is basically still in great shape because it had a very strong framework.

▶ Figure 7.28
Site section. Allied Plaza, Fountain Place. Courtesy of Office of Dan Kiley and Office of Peter Ker Walker.

▼ Figure 7.29
Site section through planter. Allied Plaza, Fountain Place. Courtesy of Office of Dan Kiley and Office of Peter Ker Walker.

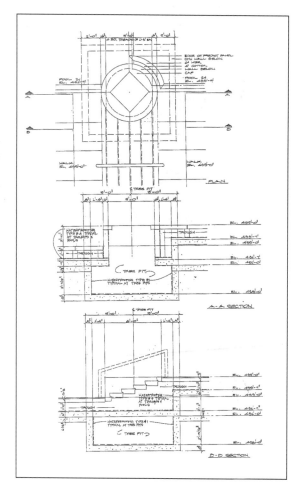

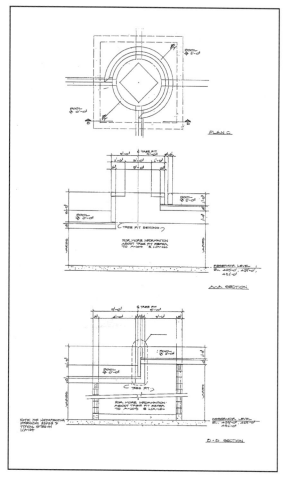

281

Figure 7.30
View of pathway. Allied
Plaza, Fountain Place.
Courtesy of James Mayeux.

◀ Figure 7.31
View of fountain pool curb
edge. Allied Plaza, Fountain
Place. Courtesy of James
Mayeux.

▼ Figure 7.32
View of stepped fountain
pool and pathway. Allied
Plaza, Fountain Place.
Courtesy of James Mayeux.

CONTRASTING SURFACES AND EDGES: EXPRESSION AND MATERIALITY IN DETAIL DESIGN

We allow materiality and the landscape detail of each project as the words spoken by the voice of each design project. Detail is the material expression of a landscape, and we always listen to the design, to figure out what the details should be.

MICHAEL VAN VALKENBURGH,
Interview with author, 1997

Figure 7.33
Section, cantilevered riverwalk. Phase I, Allegheny Riverfront Park. Courtesy of Michael Van Valkenburgh Associates, Inc.

PROJECT BACKGROUND

PROJECT
Phase I, Allegheny Riverfront Park

LOCATION
Allegheny Riverfront, Pittsburgh, Pennsylvania

PROJECT SIZE
10 acres, 4,000 by 35 feet

LANDSCAPE ARCHITECT
Michael Van Valkenburgh Associates, Inc., Cambridge, Massachusetts

Partner in charge: Michael Van Valkenburgh

CLIENT
The Pittsburgh Cultural Trust with the City of Pittsburgh Department of City Planning

ARTISTS
Ann Hamilton, Michael Mercil

ENGINEERS
Ove Arup & Partners, New York (Lead)

Frederick R. Harris, Inc. (Civil)

GAI Consultants Inc. (Geotechnical)

OTHER CONSULTANTS
Inter-Fluve (Riverbank Restoration, Hydrology)

Phillip J. Craul (Soil Scientist)

A. M. Fogarty & Associates (Cost Estimator)

Accessibility Development Associates (ADA Design Review)

BTI Consultants (Surveyors)

UDA Architects (Urban Design)

CONTRACTOR
C & M Contracting, Inc.

DESIGN PHASE(S)
1994–1997

COMPLETION
1998

COST
$ (withheld)

INTRODUCTION

The landscape architecture office of Michael Van Valkenburgh Associates can be categorized as an atelier or studio practice. Their office has a small but long-serving staff, centered on the design work, projects, and individual working processes of a named design practitioner. The day-to-day attention to detail and design issues is led by that practitioner, who, along with a few senior associates, is responsible for all project design decisions. This case study differs from the others in that the project was under implementation during the course of the interview in 1997. The advantage of this situation is the ongoing focus and intense interest in the very current problems of the detail design and site execution. The downside is the inability to observe the postimplementation use of the public spaces and to trace the eventual outcome of detail decisions.

The detail design model follows a typical pattern in this office, where an integrated approach is followed with a particular emphasis on the evolution and expansion of the detail and material language. How does a designer evolve his or her own particular detail aesthetic? For the student reader this also includes the concerns of working within a particular aesthetic vocabulary and offers an insight into the relationship between working at a broad site scale and the precision and execution of detail forms in this urban transition.

Detail themes evoke a search for continuous detail forms, with an ongoing interest in the placement of elements on a landscape surface, particularly the use of natural materials — earth, stone, wood — and their manipulation and deformation through natural forces and processes. This results in a dual concern for tectonics in detail design and sources of detail inspiration from natural processes and forces.

SITE DESCRIPTION

Phase I is a 35-by-4,000-foot strip of landfill bounded by the Allegheny River to the north, Pittsburgh's downtown to the south, the elevated Fort Wayne Railroad Bridge to the east, and Point State Park on the west, at the confluence of the Allegheny and Monongahela rivers. The site is split into two terraces, one located approximately 3 feet above the Allegheny, incorporating a former parking pier and a four-lane highway, and the other 20 feet above the river and including part of a street, which will be moved closer to the city. The lower section of the site floods annually. The program was to provide a linear park intended to reconnect the citizens of Pittsburgh with the riverfront and encourage residential development in the adjacent downtown area. Because of the 20-foot sectional grade change between the river and the city, plus the presence of two roadways, the park is divided into two linear parts, one along the edge of the water and one along the edge of the downtown. The upper park has an urban character with ordered edges and sections, whereas the lower park features a more irregular edge. The two are connected by new ramps and walkways that were designed by the landscape architects, including two 350-foot-long, cast-in-place concrete ADA-compliant wheelchair ramps, intended to form a grand civic gesture. Both parks are heavily planted with canopy-forming trees, which include red maples, sycamores, and river birch, as well as planters and vines. The lower level cantilevers 16 feet out over the river's edge and is designed with infrastructure and landscape detail elements that can withstand significant flooding.

(Adapted from a project description by Michael Van Valkenburgh Associates, Inc.)

Figure 7.34
Section through upper park and lower park. Phase I, Allegheny Riverfront Park. Courtesy of Michael Van Valkenburgh Associates, Inc.

DISCUSSIONS WITH THE DESIGNER

MICHAEL VAN VALKENBURGH, *Landscape Architect*

The interview was carried out in the office of Michael Van Valkenburgh Associates, Inc., Cambridge, Massachusetts, on October 2, 1997. Participants are identified as Michael Van Valkenburgh (MVV) and the author (Q).

An Overview of Detail and Detailing

Q: How does your office, you within the office, go about the process of details and drawings, on any project?

286

MVV: There's little separation of the conception of the design and the conception of the details, one is an extension of the other. We are frequently inventing. There are, of course, things that get repeated, but we don't have a standard set of details.

Q: So the detail design part of the process could be quite a lengthy period within any project?

MV: We're often thinking about the detail design of the project early in the process; not making decisions about detailing, and not making decisions about materiality, but just starting to corral the choices from we will later choose our final design. So what evolves early translates the conception into an idea of the felt experience a landscape will provide.

Q: Is there any occasion when the inception of a project is actually a detail? For example, one starts with a notion of a material, or use of material, or a juxtaposition of materials?

MVV: Not usually, but sometimes. The word I would use to describe what we are looking for through detailing our projects is the kind of grain, or some innate tactile quality that we want. That is especially true when we are dealing with some kind of dialectic where the landscape is meant to respond to an architectural or an urban condition and the power comes from this contrast, such as the way Olmsted uses Central Park to play against the grid of the city.

Q: When you're developing a set of design details in the office, there has to be a close relationship between you, the principal, and the very precise development of a project, in terms of people doing design development drawings. Is there an exchange backward and forward with sketches and constant review of drawings?

MVV: Part of the success of our office is the long-term rapport that has developed working with Laura Solano and Matt Urbanski of the office, and other people like Julie Bargman in times past. Those are three of the staff collaborators with whom there is a conversation between us and a reciprocal way of evolving a design. I also try to work with the more junior people in the office who are working on smaller projects.

I suppose it's really a process of revealing, of discovery, that describes what we do a lot of the time. Sometimes, you could say we just find our way intuitively. But I see intuition as one of the most important ways of operating as a designer.

Detail Language and Themes

Q: Is there, then, an identifiable detail language that you feel exists across all the projects you do, irrespective of scale? This probably gets back to some-

thing more closely to do with your own aesthetic and where you stand, not just on details, but on many things. But would you say there's a recognizable detail language that is associated with your work and the work of the office?

MVV: The detail and material language is definitely biased toward simplicity. What has started to change in our work in the last few years draws from two influences, and sometimes they overlap, and work together. They are disparate, and sometimes they stay disparate and don't collaborate. One is a modernist way of looking at the work that a detail is supposed to do, especiallt the opportunity of tectonic details. The other thing that has started to come up in our work is trying to draw details and processes from the more powerful evocations of the natural world.

I think the roots of working with the details and processes of the natural landscape goes back to the work that I did with ice in the early 1980s. But that work has translated recently into paving that is kind of exaggerated, "hyper-nature," irregular, sometimes made with orthogonal pieces, and recently using broken stone as pavement. The one thing that we normally consciously eschew is detailing with overtly historicist overtones.

Q: What about the need for things to endure physically rather than formally?

MVV: Part of that comes out in the work. Certain people like Laurie Olin try to build in an enduring way. One of the strengths of the work of some of us in the generation to follow after Olin and Pete Walker is that we really do try to build things that last, like Laurie and Pete. This has been made simpler for us with the kinds of budgets under which most of us have been making projects.

Q: What do you think is the essential relationship between the detail of the part and the whole in, say, a garden or a park?

MVV: Because I am a painter I want to think of an example from painting. There is so much about the way one places paint on the canvas, and so, in a sense, the way the paint is applied *is* the detail. The painting is partly the consequence of the process by which paint is applied, the picture has the intentions that guided the decision about applying the paint.

Detail Influences

Q: Who influenced you in terms of individuals?

MVV: Well, Corbusier's buildings, even though they haven't all lasted well. Even in the Carpenter Center at Harvard, the ramp has exquisite details. I would have to say that I've been more influenced by sculptors, the way of thinking about detailing that Martin Puryear and others have shown.

Q: But a sensibility?

MVV: It's a sensibility that comes back to that thing I said at the beginning of our conversation, I'm always thinking more about how a detail, or a material thing, is going to be experienced.

Landscape gives us the opportunity to make a journey into time. This journey should be a part of the imagination, rather than a recollection of the past. The great magic of landscape is the journey that it lets us go on. It's Gaston Bachelard's ideas about the intimate conception of psychological immensity; and how landscapes make a place that is very here but also about getting there.

Phase I, Allegheny Riverfront Park, Pittsburgh

Q: How is this exemplified in the detail design of the Pittsburgh project?

MVV: The detail I would like to focus on is the sectional detail, from the way the riveredge walk projects out over the Allegheny River. We worked on this with Ove Arup's (engineers), and this sidewalk, 15 feet at its widest place, is not only a sidewalk but a significant cantilever design. This sidewalk being not on the land, but moving out over the river and then coming back, is exactly the kind of thing we were just talking about, where the park user's experience can be much richer because of this decision we made. This sort of landscape can nourish your imagination.

Q: Its parts are composed of a surface and an edge?

MVV: An edge and its associated spatiality. The surface evolved by working with Ann Hamilton [artist] and the other people in my office to create a strongly textured surface of concrete. The textured surface of concrete was created by taking plants that would grow on the river banks and tracing their memory by pressing them into the concrete. The concrete has an imprint of the native riparian vegetation, from parts of this river upstream where it's not as urbanized as at our site.

Adjacent to that walk, at the opposite of the cantilever, is our 350-foot-long wheelchair ramp that goes from 16 feet to zero. It is a big sculptural wedge, and that is all made out of cast-in-place concrete.

Q: The dictates of what a lot people see as restrictions—for example, the ADA regulations—here are simply absorbed into the project?

MVV: Here ADA empowered us to make a bold urban move that otherwise would have been impossible. We try to not sit around and say "isn't it too bad we got picked to design a park in Pittsburgh that's a mile long but only 35 feet wide."

The first day we met with the citizens of Pittsburgh, the mayor was there and announced that there would be a 15-foot sidewalk on a park that's 35 feet wide. If you put a 15-foot-wide sidewalk in a 35-foot strip, that leaves you 10 feet of landscape on each side. So, to respond to this straitjacket Matt Urbanski said, "OK, we'll take this path and we'll run it right out over the water."

Q: It contains two of the themes that you talked about. One is the tectonic?

MVV: The expression of the cantilever, of the ramp, the folding over of the surface.

Q: The second, natural processes?

MVV: The park is beside the Allegheny River, and not beside a pond or a lake. Spatially, we brought water and land together, which has been a recurring theme in my work for a long time.

Q: On a very practical level in that project, how did you go about testing out, for example, the pressing—did you do mock-ups?

Figure 7.35
View of west ramp. Phase I,
Allegheny Riverfront Park.
Courtesy of Michael Van
Valkenburgh Associates, Inc.

MVV: Weeks and weeks of testing were conducted by Ann Hamilton and Michael Mercil in a big warehouse. Ann directed most of this work. The exciting moment in the Pittsburgh project is where you have the wall of the wheelchair ramp, the horizontal planes of the cantilever going into the river, and then the 15-foot-wide sidewalks with the grass imprint in it. At that point a robust composition of the three elements merge and are complemented by native riparian trees, rocks, and then these concrete counterweights of the cantilever. The boxes of concrete set into the stone are also the tables, and the site furniture. Remembering that, like in Mill Race Park in Columbus, Indiana, this entire park is annually under 16 feet of water. So another layer of the resolution of the detailing is its capacity to survive flood inundations.

Figure 7.36
View looking down east ramp. Phase I, Allegheny Riverfront Park. Courtesy of Michael Van Valkenburgh Associates, Inc.

Figure 7.37
Maquette of bronze rail
mounted on guardrail.
Phase I, Allegheny
Riverfront Park. Courtesy of
Michael Van Valkenburgh
Associates, Inc.

▲ Figure 7.38
Preparation of bulrush
paving sample. Phase I,
Allegheny Riverfront Park.
Courtesy of Michael Van
Valkenburgh Associates, Inc.

▶ Figure 7.39
View of boulder field and
bulrush paving. Phase I,
Allegheny Riverfront Park.
Courtesy of Michael Van
Valkenburgh Associates, Inc

ABSTRACTING NATURE'S DETAILS: A PLANTED PATH ALONG A COVE

The art of the detail, the challenge of the detailing, was to make this seem harmonious, all these contrasting layers of water's edge elements, to integrate them in a harmonious design you would never come across in nature. So it's not a copy, but it's certainly inspired by nature.

SUSAN CHILD,
Interview with author, 1997

PROJECT BACKGROUND

PROJECT
South Cove

LOCATION
Battery Park City, Manhattan, New York, New York

PROJECT SIZE
$3\frac{1}{2}$ acres

LANDSCAPE ARCHITECT
Child Associates, Boston, Massachusetts
Partner in Charge: Susan Child

CLIENT
Battery Park City Redevelopment Authority

ARCHITECTS
Cooper Eckstut Associates, New York, New York

ARTIST
Mary Miss

ENGINEERS
Mueser Rutledge (Structural)

OTHER CONSULTANTS
Philip J. Craul (Soil Scientist)

DESIGN PHASE
1984–1987

COMPLETION
1990

COST
$ (withheld)

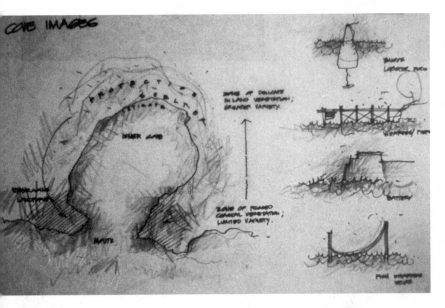

Figure 7.40
South Cove detail edge.
South Cove, Battery Park
City, Manhattan, New York.
Courtesy of Child
Associates, Inc.

INTRODUCTION

The interdisciplinary site project marks out a particular type of office practice and evolving patterns of detail design. In the case of Child Associates, landscape architects, this resulted in a rich and complex search for appropriate detail forms in concert with a collaborative team of designers and artists. The approach was integrative, combining the abstraction of natural landscape detail forms and man-made structures with broad planning and site design principles, although, as the case study demonstrates, the actual detail forms came later as a result of periods of refining and development.

Of particular interest to student readers are the concerns of detail precedents that arise from existing landscapes, particularly natural landscapes and their manipulation and evocation, and the pragmatic and tectonic concerns of working on an artificial or built ground plane. Here the detail precision and execution are related to the detail issues of substructure and a new terra firma. The focus of detail study centers on the resolution of the re-formed surface and the issues of detail form and materials of planting and site surfaces and transitions.

SITE DESCRIPTION I

South Cove, a 3½-acre park, is located on Manhattan Island at the southernmost tip of Battery Park City. Surrounding a sea cove, the park is built on a concrete platform over filled land as part of a new urban residential community. Nowhere in New York is the confrontation between the city's man-made elements and its natural setting more dramatic than at South Cove. The purpose of this landscape project was to provide a refuge from the dominant architectural and environmental forces that surround the site. The design process for South Cove was set by the Battery Park City Authority, which commissioned a collaborative team of Mary Miss, artist; Stan Eckstut, architect; and Child Associates, landscape architects. The Authority insisted on an open exchange of conceptual ideas between the three members. In the conceptual and schematic phases of design, the landscape architects proposed images of natural coves and maritime structures along the north Atlantic coast and, from this theme, abstracted the natural cove form as a metaphor and material expression for the park. This created both a detail language and expression for this new built public landscape.

In the final design, drifts of native coastal vegetation and the constructed dune-like topography of the "inner shore" evoke the earlier coastal condition of a protected cove area. Densely planted meandering groves of multistem locust and sweeps of beach grass and beach rose counter the new linear seawall and the intense built environment. The substructure grid of beams and piers that support the park is expressed in the spacing of the wood pilings in the water, the jetty, which recalls earlier maritime structures, and the geometry of the bosquet planting of the trees in the grove. The upper walkways and lower promenade merge and meander along the cove's edge, inviting exploration and giving visitors a variety of vistas of the waterfront, the Statue of Liberty in New York Harbor, and the ocean beyond.

(Adapted from a project description by Child Associates.)

SITE DESCRIPTION II

In 1973, artist Mary Miss executed a site installation on the Battery Park landfill, which now forms the general site or ground of the new Battery Park District. Deborah Nevins, in an interview with the artist, wrote of the site installation as "a series of punctured billboards composed of wooden planks, these structures on the edge of Manhattan were evocative of the uncertain nature of this leftover terrain. The viewer is obliged to line them up visually." She continues, saying that following work on a small waterfront park in Port Townsend, Washington, "The ideas and images of a place that acts as a connector between the land and the water were fresh in my mind [as I started work on South Cove]."*

Figure 7.41
Conceptual model. South Cove, Battery Park City. Courtesy of Child Associates, Inc.

*Deborah Nevins, in "An Interview with Mary Miss," *Princeton Journal* 2, Landscape (1985).

DISCUSSIONS WITH THE DESIGNER

SUSAN CHILD, *Landscape Architect*

The interview was carried out at the office of Child Associates, in Boston, Massachusetts, on December 17, 1997. Participants are identified as Susan Child (SC) and the author (Q).

Detail Development and the Office

Q: How does the office generally go about detail development on any project? Is there a single way of approaching it, or is each project taken on its own merits?

SC: Of course, there is no single way of approaching a project. Each project presents a fresh challenge and must be treated individually. During this process, there are ongoing parallel activities in the office—creative design and research—which inform the design. We search for precedents and images from our resource library to find inspiration for design and details. Our designs are usually very site specific and require unique expression. The research process stimulates ideas and the invention of new details.

Q: Are there certain ways you do things from project to project?

SC: Several projects may share similar characteristics or elements. That is because we are drawn to certain approaches—ways of looking at things, details that we tend to like, a certain aesthetic of putting materials together—a design "language" develops. For example, there are ways of using stone and paving that we like which are bound to reoccur in more than one project. However, at the time we were designing South Cove, 1984–1987, the office was relatively new and we did not have a large reservoir of built projects to draw on. South Cove was developed from tabula rasa, so to speak. It was a fresh design concept that required a totally innovative approach and a new language of details.

Q: How do you work within the office. How would a project, as it were, move through the office?

SC: I am responsible for the conceptual design and am involved throughout the entire design process to see that the concept is faithfully carried out. As a project moves from schematic into design development, a range of types of construction details and materials comes into focus. The selection of details continually narrows from this point on through project construction. Most everyone in the office usually becomes involved in the development of a project. The determination of final details may be in flux until the last moment. The design process consists of constantly evolving, testing, reassessing, improving, and refining details. The design is most successful when the dialogue is kept open until the last minute on the construction site.

Detail Design Influences

Q: What were the influences or people who influenced you, in your own training?

SC: Different people have influenced me at different times. Pete Walker had a great influence on me at the HGSD [Harvard Graduate School of Design]: his galvanizing energy, commitment to contemporary art, and incisive critiques established a standard that each design be a work of art. The works of modernists such as Mies Van der Rohe and Dan Kiley also had a great influence on me during this period. The minimalism, geometry, and asymmetry of their work opened a whole new venue to me for organizing the landscape and provided a new aesthetic vision. I was also drawn to Luis Barragan's elemental architectural forms that rooted his designs into the landscape as if they were its natural expression. What each of these artists has in common, in spite of individual imagery, is the ability to express with clarity, simple, powerful concepts with a minimum of design elements.

Q: Would you care to identify the commonalities that cut across your projects, in terms of an attention to certain themes or ideas that you keep coming back to at the detail scale?

SC: These commonalities are site specific design, the experience of passage through the landscape and simplicity of design expression. Regionalism, particularly of the Northeast, of rural New England, is a recurring theme. I know the context well, take pleasure in it, and can express it quite naturally. The design is spare, the elements are few, but require an exacting search for the right fieldstone, piece of granite, or hand-molded brick to be placed with precision on the site.

South Cove, Battery Park City, New York

Q: How did you come to participate in this collaborative effort?

SC: We were selected as the landscape architect for the design of South Cove by Amanda Burden, Vice President and Director of Art & Architecture of the Battery Park City Authority and member of the Authority's Fine Arts Commission. Amanda searched for a small landscape architecture firm which she believed had a creative approach to planting design and with whom she could work in a direct personal relationship. She selected Child Associates to collaborate with artist Mary Miss and architect Stan Eckstut. The Authority insisted on a fully open and equal collaborative design process between landscape architect, artist, and architect during the conceptual, schematic, and design development phases of the South Cove project. Cooper Eckstut was the prime and administered the project.

The Authority's mandate to our team for South Cove was to create a park for a low-rise residential community that was human in scale and green. Immediately after our initial tour of the site in January 1985, the team set to work. We each developed ideas, sketches, study models and images of precedents, independently, which we then presented to the team and advanced our work together in a three-day charrette. On the last afternoon of the charrette, the team made joint and individual presentations to the Authority for review, comment, and direction. We met in charrette this way with the Authority six times during a four-month period. The Authority's intense schedule, high aesthetic standards, and total discretion over the design provided an unusually creative environment in which to work.

Q: What immediately did you see in terms of responses to the site?

SC: When we first saw the site in January 1985, it was cold, windswept, barren, and flat—a small part of the huge 92-acre expanse of landfill. Nowhere in Manhattan was the confrontation between manmade and natural elements more dramatic than here. The cove was a long rectangular shape, an artificial cutout in a relieving platform. The task of creating a habitable sheltered space—a sense of place—in South Cove appeared immense.

The design for South Cove was wide open. As landscape architects, we asked, "What is a cove, what are the generic elements of a cove?" We contributed images to the team from the natural coastal landscape of the Northeast, coves from the rocky Maine coast to the sandy shores of Chappaquiddick Island. We created a conceptual sketch—a prototypical cove—which showed a protected inner shore with gentle terrain, soft vegetation and provided a sense of intimacy and shelter, with a bold protective character at its mouth. We also created a conceptual model for South Cove, which showed a dune topography terrain with a jetty at the mouth of the cove—the embracing landform of a cove. Both the conceptual sketch and the model included manmade elements that one also finds in coves and harbors: jetties, buoys, fish weirs, wharves, and piles. The remnants of old wharves and freestanding piles along the Hudson River shore had provided us with similar haunting images from New York's maritime past.

Q: The scale is quite small?

SC: Yes, it is, relative to the 1½ mile shorefront of Battery Park City. South Cove is a 3½ acre site supported by a relieving platform resting on a landfill. It is an arbitrary cutout, 360' long and 160'–200' wide. Our first objective was to break down its rigid edge and give the cove a more naturalistic configuration and landform.

Q: The plan has really four parts: the start of the mouth, the breaking away down at the waters edge, the modulated, topographical lines, the start of the mouth, and it has some indication of places where you can actually get through?

SC: I think that an east-west section through South Cove is very revealing. What is really important is the relationship of these elements to each other in section, through the short east-west dimension (120'). We developed a topographic change in elevation of 7' in 25' on the relieving platform and exaggerated this vertical dimension with the planting of canopy trees. The real impact of the park, both visually and experientially, comes from exploiting this vertical dimension rather than from disposition of elements in plan.

Once the imagery was established in South Cove, circulation became the primary concern. From the beginning, we wished to entice the public through the cove to explore a variety of routes, to experience the layering of elements in the cove and to discover a variety of views from different elevations. Earth and rocks were peeled back to reveal granite steps—wide stairways—climbing up between the rocks and grasses leading up to meandering paths through the locust grove to views of the River and the Statue of Liberty. A bridge over an island lures the visitor out onto a wooden jetty at the mouth of the cove. In the opposite direction a path leads out to a wild point at the southern end of the cove.

Q: Could you see under the relieving platform and the seawall?

SC: No, but when the tide was low, the surface of the concrete seawall was very exposed. There were severe monetary and regulatory constraints to altering the sea wall in a major way. However, the decision to lower the Esplanade and bring people closer to the water reduced the face of the concrete seawall, against which the eight-foot tide rose and fell, to a less daunting facade covered with a wood lattice beneath a wood railing. In keeping with the maritime vocabulary of the cove, Mary's detail for the lattice gave the wall articulation, texture, and depth and provided interesting variations in sound as the water lapped against it.

Q: You mentioned here that clearly this is an abstraction, a representation of nature. What do you think then is the role of detail in representing that? Are the details, in a sense, iconographic?

SC: The role of detail and the use of specific materials are intended to evoke a sense of a natural cove, but *not* to replicate it. It is a reference to a cove and nothing more. The details could be considered iconographic, but we have transformed their natural context and put them together in a different way that is highly intense.

We have used many elements that appear in coves and composed them in a way that they would not actually occur in nature, that is, in close proximity, in layers next to each other. For example, the plant material is not a representation but an abstraction of an exuberant and very intense natural planting which exploits the vertical dimension and unifies the park. There is something very powerful about finding this intense experience at the edge of the water. Yes, clearly the design is an abstraction.

Q: And it has associations?

SC: Our intention was to make it highly evocative. The associations are made consciously and unconsciously by the visitor, but are less important than the visitor having an intense experience associated with a cove. In the broadest sense, the park appeals, at once, to the mind, the emotions, and the senses.

Q: You mentioned that many of the elements are in a sense driven by dealing with the conditions imposed by the platform?

SC: Yes. In addition to the wood structures—the jetty, the wharf, and man-made elements such as the lights—the locations of all the natural elements in the park, such as the locust trees and the rocks, are dictated by the load-bearing requirements of the modular substructure of the relieving platform. Even the freestanding piles in the water are purposely aligned with the substructure to visually reinforce the module. The rhythmic intervals of the substructure create one underlying discipline and system of organization for the entire park.

Q: An echo of your initial response to the abandoned wharf?

SC: Yes, that haunting picture of the abandoned wharves with rotting piles on the Hudson River is vividly recalled here. This image of the piles endows South Cove with a sense of place and roots the park deeply into New York's maritime history.

Q: Where the steps meet, for example, the freestanding rocks, these junctions required a lot of close attention. How was that detail study done?

SC: The way these elements—the rocks—tumble down among the grasses in boulder-strewn fashion occasionally peeling back to reveal granite steps beneath vegetation—required careful detailing. Our task was to convince the Authority and our collaborators that what we were envisaging conceptually would, in fact, work. This included some early detail sketches by Miles Kamimoto. They were convincing because they're technically real—they work. They show the proposed relationship of the relieving platform to the land-form, to the styrofoam weight-displacement blocks, to the added soil, to the freestanding rocks and to the tree and shrub locations. The junction of these details was innovative yet credible.

Q: Did you develop the paving?

SC: We developed the concept for the paving with the team. Stan executed the final specifications. We considered many materials such as wood and granite to recall wharf construction. The Authority wanted the asphalt pavers along the lowered Esplanade. However, we finally agreed to edge the seawall with granite and to lay granite bands across the asphalt at intervals which reflected the substructure module. On the upper level, we had hoped to have something soft and entirely different underfoot like stone dust. But the Authority was forced to maintain a wide fire lane with a hard surface and also to make the grove accessible. So, eventually asphalt pavers had to be used for the paths.

Q: What informed the detail design of the planting?

SC: From the very beginning, we had a clear concept for the planting design. Our intention was to respond to the immense scale of the river and the size of the site with a simple large-scale planting plan—a massing of a few species of coastal plants in linear drifts. This would unify the site and make it appear a part of a larger context of coastal vegetation. We designed a long sweeping grove of multistemmed honey locust trees with underdrifts of shrubs—bayberry, rosa rugosa, and grasses, all seaside plants.

Multistem honey locusts and American beach grass predominate on this windswept site. They were both selected for their light and feathery quality and responsiveness to the wind. All plants were selected for their ability to survive the harsh coastal conditions.

The soil mixture and the method of planting and tree-guying were also critical elements for plant survival. Phil Craul, soil scientist, devised the soil mixture and personally supervised its preparation on site. It turned out to be superb, as is evident today. Phil also prescribed the method of planting. The importation of all new soil permitted planting by trench excavation—that is, the arrangement of trees and shrubs within large open trenches prior to the addition of topsoil. Although the multistem honey locusts had to be precisely located on the load-bearing points of the relieving platform, this method of planting, in open trenches, allowed plenty of discretion in the composition and massing of shrubs.

Q: Were you responsible for the maintenance of, the operation of it after it was completed?

SC: No, that was the responsibility of the Battery Park City Corporation, and of Tessa Huxley in particular. She has done a superb job. From time to time, we discuss the planting, but the Corporation is responsible for it. Some changes in plant material have been made for maintenance reasons, but on the whole, the design is intact and flourishing.

Q: We're referring specifically to the island in the project adjacent to the bridge?

SC: Yes, it had a beautiful planting of waving grasses, which was very soft. In the end, the grasses were hard to maintain because they collected trash and were finally replaced. The other planting changes occurred out on the wild point beyond the jetty. This was one area where we had the vegetation come right to the water's edge, the only place in Battery Park City where this occurred. The wild point was originally planted with beach grass, scrub oak, pines, a few rosa rugosa, and inkberry.

It was a relatively open, grassy, moor-like planting, with a single footpath through it. However, people walked randomly across the planting trampling the grasses. Almost all of this area has now been replanted with rosa rugosa as a barrier to trespassing. The path to the water's edge is still there, but it no longer provides the same sense of wildness and freedom as it once did.

Detail Durability and Craft

Q: What is your attitude to how things last or don't last?

SC: One hopes one builds forever, but one has either to anticipate or accept change and its effects on living and nonliving material. At Battery Park City, there are several factors that will make this park more durable than most — the Authority's ability to generously finance the project, to enlist the best technical assistance, to buy quality materials and finally to provide the best of maintenance.

Q: Is there such a thing today as craftsmanship?

SC: There are still individuals who work at a specialty developing a craft and finding new ways of doing things and using new materials. The best details on the project often derive from a craftsperson's particular experience and know-how. We always listen to the builder's suggestions. If there is a real give and take between you and the builder/craftsman, you learn from him.

Occasionally, on a public project, there is a problem in developing an innovative, well-crafted solution because of the prescribed procedures of labor unions. For instance, the idea of trench excavation was completely new to the contractor at South Cove and it took a while to convince him that it would work, but eventually he came around.

Q: What you're saying is that craftsmanship is still alive, but it takes other forms?

SC: That's right! In landscape architecture, among the specialists, Phil Craul is a hands-on specialist, a craftsman. He is fantastic and I have to give him great credit for the ultimate success of the project. He and Gerry Weinstein, who was the horticulturist, worked together. They made planting an exercise that was exciting and interesting, and I think that their enthusiasm, knowledge, and willingness to try something new eventually got the contractors excited too.

Q: Since the project was completed, have you worked on projects that had a similar multidisciplinary aspect to them?

SC: Yes, in particular, a 1¼ acre roofdeck garden for Moshe Safdie's Esplanade condominiums in Cambridge, which Phil Craul also consulted on, and North Cove Park, the "Belvedere," also in Battery Park City was a collaborative design with Mitchell/Giurgola and Martin Puryear. However, South Cove was our first collaboration, an extraordinary experience with an extraordinary client. The design of South Cove surpassed all of our aspirations, particularly in its reception by the public.

Figure 7.42
Site plan. South Cove,
Battery Park City. Courtesy
of Child Associates, Inc.

304

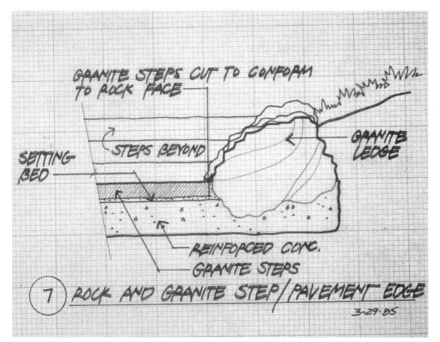

GRANITE STEPS CUT TO CONFORM TO ROCK FACE

STEPS BEYOND

SETTING BED

GRANITE LEDGE

REINFORCED CONC.

GRANITE STEPS

7 ROCK AND GRANITE STEP/PAVEMENT EDGE

3-29-85

◀ Figure 7.43
Rock and granite edge
condition. South Cove,
Battery Park City. Courtesy
of Child Associates, Inc.

▼ Figure 7.44
Illustrative section through
berm. South Cove, Battery
Park City. Courtesy of Child
Associates, Inc.

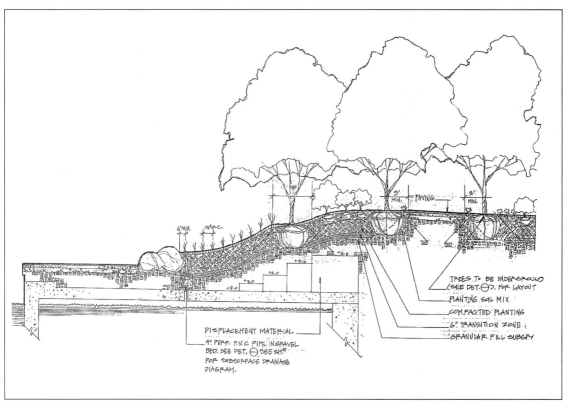

TREES TO BE UNDERGROUND (SEE DET. 7. FOR LAYOUT

PLANTING SOIL MIX

COMPACTED PLANTING

6" TRANSITION ZONE

GRANULAR FILL SUBGR'Y

DISPLACEMENT MATERIAL

4" PERF. P.V.C. PIPE IN GRAVEL BED. SEE DET. 6 SEE SH. FOR SUBSURFACE DRAINAGE DIAGRAM.

305

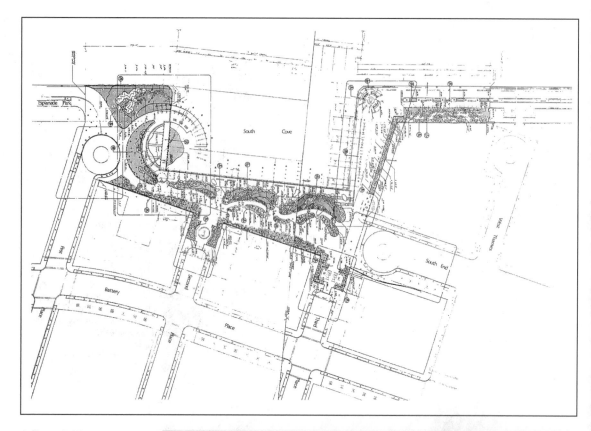

▲ Figure 7.45
Site planting plan. South
Cove, Battery Park City.
Courtesy of Child
Associates, Inc.

▶▶ Figure 7.46
View of South Cove. South
Cove, Battery Park City.
Courtesy of Child
Associates, Inc.

▶ Figure 7.47
View toward berm. South
Cove, Battery Park City.
Courtesy of Child
Associates, Inc.

BEYOND THE WALL: SURFACE DETAILS FOR PUBLIC ACCESS

Originally the proposal called for grass to extend to the wall. At that time we didn't know that there would be many thousands of people every day coming close to the wall.

HENRY ARNOLD,
Interview with author, 1996

PROJECT BACKGROUND

PROJECT
Vietnam Veterans Memorial, Washington, D.C.

LOCATION
The Mall, Washington, D.C.

PROJECT SIZE
6 acres

LANDSCAPE ARCHITECT
Arnold Associates, Princeton, New Jersey
Partner in Charge: Henry F. Arnold

CLIENT
Vietnam Veterans Memorial Fund

ARCHITECTS AND PLANNERS
Cooper-Lecky Partnership, Washington, D.C.

DESIGNER
Maya Ying Lin

ENGINEERS
Jim Cutts (Structural)
Walter Osbourne (Civil)

DESIGN PHASE
1981–1982

COMPLETION
November 1982 (project dedication)

COST
$3.9 million for construction

Figure 7.48
Base of wall under construction. Vietnam Veterans Memorial, Washington, D.C. Courtesy of Arnold Associates.

308

INTRODUCTION

Henry F. Arnold, landscape architect, is the principal of the landscape architecture office of Arnold Associates in Princeton, New Jersey. The Vietnam Veterans Memorial was one of a number of civic projects [in Washington, D.C.] on which Arnold was the landscape design consultant. These include a 40-acre park, Constitution Gardens, as a consultant to architects SOM, and, more recently, the Korean War Veterans Memorial, with architects Cooper-Lecky.

The focus of the Vietnam Veterans Memorial landscape detail study is on the graded grass and subbase that forms the ground surface between the public walkway and the wall. The issues of detail design evolution and the compromise between the pragmatic concerns of circulation, the foot traffic of 5 million annual visitors and the resultant weathering, and the original site conceptual ideas are examined.

The general discussion and analysis focuses on the landscape detail process, the roles of the original competition designer and landscape archi-

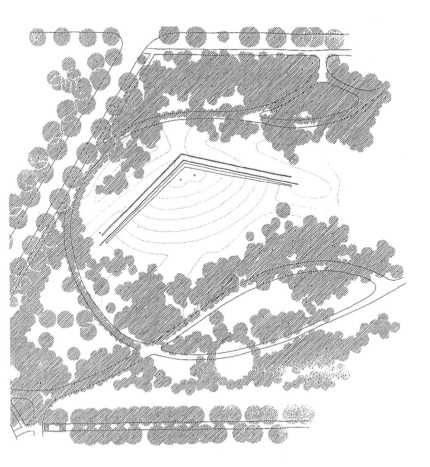

Figure 7.49
Conceptual site plan.
Vietnam Veterans
Memorial, Washington,
D.C. Courtesy of Arnold
Associates.

tect, and the changing detail interpretation of the cutting of the earth, the walkway and the surface connections.

For the student reader, the detail process illustrates the need to address equally the poetic and pragmatic concerns. Of particular interest is how the subtle changes to the ground surfaces caused by weathering have not diminished the overall integrity of the few key landscape details: the transition of wall to ground, the wall top or warning device, and the integration of path and topography.

From the Designers Competition Statement by Maya Ying Lin:

> The memorial is composed not as an unchanging monument, but as a moving composition, to be understood as we move into and out of it; the passage itself is gradual, the descent to the origin slow.

From the Report of the Vietnam Veterans Memorial Design Competition, May 1, 1981:

> Of all the proposals submitted, this most clearly meets the spirit and formal requirements of the program. It is contemplative and reflective. It is superbly harmonious with its site, and yet frees the visitors from the noise and traffic of the surrounding city. Its open nature will encourage access in all occasions, at all hours, without barriers. Its siting and materials are simple and forthright.

DISCUSSIONS WITH THE DESIGNER

HENRY ARNOLD, *Landscape Architect*

The interview was carried out at the office of Arnold Associates, Princeton, New Jersey, on June 13, 1996. Participants are identified as Henry Arnold (HA) and the author (Q).

An Overview of Detail and Detailing

Q: How do you go about detail design in the office? What is the process? Do you personally establish every detail condition yourself?

HA: There are two approaches to producing details. One is just straightforward, functional problem solving, and that's important in most detailing, but there's also decorative detailing, and on most projects the problem-solving functional and decorative detailing are part of the same thing. Generally in our office, details evolve in developing a design. We start out by looking at the broadest issues of design, we don't even think about details. We look at the major overall spatial implications of a project.

For example, we start by defining the spaces that are important in this project.

We always start without any preconceptions about the overall design, or about how to do a detail. Later, as we're developing the concept, we see how certain kinds of details work with that concept.

There are several things that greatly influence detail design that formerly were not constraints. One of them is safety codes—the ADA [Americans with Disabilities Act] and OSHA [Occupational Safety and Health Administration] regulations. It's rare that you get to design a public project, and even a private project, where the codes don't change the design approach to detailing. The other contemporary condition that has an impact on detailing is the desire for historical versimilitude. There is emphasis on reproducing historic details such as old-fashioned light fixtures that represent a selected historical period. This poses problems for the designer. How does one combine the required 150 watt mercury vapor lamp with a fixture that was designed to have a gas lamp, and maintain visual integrity within the space? Where clients place an emphasis on historical accuracy in detailing a project, finding an acceptable design solution may depend upon careful historical research combined with inventive adaptation.

Simply copying old details may produce an inappropriate, even comical design solution. This reinforces my conviction that landscape design details should be developed to solve specific conditions in the present day context, using the most appropriate technology in a sensitive way.

Q: How do you deal with a water edge, a promenade, one of the places in which you can really accuse people of using historicist details?

HA: Twenty years ago, when we were doing the Trenton Marine Terminal Park we designed a railing of precast concrete and stainless steel cables. The simple form was visually open when sitting in the park and comfortable to lean on. If this design were done today were would have to produce a very different design to meet code requirements. Today's railing would be less transparent and probably less elegant. A more recent design illustrates this point. A railing we developed along the DNR Canal in Lambertville, New Jersey, resolved the historical context with code requirements by adding wire fabric panels to an old industrial railing design. The resulting railing has an appropriate industrial appearance in what we felt was an acceptable compromise even though it is not a historic facsimile.

Q: So that's an additive detail using standard elements?

HA: Yes, the existing railing system was a pipe rail with stanchions. The stanchions were precast pieces with cast iron fittings. We also used pipes and standard fittings in the design of metal bollards.

311

Q: Is there anything in the new technology that you're using that has changed the way you do and think about detailing? In particular, I know that you use computer applications, or is that simply a device to help you produce drawings faster?

HA: In our office, the computer is more useful in production than design. It can be a time-saving tool especially in drawing details. Projects require more careful documentation than may have been the case in the past where skillful craftsmen executed details without elaborate drawings. When Central Park was built Olmsted did much of the detail design in the field.

Materials

HA: There are certain details that were repeatedly used in many of our designs because they work well both visually and functionally. One example is a form of crushed stone pavement that we refer to as "stone screenings pavement" to differentiate it from loose gravel or crushed stone that does not make a firm, easily maintained walking surface. We have to be careful to make this distinction, because our clients are often familiar with places where this detail was not properly specified or installed. We have never found a better material for paving around trees in large urban tree groves with extensive pedestrian traffic. We have tried scores of other paving materials and systems in this type of space. None of them can approach properly detailed "stone screenings pavement" for simplicity, utility, appearance, and cost. It is comfortable to walk upon, poses no tripping hazard, has a natural looking irregular surface pattern, allows air and water to percolate to the tree roots below, and is firm enough to support wheelchairs and bicycle traffic. These qualities make "stone screenings pavement" the ideal material for urban outdoor pedestrian spaces shaded by trees. I do not know of anyone else who has specified this type of pavement as we have detailed it, yet the results on our projects have been very successful.

In site detailing one has to consider things like weathering, erosion, oxidation, freezing and thawing, thermal expansion, rainfall runoff, human behavior and scale, the geometry of vehicular movement, and maintenance operations. All those things have an impact on how you detail the landscape as opposed to interior spaces.

For example, exterior steps need a much shallower tread-riser ratio than interior steps to feel comfortable. If you ever took a set of interior steps and put them in a landscape, they would feel awkward and out of place.

Q: That's often what happens.

HA: Sometimes on newer sites. When you go back to the old projects, very often you'll find that the steps are much more shallow and generous, and have that feeling of being part of the landscape. The designers followed good tread–riser ratio rules: the Olmsted rule and the Boston rule. These vary a little bit from each other, but maintain a gentler rise than most indoor stairs.

Q; Are certain steps more comfortable?

HA: One that I like is a 5-inch riser and a 15-inch tread. That's a good general standard you might use as a point of departure, and for a different project you might vary it to fit shallower, or steeper conditions.

They all have a general proportion where the tread increases in width in relation to riser decrease. I suppose tall people like one rule and short people like another rule.

Q: In each project, you are able to push forward your own detail experimentation?

HA: We develop details to fit the particular circumstances. I would call it innovation, not experimentation. For Mercer County Cemetery Park we worked with a graphic designer to develop a monitor and some marker signs, and they have a character that fits well with the configuration of gravestones and path benches. We also designed concrete and metal bands that act as an architectural screen between the parking lot and cemetery gathering area. Our goal is to improve the details on each new project based on our experience in detailing earlier projects, and observing how they perform over time.

Vietnam Veterans Memorial, Washington, D.C.

Q: How did your involvement in the project start, and how did the group work together?

HA: I was brought in as landscape architect by Maya [Lin]. I had been recommended by SOM and Cooper-Lecky because of my previous work with them in Washington. Maya was involved throughout the project. She was not consulted on the details which were added later, namely the widening of the paving with a cobblestrip, the lights and the crowd control barriers.

On the Memorial one of the important problems that wasn't completely resolved in the original concept, was how you bring in hundreds of thousands of people and still maintain the integrity of the design.

Detail Design

Q: What was the scope of your detail design work?

HA: Grading, subsurface drainage, grass and planting; the architects did the wall itself, the path, and the lights. My drawings and specifications became part of the architectural documents.

Q: A lot of people might argue that a landscape architect could have done everything on this project.

HA: I agree. Requiring the collaboration of an architect is an indication of the lack of understanding about what landscape architects do. The Korean War Veterans Memorial project [designed for the Washington Mall by Cooper-Lecky with Arnold Associates as landscape architects in 1996] comes a lot closer to a complete landscape architectural project. Our design for the Memorial Grove of pleached linden trees was incorrectly constructed and subsequently changed by the Corps of Engineers. At this time the revised design awaits completion.

Schematic Design

HA: The conceptual design was very cleanly expressed by the wall with the names on it and the grass running up to the top and base of the wall, creating a fault-like rift. Some kind of paving system was needed near the wall.

We looked at how people would survey the wall. Most people wouldn't walk or stand right up at the face of the wall, but they would stand a couple of feet back so that they could read the names, and that gave us a clue to where a walk should be and how wide it should be.

The walk was moved farther away; that would leave a little strip of grass against the wall, which I thought was very important. There was also a narrow granite gutter at the bottom of the wall that makes a neat transition between the grass and the wall.

There were so many people who came and gave offerings at the foot of the wall that the grass did not survive in the strip between the wall and the pavement.

We knew that reinforcement of the grass system was going to be important, because not everybody was going to stay on the walk. We put in a reinforcing mat and detailed a granular lawn base with underdrainage for the turf so that the grass could bear more traffic. Before the dedication in November [1982], there had not been enough time to establish roots. It was put in place only 10 days before the ceremony, and the sod had not knitted. There were more than 4 inches of rain in the 48 hours before the dedication, and the water did not have time to seep away. Thousands of people churned up all the sod. If the sod had been in place for 6 weeks and there had not been heavy rain immediately before the dedication, the lawn would have survived. Later the turf was replaced. It was further reinforced near the wall using granite block with grass joints.

Detail Development

HA: Two details were added to the original design. The top of the wall required a very special detail in order not to have a railing or a fence. This was a low curb 6 feet from the top of the wall, a safety feature, 6 to 8 inches in height, as a warning device if somebody approached it. This curb could not be seen from anywhere except from a distance beyond the top of the memorial. The purpose was to warn people who might be running or chasing a frisbee that they were coming to a drop. Another detail came about as a later addition in response to the long hours that people were spending at the wall. A continuous string of lights housed in flat turtle-like stone fixtures were added within the granite block strip. In an effort to restrict the crowds of people to the paved walk, a portable barrier consisting of a chain with metal stanchions was added even later. This detail is particularly unflattering to the memorial even if it is portable and removed at uncrowded hours.

In retrospect, I do not see how this requirement to control such large crowds could have been anticipated, and if it were, what kind of acceptable design solution might have been incorporated in the original concept.

Bringing the grass near to the wall at the base as well as the top was necessary in carrying out the concept of a rift in the ground. Further widening of the lower stone paving would only have weakened the concept.

Q: You would need a handrail now.

HA: At this time there was no code requirement for a handrail along the path in front of the wall. If this had been a requirement it would have produced an unacceptable alteration to the design.

Concluding Remarks

Landscape design details should express and strengthen the concept. Rather than trying to introduce novelty, it is my intent to execute details that increase coherence. Very often age-old ways of detailing the ground and structures in the landscape are a satisfactory way to achieve unity in a design. Improving on old details can be as successful in realizing an effective design as inventing new detail designs. Just as often the contrast of new materials and building methods can provide satisfying unity to the design. Historical continuity might be better achieved by contrasting the old with the new, instead of imitating a past style. I see no incongruity in placing well designed modern benches or light fixtures on the most venerated of historic sites, if it is done in a sensitive manner. Landscapes are evolving forms. Pretending that a particular site is frozen in time, revealing only evidence of one historic period, seems less honest. Adding contemporary details can reveal the evolution of the place over time. In this way the landscape better reflects the continuing process of historic change.

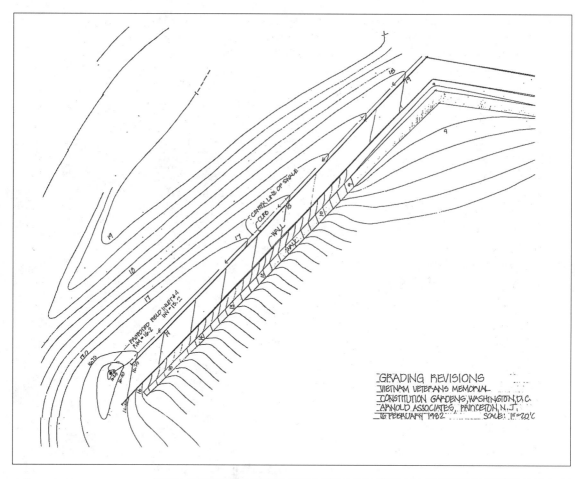

GRADING REVISIONS
VIETNAM VETERANS MEMORIAL
CONSTITUTION GARDENS, WASHINGTON, D.C.
ARNOLD ASSOCIATES, PRINCETON, N.J.
16 FEBRUARY 1982   SCALE: 1"=20'C

▲ Figure 7.50
Grading revisions. Vietnam
Veterans Memorial,
Washington, D.C. Courtesy
of Arnold Associates.

▶ Figure 7.51
Reinforced turf detail.
Vietnam Veterans Memorial,
Washington, D.C. Courtesy
of Arnold Associates.

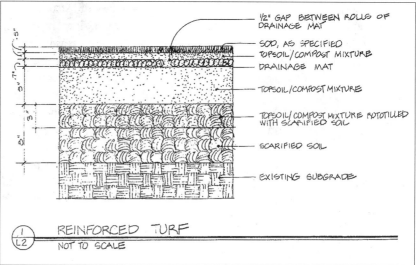

½" GAP BETWEEN ROLLS OF DRAINAGE MAT
SOD, AS SPECIFIED
TOPSOIL/COMPOST MIXTURE
DRAINAGE MAT
TOPSOIL/COMPOST MIXTURE
TOPSOIL/COMPOST MIXTURE ROTOTILLED WITH SCARIFIED SOIL
SCARIFIED SOIL
EXISTING SUBGRADE

REINFORCED TURF
NOT TO SCALE

316

◄◄ Figure 7.52
View of implementation.
Vietnam Veterans Memorial,
Washington, D.C. Courtesy
of Arnold Associates.

◄ Figure 7.53
View of implementation.
Vietnam Veterans Memorial,
Washington, D.C. Courtesy
of Arnold Associates.

◄ Figure 7.54
View of implementation.
Vietnam Veterans Memorial,
Washington, D.C. Courtesy
of Arnold Associates.

▼ Figure 7.55
View of surface and light
fixture beyond the wall.
Vietnam Veterans Memorial,
Washington, D.C. Courtesy
of Arnold Associates.

317

LANDSCAPE DETAILS OF CULTURE, TRADITION, AND ABSTRACTION

I like to work with surfaces, the way you work out the directionality, and especially if you start to play with those horizontal surfaces on the grass and in the park, they start to establish a very beautiful structure.

MARIO SCHJETNAN,
Interview with author, 1996

PROJECT BACKGROUND

PROJECT
Parque Ecológico, Xochimilco

LOCATION
Xochimilco, Mexico City, Mexico

PROJECT SIZE
700 acres, 278 hectares

LANDSCAPE ARCHITECT
Partners in Charge: Mario Schjetnan and José Luis Pérez
Grupo Diseño Urbano, S.C., Mexico City

CLIENT
Federal District of Mexico and Delegacion Xochimilco

ARCHITECTS AND PLANNERS
GDU, Mexico City

ENGINEERS
Garza Maldonado y Asociados/RCL Ingenieros

OTHER CONSULTANTS
Alejandro Cabeza, Landscape Architect, and Eduardo Basurto, Architect

DESIGN PHASE
1990

COMPLETION
June 1993

COST
$ unknown

Figure 7.56
View of landscape surfaces.
Parque Ecológico,
Xochimilco, Mexico City.
Courtesy of Grupo Diseño
Urbano.

318

INTRODUCTION

Mario Schjetnan, landscape architect, is a partner with José Luis Pérez in the landscape architecture office of Grupo Diseño Urbano, S.C., in Mexico City. The Parque Ecológico Xochimilco is one of a number of large-scale, complex landscape restoration planning and design projects carried out by the designer. They include the conservation of water bodies, the restoration of wetland areas, agricultural districts, large park and recreational zones, with circulation, site structures, and cultural museum buildings.

As an expression of the art of landscape detail and the detail design processes, this final case study illustrates a clear approach to the production of detail form through the abstraction of natural and cultural sources. This includes the designer's selection and assembly of site materials and the association of detail forms within a familiar and understood cultural context— in short, the development of vernacular detail form that acknowledges the influences of working within a detail design *tradition*. This is exemplified by the designer's reference to the historic uses of local materials, the continued use of detail precedents from both ancient and twentieth-century built forms of Mexico, and the evolution of detail forms within an accepted detail language, albeit all with a contemporary interpretation.

What does this offer for the student reader as a potential model in detail design? Does the use of detail themes and motifs concerned with the layering of natural and man-made elements support the development of more complex and durable detail forms? Finally, what does the designer bring to the detail design process today in terms of a contemporary viewpoint on the issues of detail *precision* and the detail *execution* of the parts?

The general discussion focuses on the landscape detail process and the role that cultural detail precedents play in creating new and imaginative detail forms.

SITE DESCRIPTION

Xochimilco, the last remnant of the original form of lakeside agricultural life in Mexico, is situated to the south of the Valley of Mexico. Declared a World Heritage Site by the United Nations Educational, Scientific, and Cultural Organization (UNESCO) in 1987, it is part of a plan to repair and restore this vast pre-Hispanic built landscape.

The Ecological Recovery Plan of Xochimilco, carried out over an area of 3,000 hectares, consists of the following design activities: historic preservation and restoration of the historic *chinampas* ("agricultural islands" of fertile dredged soil held by mats of plant roots and with vertical *salix* trees to bind them all together), ecological management through the clearing and cleaning

319

of 140 kilometers of canals and lagoons, and economic development and technical support for 700 hectares of agricultural production. Complementing these activities, the designers, as part of the plan, carried out specific projects and the architectural supervision of a 278-hectare cultural and regional park that includes a botanical, cultural, and recreational park, around a new 100-acre lagoon. This contains an entrance plaza and information center, an embarcadero for boat trips, a bridge connecting the park to the agricultural production area, a 167-hectare sports park, and a plant and flower market. The center of this area is a demonstration area, where the botanical garden recreates the ancient agricultural method of this region, the *chinampas.*

In the entrance plaza is located an information building with video displays, exhibitions, an archeological museum and observation terrace overlooking the Xochimilco region, with a restaurant, offices, and support services. Outside are a water tower and seven water aqueducts feeding into a

Figure 7.57
Sketches of site detail forms.
Parque Ecológico,
Xochimilco, Mexico City.
Courtesy of Grupo Diseño
Urbano.

320

lagoon. The park as a whole is a complex of lagoons and wetlands. The local recreation area at the edge of the lagoon includes a terrace with a place for concerts, an area for park visitors to spend a day in the country, and a pergola walk flanked by flower gardens. The distinctive water aqueducts and flower pergola walk were the focus of detail design study.

DISCUSSIONS WITH THE DESIGNER

MARIO SCHJETNAN, *Landscape Architect*

The interview was carried out in Cambridge, Massachusetts, on March 14, 1996. Participants are identified as Mario Schjetnan (MS) and the author (Q).

An Overview of Detail and Detailing

Q: How important in the office is the development of an idea right down to the detail?

MS: Very! We take projects from conceptual design and the program, to the final details and to the supervision of the work. Generally, I conceptualize the

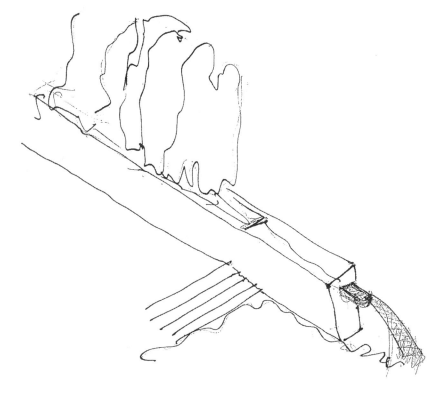

Figure 7.58
Sketch of water channel.
Parque Ecológico,
Xochimilco, Mexico City.
Courtesy of Grupo Diseño
Urbano.

321

project, I trace in sketches; these details are refined in the office by the staff and presented to the client and to people who, in turn, criticize, modify, or approve it. Then we go to working drawings.

Q: Is there anything you could encapsulate as being a "Mexican" way of detailing?

MS: Yes, because of the people who are in the detail process in Mexico. I have people who have done their careers partly in engineering and partly in architecture. I also have architects and landscape architects. So there is a mixture of people who are in charge of the technical aspects of the process of design. I then have design sessions in my house. I appoint people to work in my house, to review the process of detail design, and then we send this to be assessed, to quantify materials, to approve technically their costs, and to write the specifications. I like to be in the construction itself. I have created a group in my own office to supervise the projects on-site, and this has given us control to oversee the production of details.

Combining Crafts and Industry in Detail

Q: Is there something we could identify as a "Mario Schjetnan" way of detail design that may be even different from other landscape architects and architects in Mexico?

MS: I have always searched, in my work, to have a combination of crafts and the industrial. I read many many years ago an article by Kenneth Frampton, in which he said that the humanity of building is instilled by the making of it. It's definitely building which establishes a communication with hand, the communication with labor.

We are very fortunate in Mexico, because we have wonderful local craftsmen—of stone, stucco, carpentry, and of metal. We have another advantage, we have had four years of workshops in detailing in the School of Architecture at the National University of Mexico, detailing of different complexities. Then we had to go to building sites to make reports of details and construction processes.

Working with Industry

Today we have continual meetings on new materials with manufacturers. We have now developed a very interesting vocabulary for the construction of vaults in metal. These are industrialized vaults which I had seen and are very interesting for some of the kiosks and entrances. I have even used them for workshops in a cultural center. I did research, going to the factory. We have also worked directly with the production of pavements with a base of volcanic basalt stone. The stone has been used traditionally in Mexico City since the sixteenth century. We worked for one year directly with the manufacturer of the pavement. Now it has been adopted in the sidewalks of the Historical Center in Mexico City. We use the stone as a base, not just to have a tint in the pavement, but to use it pulverized.

Regarding the footpaths of the park at Xochimilco, we used a red volcanic gravel. It is a wonderful stone, called *tezontle*. Its red color never fades; it's permanent. I have been fascinated by this color since my childhood days.

In the highlands of Mexico that's how they used to construct the shoulders on the roads. Then we worked out whether it was possible to use it with concrete for the buildings and benches, to chip the stone to bring out the color by machine, by an industrialized system, like a hammer, or by punching it. We found out it was not possible. So in the end we came back to the hand chipping, in panels or slabs.

Site Construction

Q: How did you learn about construction?

MS: I love the process of construction. My father was an architect and was very conscientious about his detailing. He was not, how should I say, an avant-garde designer, although early in his career he was a very interesting modernist architect. He was always interested in technology, and he designed his own piping systems, he designed his own watering systems for golf courses. In this way I learned the philosophy, the process; I started to build very early.

In my fourth year of architecture I started to build gardens. I did a model garden for an exhibit. It was a very small garden, it was about 100 square meters, and I was in charge of the plants, the water, the shingle, the pavement. It was a very important starting point for having a love for the process of construction.

Xochimilco Park, Mexico City

Q: It is clear that there are very different details being used here that I haven't seen used on your other projects. I'm thinking of the flower promenade. Was that language developed just for the project?

MS: I think that it came from the idea of creating for the first time an enormous promenade, a *paseo* to guide you into the park to the embarking dock. I was fascinated by the pergolas of Europe, and I said, I can't build at that scale, but I have a procession and need to make it look as if it is continuous. I developed this concept of a series of arches, not connected, each is a complete arch. It is not a whole pergola, but it looks like one entity.

Materials and Construction

Q: The bases are circular concrete columns?

MS: Those came out of a very practical decision. I had to build biformed arches, which were done in a shop, in a factory, and they're all the same in size. The columns were poured on-site with cardboard forms, which are very inexpensive, then we filled them with foam to make them lighter. This is very cheap, and is typical structure in Mexico.

Q: For that arch, was the metal an off-the-shelf item, a standard arch?

MS: We created what we called a central form, and that can be built by any kind of metal workshop in Mexico. I was very worried about climate; there is a lot of salt and humidity which can attack the metal. It's simpler if you want to cover it with vines. It's more difficult if you want them to grow around the columns, no? It would be more logical to bring the metal down. I was very worried, however, that the concrete columns would appear too heavy, if I should just bring them up like a pilaster to about 3 feet in height. Curiously, in the next project in El Cedazo Park in Aquascalientes I did half-size columns with a square metal arch, and it does look rather nice!

Surfaces

The checkered pattern of the plaza at Xochimilco I did not invent, I copied it from the National University of Mexico campus; I was always fascinated with this checkered pattern.

Q: Where the grass eventually goes into the grass panels?

MS: The grass panels are structured with loose stone; therefore, you can walk on top of this grass and the grass stays. You can mow it very easily, and at the same time you establish a beautiful combination. I think it's one of the great inventions for large-scale plazas, not to have a large area of hard material, but at the same time not to have a large area of grass, which would be difficult to maintain. It's a mix, and it establishes a directionality of axis and establishes also a way to walk.

Detail Influences

Q: What contemporary designers' work have you liked, not so much for the ideas, but in terms of the actual finished details of the project?

MS: I learned from the Noguchi gardens in Paris. I was fascinated by the way he worked with stone and materials. Or from the plasticicity of plant material of Roberto Burle Marx. I was always fascinated by Louis Kahn, the connection between brick and travertine, which ties the contemporary with the temporal. For instance, if you go and see the gardens and patio of the Salk Institute buildings, the connection between concrete and travertine, the juxtaposition of the poured and the cut, the very precise travertine with the little marks in it. With Barragan it was the detailing of how he works with these clean surfaces against other materials. I used to talk with him about this horizontality against verticality, this cleanness.

He would use crushed limestone, which is normally used as base for highways. He used it for his plazas, the detailing of his surfaces of water, the crushing of the stones by hand to create patterns on the plaza, the continuation of water with surface.

Observation of Detail

When I went to Rome in 1968 I started to see those things, the surfaces of the streets in Rome which have brick, and then the detailing of the signs of the streets are in travertine marble.

The most important thing for a landscape architect is to have eyes, and to store that information graphically.

You start to see an interesting combination of chipped marble with polished marble in a location, and you store that information, and you'd like to do something like that at some time, and you start to think of uses.

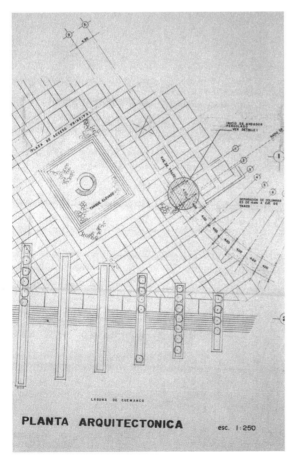

Figure 7.59
Site plan. Parque Ecológico, Xochimilco, Mexico City. Courtesy of Grupo Diseño Urbano.

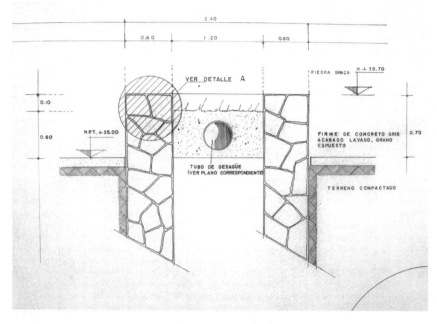

▲ Figure 7.60
Water channel. Parque
Ecológico, Xochimilco,
Mexico City. Courtesy of
Grupo Diseño Urbano.

▶ Figure 7.61
Pergola structure. Parque
Ecológico, Xochimilco,
Mexico City. Courtesy of
Grupo Diseño Urbano.

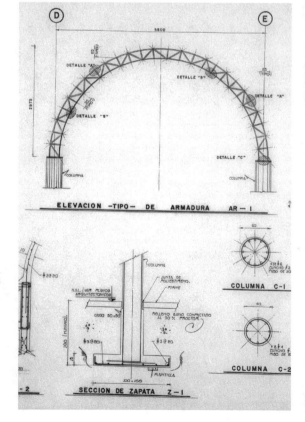

▲ Figure 7.62
View of pergola. Parque
Ecológico, Xochimilco,
Mexico City.

◀ Figure 7.63
View of water channel.
Parque Ecológico,
Xochimilco, Mexico City.

CHAPTER 8

POSTSCRIPT: POETICS AND PRAGMATICS

An art form has neither beginning nor end, and the art itself is in the making and not the completion.

SIR GEOFFREY JELLICOE AND SUSAN JELLICOE,
The Landscapes of Man, *1975*

THE EARLY LESSON

Let me reiterate: landscape detail is a design activity. It is not to be confused with the activity of producing construction drawings nor the implementation of projects on-site. Therefore, how a landscape element appears on-site in its final detail form is as much a result of earlier conceptual thinking as it is of the ongoing solution of site problems and concerns.

In the introductory section of this book, I described my early experience in a design office of watching an accomplished designer instinctively start a project by drawing out both the framework of the plan *and* the detail form simultaneously. The swift actions of moving from concept to detail, detail to landscape, landscape to detail, were recorded in precise pencil sketches on a single sheet of paper. The drawing remained pinned on the wall for the duration of the project as both the initial conceptual workings on the project and a record of the results of that period of intense creative activity. The sketch drawings also became the reference point to which the entry-level employees constantly returned to confirm that further design and detail decisions were consistent. This was not an isolated event in the history of the office, but was carried out, on each and every project, as a working habit, irrespective of project size, type, budget, or client.

The lesson presented to this entry-level graduate in this design office at that time was that it was possible to conceive of detail forms at the same time as considering the major structure and arrangement of program and space. This meant that the search for detail form was a design activity, and a significant one to the project at that. It also presented a holistic view of design and detail across all manner of scales and work types, and one in which the designer was able to patiently and purposefully map out a clear direction for the project and develop a cohesive view of its entire detail language.

As I observed earlier, these key detail forms remained unchanged while the project, like any other piece of design work, underwent dynamic shifts and changes in the structuring and organization of space and forms. For many designers, landscape detail is too often seen as the final action in this dynamic process of design, whether detail is understood as a design or a construction element—in short, simply a concluding act of documentation that resolves all known issues at a detail scale within a set of defined spatial parameters. To present and repeat the early lesson within this book is important in reinforcing the significance of landscape detail in any project, and in rethinking the way in which detail and landscape are considered within the landscape design process. It also brings alive the vitality of the creative act which was witnessed that day, the sense of producing detail form as a mental process through those initial pencil strokes on paper, bringing intellectual and physical concerns together, both the poetic and the pragmatic.

LESSONS FROM THE CASE STUDIES

The Case Studies in Part Three illustrate a series of separate and distinctive viewpoints about the art of landscape detail. Together they demonstrate many of the approaches and themes introduced in Part One, "Fundamentals." A number of the practices reviewed in Part Two were also present and discussed. However, none replicates exactly the detail process that was described at the beginning of the book. This is not a failing; it is simply that the process of detail design is a result of individual choices, motivations, and training.

It is necessary, in closing, to consider two points that have not been directly mentioned but have an important bearing on the subject of landscape detail for students and young practitioners: first, the individual character of the case studies and, second, the relationship between thinking and making. Here we return to the question raised in the introduction regarding the nature of landscape design, detail, and the discipline of landscape architecture as a fine or mechanic art.

CHARACTER OF THE CASE STUDIES

The case studies did not depict the entire nature of the design process or the scope of work in the design projects in question. It is therefore important to recognize that although the designer's voice has been the dominant force throughout the case studies, there are, in fact, others who bring an important dimension to the entire efforts in detail design. In many cases, the voice of the client was absent, as were those of other consultants or groups who were involved in aspects of the detail design, whether as engineer, architect, consultant, surveyor, or cost estimator. In addition, those who built the project and the final users of the project were heard only through the words of the designer.

FINE ART AND MECHANIC ARTS?

We now return to a central question that was raised earlier—is landscape design a fine art, a mechanic art, or both? Here the roots of landscape architecture were described as being derived from the categories of the "mechanic" and "fine arts." Although the broad term *technology* is now applied generally to this area of teaching and practice, it is useful to speculate about the relationship between the terms *mechanic* and *fine arts* as they were outlined in the initial chapters and demonstrated during the case studies.

In the case studies we have heard from accomplished designers about their own particular ways of working and making at the detail scale. No one exactly replicates the process that I described earlier. Some, for example, rely on different strategies to produce detail form, using research of historical design detail precedents to develop new detail proposals (Laurie Olin) or drawing on sources from other artistic activities, including painting and sculpture (Martha Schwartz). Others relinquish the need even to draw (Dan Kiley), conceiving of the total project internally while allowing colleagues to direct the pencil or execute the cardboard models for them. As a result of the multidisciplinary nature of the work, there is also the interchange between different hands at the early stages of a project whereby the process that we have described may be replicated across a range of participants (Susan Child). Finally, there are examples in which the two—that is, design and detail form—are presented at first as being totally disconnected, the detail forms appearing to follow at a much later time in the process.

It is important to recognize that these are not necessarily models to follow in your own design work, but that they reflect how these individual designers, in their respective practices, have been able to address the opportunities afforded by this aspect of design within their own design experience, backgrounds, training, and detail influences.

It is important to note here that there is sometimes a disjunction between what a designer says and what he or she actually does. Here we return to the issue discussed in Chapter 1 regarding the multiple definitions of the term *detail* as they are currently used. In many cases the designer was referring to "landscape details" as the final working *drawings* of detail forms and the descriptions and specifications that make up a series of detail *instructions*. In

330

all these cases there was still an inherent separation between the act of design, or conception of ideas about design and detail form (thinking), and the final process of implementation (making). Landscape detail was still considered in the same light as issues of construction techniques and site operations. In the case study interviews, it is interesting to note a common remark by the designers regarding the influence of their early experiences around building and construction ("My father was an architect and was very conscientious about his detailing"; "From childhood on, I grew up around construction projects") as validation of their concerns for detail form. In some cases this has served to maintain the separation between the twin aspects of the "mechanic" arts and the "fine" arts.

We are left with a series of paired conditions that were present in discussions of the subject of landscape detail:

Mechanic Arts	Fine Arts (before the mid-nineteenth century)
Technology	Design (the contemporary version)
Making	Thinking
Practical	Theoretical or Conceptual

By considering landscape detail (the fine grain) at the same time as, and of equal importance to, the overall concept (the broader picture), the paired sets of opposites can be united into a complete portrayal of landscape design. Here, through the search for landscape detail form, the concerns of the mechanic arts and technology, the practical and mundane, are considered an intellectual process of design exploration and, again, through landscape detail, the concerns of form, structure, and expression are focused on "making" as an aspect of fine arts and design, the theoretical and the ideal. The mechanic and fine arts are united in landscape detail.

FINAL REMARKS

The case studies and the remarks in this postscript are offered for students and young practitioners. They do not present a set of guidelines or rules that will result in successful details (however we may care to measure the notion of success). That is not the nature of landscape design, nor of landscape detail.

Progressive landscape detail still requires individuals to have developed individual design talent with the capacity to work productively in the landscape field. Nor does landscape detail absolve the designer of having to grasp the total range of knowledge and skills in all other areas of landscape architecture design, technology and construction, law and business practices.

The case studies provide, instead, a way of understanding landscape design through its detail and, at the same time, a way of looking at landscape detail through design. In this, the purpose is to project landscape detail beyond its current role, as a complement to other parts of the landscape design and planning processes, and to establish it as an identifiable subject on its own—a subject deeply concerned with the intellectual activity of design, both as a daily form of practice and a personal aesthetic language.

Landscape detail is also a way of rediscovering what has already been recognized in the landscape design work of previous historical periods but today continues to elude our full appreciation. Making landscape detail form requires the lifetime investment of energy, resources, and patience of any designer.

Commitment to serious detail investigation requires an obsessive mind, as well as broad attention given to landscape detail's particular design challenges. It also demands a clear intellectual focus and a deep understanding of design history, with as much practical site experience and travel to built landscapes in varied cultures and climates as any designer can muster in a professional lifetime.

In return, an art form is produced which combines poetic ideas with pragmatic common sense and is both intricate and strong in its formation, resolution, and execution. The fundamentals, practices, and case studies presented in *The Art of Landscape Detail* demonstrate that landscape detail is an art form of the highest order.

CASE STUDY REFERENCES AND ACKNOWLEDGMENTS

THE FOLLOWING LISTS present an abbreviated selection of current articles and essays about the case study projects, either written as magazine articles or included in books and monographs. Included also are a selection of articles written by or about the principal designers that particularly focus on their working methods, interests, and main design philosophies. Other projects of the designers that are of interest, in terms of the continuation of detail themes and motifs, are noted. These should form a starting point for students in studying and carrying out further site evaluations and research.

Acknowledgements are given for individuals and design office members who provided background and technical information or assisted in retrieving project drawings, sketches, and photographs, as well as those who revisited projects and provided slides and photographs.

CASE STUDY A

BRYANT PARK RESTORATION AND IMPROVEMENT, *New York*

Project References

Amateau, Albert, and Steven Saltzman. "Bryant Park Plans Proceed." *Metropolis* 9, no. 6 (Jan.–Feb. 1990): 13–14.

Biderman, Daniel. "Up From Smoke: A New, Improved Bryant Park." *NY Affairs* 6, no. 4 (1981): 97–105.

Kahn, Eve. "Panacea in Needle Park." *Landscape Architecture* 82, no. 12 (Dec. 1992): 60–61.

Kay, Jane Holtz. "The New/Renewed Urban Parks: Over-design by Committee?" *Landscape Architecture* 82, no. 12 (Dec. 1992): 38–39.

"Poets Park." *Landscape Architecture* 79, no. 2 (March 1989): 13.

Simson, Lusby. "Bryant Park, Sixth Avenue, 40th to 42nd Streets." *Architecture and Urbanism* (Dec. 1994, extra edition): 196–199.

Smith, C. Ray. "Bryant Park Restoration." *Occulus* 50, no. 6 (Feb. 1988): 12–15.

Thompson, J. William. *The Rebirth of New York's Bryant Park.* Washington, D.C.: Spacemaker Press, 1997.

Urbach, Henry. "Reclaiming Public Parks." *Metropolis* 7, no. 6 (Jan.–Feb. 1988): 20–21.

Articles on or by the Designer

Olin, Laurie D. "Toppling the Walls Between Building and Landscape." *Landscape Architecture* 80, no. 8 (Aug. 1990): 128.

Olin, Laurie D. "Form, Expression and Meaning in Landscape Architecture." *Landscape Journal* 7, no. 2 (fall, 1989–1990. Special issue: "Nature, Form, and Meaning." ed. Ann Whiston Spirn): 149–168.

Olin, Laurie D. "Ecology and Design of the Landscape." In *Ecological Design and Planning,* ed. George F. Thompson and Frederick Steiner. New York: John Wiley & Sons, 1997.

Olin, Laurie D. "Design of the Urban Landscape." *Places* 5, no. 2 (1988): 142–168.

Olin, Laurie D. *Transforming the Common Place: Selections from Laurie Olin's Sketchbooks.* Cambridge: Harvard University Graduate School of Design; Princeton: Architectural Press, 1996 (see sketches of Bryant Park, pp. 10–13).

Olin, Laurie D. "The Museum of Modern Art Garden: The Rise and Fall of a Modernist Landscape." *Journal of Garden History* 17, no. 2 (April–June 1997): 140–162.

Steiner, Frederick R., and Todd Johnson. "Perfecting the Ordinary." *Landscape Architecture* 82, no. 3 (Mar. 1992): 68–77 and cover.

Related Projects

ASLA Awards. "Battery Park Esplanade, I and II." *Landscape Architecture* 78 (Nov. 1988): 42–43.

Dietsch, Deborah. "Americans in London." *Architecture* 79, no. 9 (Sept. 1990): 64–71.

"Harbouring Views: Wagner Park." *World Architecture* 57 (June 1997): 76. (Battery Park City, New York.)

"New York Public Library Fifth Avenue Terrace." *Landscape Architecture* 78, no. 7 (Nov. 1988): 48–49.

Webb, Michael. "Common Ground: Pershing Square." *Deutsche Bauzeitung* 128, no. 6 (1994): 140–142.

Welborne, H. "Discovering Common Ground in Downtown LA." *Urban Land* 53, no. 12 (Dec. 1994): 29–33.

Acknowledgments
Alistair Mcintosh and Christopher Allen, both formerly of Hanna/Olin Ltd., Philadelphia. Robert Bedell, The Olin Partnership, Philadelphia.

CASE STUDY B

CHRISTOPHER COLUMBUS WATERFRONT PARK, *Boston*

Project References

Simo, Melanie. *Sasaki Associates: Integrated Environments.* Washington, D.C.: Spacemaker Press, 1997.

Articles on or by the Designer

Dawson, Stuart. "Dallas Arts District." *Urban Design International* 4, no. 3 (spring 1983): 20–23.

Further Projects

Campbell, Robert. "A Mosaic of Parks." *Landscape Architecture* 79, no. 4 (May 1989): 70–73.

Thompson, J. William. "Waterfront Park." *Landscape Architecture* 81, no. 2 (Jan.–Feb. 1991): 44–47.

Thompson, J. William. "Embarcadero: Free from the Freeway." *Landscape Architecture* 83, no. 6 (June 1993): 60–61.

Walker, Peter, and Melanie Simo. "The Modernization of the Schools" and "The Corporate Office, First Wave." *Invisible Gardens: The Search for Meaning in the Modern Landscape.* Cambridge: MIT Press, 1994.

Acknowledgments
Alan Ward, Alistair McIntosh, both of Sasaki Associates, Watertown, Massachusetts.

CASE STUDY C

THE CITADEL GRAND ALLÉE, *Commerce, California*

Articles on or by the Designer

Jones, Michael. "Martha Schwartz." *Landscape* 40 (Summer 1989): 8–13.

Schwartz, Martha. "Seeing and Making the Landscape Whole." *Progressive Architecture* 72, no. 8 (Aug. 1991): 92–95.

Schwartz, Martha. "Landscape and Common Culture Since Moderism." In *A Critical Anthology of Modern Landscape Architecture,* ed. Marc Trieb. Cambridge: MIT Press, 1993.

Schwartz, Martha. "Transfiguration of the Commonplace." Washington, D.C.: Spacemaker Press, 1997.

Vickers, Graham. "Martha Schwartz/Inc." *World Architecture* 36 (1995): 80–83.

Further Projects

Anderton, Francis. "Avant-gardens." *Architecture Review* 186, no. 1111 (Sept. 1989): 32–41.

"From Trolley Tracks to Linear Park." *Architecture California* 11, no. 2 (Sept.–Oct. 1989): 30–31. (Marine Linear Park in San Diego, California.)

Johnson, Jory. "Martha Schwartz's Splice Garden: A Warning to a Brave New World." *Landscape Architecture* 73, no. 4 (July–Aug. 1988): 100.

Mays, Vernon. "A Park as Art in Concord (California)." *Progressive Architecture* 69, no. 4 (April 1988): 27.

"Necco Garden, Cambridge, Massachusetts." *Progressive Architecture* (Oct. 1989): 126–127.

Acknowledgments
David Meyer and Ken Smith, formerly Schwartz, Smith Meyer, San Francisco, California.

CASE STUDY D

ALLIED PLAZA, FOUNTAIN PLACE, *Dallas, Texas*

Project References

"Allied Bank Tower at Fountain Place." *Places* 4, no. 4, 34–35.

Gillette, Jane Brown. "Kiley Revisited." *Landscape Architecture* 88, no. 8 (Aug. 1998): 58–61, 86–89.

Kiley, Aaron. *Fountain Place* (video tape recording). London: Gardner Communications, Pidgeon Audio-Visual, 1988.

Price, Martha. "Dallas (Texas) Oasis." *Architectural Review* 184, no. 1098 (Aug. 1988): 70–71.

Rome, Richard. "The Dallas Waterfronts." *Cite* 29 (fall 1993): 31–32.

Zapatka, Christian. *The American Landscape.* New York: Princeton Architectural Press, 1995. (Contemporary landscape architects and a sculptor: *Daniel Urban Kiley, Peter Walker, Ron Wigginton, Hargreaves and Associates, Mary Miss.* Contains description and illustrations of Fountain Place, p. 187.)

Articles by or on the Designer

Byrd, Warren T., and Reuben M. Rainey, eds. "The Work of Dan Kiley: A Dialogue on Design Theory." *Proceedings of the First Annual Symposium on Landscape Architecture.* Division of Landscape Architecture, School of Architecture. Charlottesville: University of Virginia, 1983.

Dean, Andrea Oppenheimer. "Modern Master." *Landscape Architecture* 86, no. 2 (Feb. 1996): 74–79.

Guthheim, Frederick. "Landscape Design: The Works of Dan Kiley." *Process Architecture* 33 (October 1982): 1–47.

Karson, Robin. "Conversation with Kiley." *Landscape Architecture* 76, no. 2 (March–April 1986): 50–57.

Kiley, Dan. "Landscape in the Urban Environment" (with Garrett Eckbo and James Rose). *Architectural Record* (May 1939).
  "Landscape in the Rural Environment" (with Garrett Eckbo and James Rose). *Architectural Record* (May 1939).
  "Landscape in the Primeaval Environment" (with Garrett Eckbo and James Rose). *Architectural Record* (Feb. 1940).
(reprinted in *A Critical Anthology of Modern Landscape Architecture,* ed. Marc Treib. Cambridge: MIT Press, 1993.)

Kiley, Dan. "A Way with Water." *Landscape Design* no. 208 (March 1992): 33–36. (Article by Dan Kiley on the use of water in his projects, including Fountain Place.)

Kiley, Dan. "What Is Design" (Dan Kiley: Landscape Design II: In Step with Nature). *Process Architecture* 108 (1993): 36–45.

Walker, Peter, and Melanie Simo. "The Lone Classicist." *Invisible Gardens: The Search for Modernism in the American Landscape.* Cambridge: MIT Press, 1994, 170–197.

Further Projects

Dillon, David. "The People Commandeer a Plaza." *Landscape Architecture* 81 (Jan. 1991): 44–46. (First Interstate Plaza, Dallas.)

Acknowledgments

Peter Ker Walker, Burlington, Vermont; Jane Amidon, Office of Dan Kiley, Charlotte, Vermont; Mary Daniels, Francis Loeb Library, Graduate School of Design, Harvard University; Peter Lindsay Schaudt, Chicago, Illinois.

CASE STUDY E

ALLEGHENY RIVERFRONT PARK, *Pittsburgh*

Project References

Miller, Donald. "Pittsburgh Riverfront Project." *Public Art Review* (spring/summer 1997): 28–29.

P/A Awards. "Allegheny Riverfront Park." *Progressive Architecture* 86, no. 1 (Jan. 1997): 92–93.

Articles on or by the Designer

Brown, Brenda. "Avantgardism and Landscape Architecture." *Landscape Journal* 10, no. 2 (fall 1991): 134–154.

Brown, Jane Gillette. "Michael." *Landscape Architecture* 88, no. 2 (Feb. 1998): 66–73, 86–90.

Fleming, Lee. "Long-term Dividends." *Garden Design* 12, no. 4 (Sept.–Oct. 1993): 38–49.

Hodge, Brooke, ed. *Design with the Land: Landscape Architecture of Michael Van Valkenburgh.* New York: Princeton Architectural Press, 1989.

Johnson, Jay. P/A Profile. "Michael Van Valkenburgh." *Progressive Architecture* 70, no. 7 (July 1989): 72–77.

Otis, Denise. "On the Cutting Edge: Michael Van Valkenburgh." *Garden Design* 16, no. 1 (Jan.–March 1997): 72–81.

Van Valkenburgh, Michael. "Notations of Nature's Processes." *Landscape Architecture* 76, no. 1 (Jan.–Feb. 1986): 40–45.

Further Projects

"In the Works: Harvard Yard." *Planning* 59, no. 10 (Oct. 1993): 50.

Linn, Charles. "Building Types Study 711: Parks and Recreational Facilities." *Architectural Record* 181, no. 11 (Nov. 1993): 108–117.

Madec, Phillipe. "French Connection." *Landscape Architecture* 84, no. 10 (Oct. 1994): 90–95.

Acknowledgments

Laura Solano, office of Michael Van Valkenburgh Associates, Inc., Cambridge, Massachusetts.

CASE STUDY F

SOUTH COVE, BATTERY PARK CITY, *New York*

Project References

Antonelli, Paolo. "Public Art: A Battery Park City, NY." *Domus* (Jan. 1991): 78–84.

Gastil, Raymond W. "On the Waterfront Art/Architecture." *Progressive Architecture* (Sept. 1988): 24–25.

Howett, Catherine. "Battery Park City." *Landscape Architecture* (May 1989): 51–58.

Karson, Robin. "Battery Park City—South Cove." *Landscape Architecture* 76, no. 3 (May/June 1986): 48–53.

Lanecker, Heidi. "Waterfront Connection: The South Cove Belvedere." *Architecture* 84, no. 8 (Aug. 1995): 56–61.

Princenthal, Nancy. "On the Look-Out (South Cove)." *Art in America* (1988): 158–161.

Articles on or by the Designer

Griswold, Mac. "Simple Gifts: A Profile." *Garden Design* 12, no. 5 (Nov.–Dec. 1993): 40–47.

Thompson, J. William. "Stakin' Out Turf." *Landscape Architecture* 82, no. 7 (July 1992): 48–49.

CASE STUDY G

VIETNAM VETERANS MEMORIAL, *Washington, D.C.*

Project References

Campbell, Robert. "An Emotive Place Apart." *AIA Journal* 72, no. 5 (May 1983): 150–151.

Charney, Wayne. "Et in Arcadia Ego: The Place of Memorials in Contemporary America." *Reflections*—Journal of the School of Architecture, University of Illinois, Urbana-Champaign—6 (July 1989): 86–95.

Freeman, Allen. "An Extraordinary Competition: The Winning Design for the Vietnam Memorial." *AIA Journal* 70, no. 9 (Aug. 1981): 47–53.

Freeman, Allen. "Vietnam Veterans Memorial Competition." *Architectural Record* 169, no. 8 (June 1981): 47.

Howett, Catherine. "The Vietnam Veterans Memorial: Public Art and Politics." *Landscape* 28, no. 2 (1985): 19.

CASE STUDY H

PARQUE ECOLÓGICO XOCHIMILCO, *Mexico City*

Project References

Kolstad, Kirsten. "Xochimilco Ecological Park." *Arkitektnytt* (Oslo) 3 (Feb. 1995): 1, 40–41.

Meier, Rudolf. "Xochimilco Ecological Park." *Garten+Lanscahft* 106, no. 6 (June 1996): 11–15.

"Parque Natural de Xochimilco." *Escala* 26, no. 164 (1994): 41–43 (in Spanish).

Schjetnan, Mario. "The Ecological Park of Xochimilco." *Lotus International* 91 (1996): 110–131.

Thompson, J. William. "Aztec Revival." *Landscape Architecture* 84, no. 4 (April 1994): 62–65.

Articles on or by the Designer

Schjetnan, Mario. "Luis Barragan: The Influential Lyricist of Mexican Culture." *Landscape Architecture* 70 (Jan. 1982): 68–75.

Schjetnan, Mario. "Monumental Spaces." *Landscape Architecture* 79, no. 6 (Aug. 1982): 50–53.

"Through Murk and Dust: Mexico's Landscape Architects Move Onstage." *Landscape Architecture* 66 (Nov. 1976): 82–119.

Further Projects

ASLA Awards. "Parque Tezozomoc." *Landscape Architecture* 79, no. 9 (Nov. 1989): 49–51.

Thompson, J. William. "Landscape as Myth and Culture." *Landscape Architecture* 84, no. 1 (1994): 72–75.

Acknowledgments
Louise Wyman and Bertha Pantoja, both formerly of Harvard University Graduate School of Design.

BIBLIOGRAPHY

LANDSCAPE DETAIL AND DETAIL PRACTICES

Blanc, Alan. *Landscape Construction and Detailing*. New York: McGraw-Hill, 1996.

Cantor, Stephen. *Innovative Design Solutions in Landscape Architecture*. New York: Van Nostrand Reinhold, 1996.

Carpenter, Jot D., ed. *Handbook of Landscape Architectural Construction*. Mclean, Va.: The Landscape Architecture Foundation, 1976.

Ciaccio, David J. *Site Sections and Details: A Reference Guide to Site Construction Details*. New York: Van Nostrand Reinhold, 1984.

DeChiara, Joseph, and Lee E. Koppelman. *Time Saver Standards for Site Planning*. New York: McGraw-Hill, 1984.

Dines, Nicholas T., and Charles W. Harris. *Time Saver Standards for Landscape Architecture*. 2d ed. Kyle D. Brown, ed. New York: McGraw-Hill, 1997.

Dines, Nicholas T., and Charles W. Harris. *Time Saver Standards for Landscape Construction Details*. CD-ROM. New York: McGraw-Hill, 1997.

Hubbard, Henry Vincent, and Theodora Kimball. *An Introduction to the Study of Landscape Design*. New York: Macmillan, 1917.

Landphair, Harlowe, and Fred Klatt. *Landscape Architecture Construction*. 2d. ed. New York: Elsevier, 1979.

Littlewood, Michael. *Landscape Detailing*. 3d ed. Vol. 1, *Enclosures*. Vol. 2, *Surfaces*. Oxford: Butterworth Architecture, 1993.

Littlewood, Michael. *Tree Detailing*. New York: Van Nostrand Reinhold, 1988.

McCluskey, Jim. *Roadform and Townscape*. 2d ed. Oxford; Boston: Butterworth-Heinemann, 1992.

Munson, Albe. *Construction Design for Landscape Architects.* New York: McGraw-Hill, 1974.

Nelischer, Maurice, ed. *Handbook of Landscape Architectural Construction.* 2d ed. Washington, D.C.: Landscape Architecture Foundation, 1985.

Newton, Norman T. *Design on the Land: The Development of Landscape Architecture.* Cambridge: Harvard University Press, 1971.

Pinder, Angi and Alan. *Beazley's Design and Detail of the Space Between Buildings.* London: E. & F. N. Spon, 1990.

Reid, Grant W. *From Concept to Form in Landscape Design.* New York: Van Nostrand Reinhold, 1993.

Robinette, Gary O. *Landscape Architectural Site Construction Details.* Reston, Va.: Environmental Design Press, 1976.

Rubenstein, Harvey. *A Guide to Site Planning and Landscape Construction,* 3d. ed. New York: John Wiley & Sons, 1996.

Walker, Theodore D. *Site Design and Construction Detailing.* 3d ed. New York: Van Nostrand Reinhold, 1992.

Weddle, A. E., ed. *Landscape Techniques: Incorporating Techniques of Landscape Architecture.* London: Heinemann, 1979.

Weinberg, Scott, and Gregg A. Coyle, eds. *Materials for Landscape Construction.* 1st ed. Vol. 4, *Handbook of Landscape Architectural Construction.* Washington, D.C.: The Landscape Architecture Foundation, 1992.

BACKGROUND SOURCES ON OTHER DETAIL PRACTICES AND SOURCES

Albertini, Biancia, and Sandro Bagnoli. *Carlo Scarpa: Architecture in Details.* Cambridge: MIT Press, 1988.

Alexander, Christopher. *A Pattern Language.* New York: Oxford University Press, 1977.

Allen, Edward. *Architectural Detailing: Function, Constructibility, Aesthetics.* New York: John Wiley & Sons, 1993.

Allport, Susan. *Sermons in Stone: The Stone Walls of New England and New York.* New York: W. W. Norton, 1990.

Alphand, Adolphe. *Les Promenades de Paris.* J. Rothschild, ed., Paris 1867–73. Reprint, Princeton: Princeton Architectural Press, 1984.

Balachowski, Joseph D. *HABS/HAER Guidelines: Recording Structures and Sites with Measured Drawings.* Washington, D.C.: U.S. Department of the Interior, National Park Service, Cultural Resources, Historic American Building Survey (HABS), Historic American Engineering Record (HAER), 1994.

Beall, Christine. *Masonry Design and Detailing,* 4th ed. New York: McGraw-Hill, 1998.

Bell, Simon. *Elements of Visual Design in the Landscape.* London: E. & F. N. Spon, 1993.

Birnbaum, Charles A., and Lisa E. Crowder, eds. *Pioneers of American Landscape Design: An Annotated Biography.* Washington, D.C.: Preservation Assistance Division, Historic Landscape Initative, U.S. Department of the Interior, National Park Service, Cultural Resources, 1993.

Brand, Stewart. *How Buildings Learn: What Happens After They're Built.* New York: Viking, 1994.

Brett, David. *C. R. Mackintosh The Poetics of Workmanship.* Cambridge: Harvard University Press, 1992.

Brunskill, R. W. *Illustrated Handbook of Vernacular Architecture.* London: Faber and Faber, 1972.

Burns, John A., ed. *Recording Historic Structures.* Washington, D.C.: AIA Press, 1989.

Bye, A. E. *Art into Landscape, Landscape into Art.* Mesa, Arizona: PDA Publishers, 1983.

Canadian Mortgage and Housing Corporation. *Landscape Architectural Design and Maintenance.* Ottawa: CMHC Development Evaluation and Advisory Services Division, 1982.

Cartwright, Richard M. *The Design of Urban Space: A GLC Manual.* London: Architectural Press Ltd. Published in the United States by Halsted Press, a division of John Wiley & Sons, 1980.

Dickinson, Duo. *Expressive Details.* New York: McGraw-Hill, 1997.

Dubé, Richard L. *Natural Pattern Forms: A Practical Sourcebook for Landscape Design.* New York: Van Nostrand Reinhold, 1997.

Fitchen, John. *Building Construction Before Mechanization.* Cambridge: MIT Press, 1986.

Ford, Edward R. *The Details of Modern Architecture.* Cambridge: The MIT Press; vol 1., 1990; vol. 2, 1996.

Frampton, Kenneth. *Studies in Tectonic Culture: The Poetics of Construction in Nineteenth and Twentieth Century Architecture.* Cambridge: MIT Press, 1995.

Freidberg, Paul F. *Hand-Crafted Playgrounds.* New York: Random House, 1975.

Goodman, Nelson. *Ways of Worldmaking.* Hassocks, Sussex: Harvester Press, 1978.

Gutdeutsch, Götz. *Building in Wood: Construction and Details.* Basel; Boston: Birkhäuser, 1997.

Hornbostel, Caleb. *Construction Materials: Types, Uses, and Applications.* New York: John Wiley & Sons, 1991.

Jacobs, Allan B. *Great Streets.* Cambridge: MIT Press, 1993.

Levick, Melba. *Barcelona: Architectural Details and Delights.* Barcelona: Ediciones Poligrafa; New York: Harry N. Abrams, 1993.

Liebing, Ralph W. *Architectural Working Drawings.* 3d ed. New York: John Wiley & Sons, 1990.

Loss, John, and Earle W. Kennett. *Performance Failures in Buildings and Civil Works.* Bethesda, Maryland: University of Maryland, 1991.

Lynch, Kevin, and Gary Hack. *Site Planning.* 3d ed. Cambridge: MIT Press, 1986.

McKaig, Thomas. *Building Failures: Case Studies in Construction and Design.* New York: McGraw-Hill, 1962.

Mostafavi, Moshen, and David Leatherbarrow. *On Weathering: The Life of Buildings in Time.* Cambridge: MIT Press, 1993.

Murphy, Richard. *Carlo Scarpa and the Castelvecchio.* London; Boston: Butterworth Architecture, 1990.

O'Gorman, Patricia W. *Patios and Gardens of Mexico.* New York: Architectural Book Publishing, 1979.

Olgay, Victor. *Design with Climate: Bioclimatic Approach to Architectural Regionalism.* Princeton: Princeton University Press, 1963.

Patterson, Terry L. *Construction Materials for Architects and Designers.* Englewood Cliffs, N.J.: Prentice Hall, 1990.

Petroski, Henry. *To Engineer is Human, The Role of Failure in Successsful Design.* New York: St. Martin's Press, 1985.

Petroski, Henry. *Design Paradigms: Case Studies of Error and Judgment in Engineering.* Cambridge, England; New York, NY: Cambridge University Press, 1994.

Plumridge, Andrew, and Wim Meulenkamp. *Brickwork, Architecture and Design.* New York: Harry N. Abrams, 1993.

Pye, David. *The Nature and Art of Workmanship.* New York: Van Nostrand Reinhold, 1972.

Radde, Bruce. *The Merritt Parkway.* New Haven: Yale University Press, 1993.

Ramsey, Charles G., and Harold R. Sleeper. *Architectural Graphic Standards.* James Ambrose, ed. 6th ed. New York: John Wiley & Sons, 1970.

Richardson, Barry A. *Defects and Deterioration in Buildings.* London: E. & F. N. Spon, 1991.

Roberts, Ann R. *Mr. Rockefeller's Roads: The Untold Story of Acadia's Carriage Roads and Their Creator.* Camden, Me.: Down East Books, 1990.

Rogers, Elizabeth R. *Rebuilding Central Park: A Management and Restoration Plan.* Cambridge: MIT Press, 1987.

Stevens, David. *Roof Gardens, Balconies and Terraces.* New York: Rizzoli, 1997.

Templer, John. *The Staircase, Studies of Hazards, Falls, and Safer Design.* Cambridge: MIT Press, 1992.

Vandenberg, Maritz. *Glass Canopies.* Detail in Building Series. Great Britian: Academy Group Ltd., 1996 (see also *Soft Canopies* and *Staircases* by same author and publisher.)

Wakita, Osamu A., and Richard M. Linde. *The Professional Practice of Architectural Detailing.* 2d ed. New York: John Wiley & Sons, 1987.

White, Stanley H. *A Primer of Landscape Architecture.* Unpublished manuscript. University of Illinois, 1956.

Whyte, William H. *Rediscovering the Center.* New York: Doubleday, 1988.

Yanagi, Muneyoshi. *The Unknown Craftsman: A Japanese Insight into Beauty by Soetsu Yanagi.* New York: Kodansha International, 1989.

Zimmerman, Scot, and Judith Dunham. *Details of Frank Lloyd Wright: The California Work, 1909–1974.* San Francisco: Chronicle Books, 1994.

Zwerger, Klaus. *Wood and Wood Joints: Building Traditions of Europe and Japan.* Boston: Birkhauser Verlay, 1997.

INDEX

Page numbers in italic refer to illustrations.